Transforming Pastoral Leadership

Transforming Pastoral Leadership

Reimagining Congregational Relationships
for Changing Contexts

❇

Quentin P. Kinnison

Foreword by
Mark Lau Branson

PICKWICK *Publications* · Eugene, Oregon

TRANSFORMING PASTORAL LEADERSHIP
Reimagining Congregational Relationships for Changing Contexts

Pickwick Publications
An Imprint of Wipf and Stock Publishers
199 W. 8th Ave., Suite 3
Eugene, OR 97401

www.wipfandstock.com

Paperback ISBN 978-1-62564-703-0
Hardcover ISBN 978-1-4982-8684-8

Cataloging-in-Publication data:

Names: Quentin P. Kinnison.

Title: Transforming pastoral leadership : reimagining congregational relationships for changing contexts / Quentin P. Kinnison.

Description: Eugene, OR : Cascade Books, 2016 | Includes bibliographical references and index.

Identifiers: ISBN 978-1-62564-703-0 (paperback) | ISBN 978-1-4982-8684-8 (hardcover)

Subjects: 1. Pastoral theology. 2. Pastoral care. 3. Christian leadership. I. Title.

Classification: BV4011.3 K46 2016 (print)

Manufactured in the USA.

BIBLE PERMISSIONS

Scripture quotations taken from the New American Standard Bible®, Copyright © 1960, 1962, 1963, 1968, 1971, 1972, 1973, 1975, 1977, 1995 by The Lockman Foundation. Used by permission.

Scripture taken from the HOLY BIBLE, NEW INTERNATIONAL VERSION®. NIV®. Copyright © 1973, 1978, 1984 by International Bible Society. Used by permission of Zondervan. All rights reserved worldwide.

New Revised Standard Version Bible, copyright 1989, Division of Christian Education of the National Council of the Churches of Christ in the United States of America. Used by permission. All rights reserved.

Scripture taken from the New Century Version®. Copyright © 2005 by Thomas Nelson. Used by permission. All rights reserved.

CHAPTER PERMISSIONS

Chapters 2 and 3 contain material previously published as "The Pastor as Expert and the Challenge of Being a Saltwater Fish in a Freshwater Tank." *Journal of Religious Leadership* 13/1 (Spring 2014) 1–30. It is used here with permission.

Chapters 4 and 5 contain material previously published as "Shepherd or One of the Sheep? Re-visiting the Biblical Metaphor of the Pastorate." *Journal of Religious Leadership* 9/1 (Spring 2010) 59–91. It is used here with permission.

Chapter 6 contains material previously published as "The Social Trinity and the Southwest: Toward a Local Theology in the Borderlands." *Perspectives in Religious Studies: Journal of the National Association of Baptist Professors of Religion* 35/3 (Fall 2008) 261–81. It is used here with permission. This material was also condensed and published in part in Lane, Julie M., and Quentin P. Kinnison, *Welcoming Children with Special Needs: Empowering Christian Special Education with Purpose, Policies, and Procedures.* Bloomington, IN: WestBow, 2014. It is used here with permission.

COVER ART PERMISSION

"The Good Shepherd" by artist He Qi. He Qi ©2014 All Rights Reserved. www.heqiart.com. It is used here with permission.

To Cindy—my partner, friend, and love.

So all the elders of Israel gathered together and came to Samuel at Ramah. They said to him, "You are old, and your sons do not follow your ways; now appoint a king to lead us, such as all the other nations have."

But when they said, "Give us a king to lead us," this displeased Samuel; so he prayed to the LORD. And the LORD told him: "Listen to all that the people are saying to you; it is not you they have rejected, but they have rejected me as their king. As they have done from the day I brought them up out of Egypt until this day, forsaking me and serving other gods, so they are doing to you. Now listen to them; but warn them solemnly and let them know what the king who will reign over them will claim as his rights."

—1 SAMUEL 8:4–9 (NIV)

"I am the good shepherd. The good shepherd lays down his life for the sheep. The hired hand is not the shepherd and does not own the sheep. So when he sees the wolf coming, he abandons the sheep and runs away. Then the wolf attacks the flock and scatters it. The man runs away because he is a hired hand and cares nothing for the sheep.

"I am the good shepherd; I know my sheep and my sheep know me—just as the Father knows me and I know the Father—and I lay down my life for the sheep. I have other sheep that are not of this sheep pen. I must bring them also. They too will listen to my voice, and there shall be one flock and one shepherd."

—JOHN 10:11–16 (NIV)

Do not conform to the pattern of this world, but be transformed by the renewing of your mind.

—ROMANS 12:2a (NIV)

Table of Contents

List of Illustrations

Figure 1: Practical Theology's Praxis-Oriented Cyclical Interaction of Practice and Theory

Figure 2: Branson's Leadership Triad

Figure 3: Latent Conflict Perceived in Relational Sphere

Figure 4: Resolve Conflict by Strengthening Agreement

Foreword

MARK LAU BRANSON

IN THE CONTEXT OF discontinuous societal changes, church leaders have struggled to understand and respond to what theologian/missiologist Alan Roxburgh called "the great unraveling" that is being experienced by churches, denominations, and other ecclesial networks. Modernity taught us that we could rely on experts and their rationalized approaches to goals, strategies, and management. As the older generation continues to experience the waves of cultural disequilibrium, a younger generation has never known a time of stability. Both traditional churches and newer mega-churches "default toward privileging expert and professional perspectives."[1] This doubling down on modernity, Quentin Kinnison notes, is an unreflective reaction that leaves clergy isolated and laity disenfranchised. Habits of consumerism keep people moving on to the next provider of religious services, churches perpetuate hierarchical management structures in hopes of controlling the unraveling, franchise systems of denominations and networks keep selling their magic programs, anxiety leads to fear and blame, and disillusionments means fewer people have enough trust to continue their participation.

Roxburgh notes, "the ordinary people of God have been socialized to assume they have neither the capacities nor the training to discern what God might be doing in the midst of the unraveling."[2] This is where Kinnison provides a map that we need. Rather than the perpetual emphasis on clergy-centric churches, he reconsiders the metaphors and practices that offer us different modes of common life that focus on discerning and participating in God's initiatives.

1. Roxburgh, *Joining God*, 34.
2. Ibid.

As an alternative to perpetuating the habits that lead to illusions about super-clergy and the resulting deskilling of laity, Kinnison lures us to biblical and theological work that shapes alternatives. While he notes important interconnected challenges—becoming aware of our contexts, rethinking what we mean by spirituality, rethinking our organizational habits—Kinnison focuses on the options we have for reconsidering the praxis of leadership.

Along with his insightful naming of cultural challenges, unhelpful ecclesial habits, and the resulting dysfunctional systems that churches experience, Kinnison reorients our understanding of a primary metaphor—shepherd—and then helps us imagine how the Trinity gives us new practices. This is what practical theology is supposed to do—name our situation, analyze some important causes and consequences, engage biblical and theological reflection, and propose new options for us to engage. Roxburgh names unraveling as a time of hope, and Kinnison explores key elements of leadership that are essential to that hope.

Church participants have diverse skills, varying levels of maturity, differing experiences, and varied motivations. But difference is not a problem to be solved. Our Christian heritage emphasizes not only the benefits of assorted gifts and cultures, but the Godhead, in whose image we are made and whose likeness is to be expressed by the church, includes otherness. So if we are to celebrate, encourage, and benefit from this variety, and we reject the functional rationalism that just plugs volunteers into management plans governed by experts, how else can we imagine leadership?

If a church's being and agency is centered in *missio Dei*, which requires that passions and labors be oriented toward collaborative participation, then we need modes of corporate life that draw on all participants—not only in the doing but also in the visioning/discerning. This is why Kinnison calls for a polycentered approach to leadership. In their work on the relationship between learning and leading, Stephen Preskill and Stephen Brookfield name our challenge:

> It is unreasonable to ask community members to give up their own ambitions and support group goals if they have not had significant input into the construction of those goals. Only when a group's aims and decisions are constructed through a process to which everyone has made a contribution can individuals be expected to set aside their self-interest to support the group's communal yearnings and take responsibility for the consequences of their actions.[3]

3. Preskill and Brookfield, *Learning*, 85.

In Kinnison's approach, this is not just a matter of democratic decision-making (which has its own role and benefits) but such participatory approaches emphasize the Holy Spirit's desire to engage the whole people of God. This collaboration is in the entire mix of activities—observing, listening, reflecting, discussing, imagining, experimenting, evaluating, and, yes, leading.

But habits are deep, and churches easily default to expert systems and clergy-centrism. There are even societal factors, as Preskill and Brookfield note, so that "anything collective is viewed as somehow un-American."[4] What Kinnison proposes will need to be approached in experimental, de-centered ways because "the unconventional nature of collective leadership means it triggers automatic resistance from the forces of tradition and the inertia of entrenched practices."[5] Aware of this, Kinnison provides some approaches that make such adaptive moves more likely to gain traction. The emphases on mutuality, openness to the other, diversity, and shared meaning-making, all rooted in the Trinity, will make it more likely that life together and with neighbors is shaped and moved by love.

Kinnison emphasizes that this is a journey of discernment, which is not something done in the backroom or among experts, but by all, in the midst of missional life. This is a holy calling, not just a structural shift. Alan Roxburgh reminds us, "The Spirit is working in the ordinariness of men and women of faith in local contexts . . . It has been, and always will be, in the local and among ordinary people that the Spirit midwifes new life that forever lies outside the reach of strategic plans, mission statements and existing defaults. Jesus promises to always be with us, ahead and around us on this journey."[6] As a theologian, professor, and experienced church leader, Kinnison provides thoughtful, promising guidance for those of us who believe this journey is the very vocation of the church and, therefore, of our own lives.

Mark Lau Branson, Ed.D., is Homer Goddard Professor of Ministry of the Laity at Fuller Theological Seminary, and author of Memories, Hopes, and Conversations *and (with Juan Martínez)* Churches, Cultures, and Leadership.

4. Ibid., 83.

5. Ibid., 92.

6. Roxburgh, *Structured for Mission*, 156.

Acknowledgements

I am blessed.

I am blessed by an amazing spouse, Dr. Cynthia Kinnison, who offered her wisdom, editing skills, and encouragement to the shaping of this manuscript. Her prodding and gentle nudges helped me stay on task despite knowing it would lead to her endless reading and rereading of this work. Thank you for your graciousness in this process.

I am blessed by a witty and smart child who kept me grounded on the important tasks of playing and storytelling, Thank you, Carissa.

I am blessed by my parents, Paul and Norma Kinnison. Mom was my first theology professor, teaching me to think carefully and critically about God's work in his world. Dad was the cheerleader, always rooting and encouraging me, and his editing skills are greatly appreciated. I am thankful for my sister, Vandi, who although she left us too soon reminds me by her life that our theology and actions are intertwined.

I am profoundly grateful to my mentors. My doctoral mentors, Drs. Mark Lau Branson and Juan Francisco Martínez, started this book's journey while welcoming me as a colleague and a friend along the way. Pastoral leaders Jim Harvey, and Don Browning and college professors Drs. Mike Baird, Clark Youngblood, and D. C. Martin shaped my formative understandings in ways that are reflected in these pages.

My friends and colleagues at FSBC Glendale and FSBC Phoenix labored together, struggling with questions this work addresses, especially David Johnson, Gordon Christopher, Karen and Steve Massingill, Pam Hill, Joe Curtis, John and Kathy Keller, Shannon and Kenny Carter, Chris and Kim Potts, and so many others. I am grateful for their loving friendship in the midst of hard struggles. Likewise, I thank my wonderful colleagues at Fresno Pacific University (faculty, staff, students, and administrators) who challenge me to further understand God and God's Kingdom at work in our world.

I am blessed. To each and all of you I say as Paul says it, "I thank my God every time I remember you."[1]

---

1. Phil 1:3, NIV.

Introduction

This book is largely about congregational leadership, cultural captivity, and how pastoral leaders and congregations can adapt practices and roles for the purpose of engaging God and God's mission in the changing world. The book is divided into three parts, with each part holding a distinct part of the material. Part one will look at the social and historical forces that have shaped our current practices and the current cultural implications of having been so shaped. Part two will investigate the biblical and theological lost memories that, when reclaimed, can offer us guidance on how to live in this disorientation. In conclusion, part three will look at ways of employing alternate practices and tools around leadership and congregational life that free us to experience the work of God's Spirit and to be reshaped accordingly.

The work of interpreting practices and roles occurs within a scaffolding that helps access resources for doing the interpretation needed for change, by drawing attention to the details that inform understanding and shape our activity. The scaffolding I find helpful in engaging the topic of pastoral leadership adaptation in congregational contexts is an integrative methodology framed by Thomas Groome's shared Christian praxis and informed by Don Browning, Ray Anderson, Mark Lau Branson, and others. Shared Christian praxis is part of the larger field of practical theology, and this work serves as a practical theology of leadership.[1]

A Brief Practical Theology Primer

Simply put, practical theology is the interaction between the theoretical (theology, philosophy, etc.) and the practical (practices, social science,

1. For a history of practical theology's development as a discipline, see Forrester, *Truthful Action*, 33–43. Also, Heitink, *Practical Theology*.

etc.) that shapes both. Academic theologians generally considered "theology proper" as the study of God and "pastoral/practical" theology as the application of theological theory in everyday contexts. In this paradigm, theory exists apart from the church for which it exists. Practical theology becomes the pragmatic application of theoretical theology in the church's work. Accordingly, academic theology risks "becoming a ghetto incapable of communicating with the culture and society in which it is embedded" and this kind of "practical" theology becomes an overly pragmatic skill set tending to "dodge or marginalise fundamental issues which are admittedly difficult to handle and almost impossible to resolve."[2] Theory or action not properly informed by the other is insufficient at best and false at worst.[3] The mutually informing interaction between theory and action is described as praxis: the cyclical process of practice informing theory, which in turn informs and revises practice (see figure 1).[4]

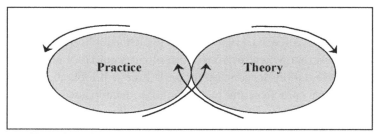

Figure 1: Practical Theology's Praxis-Oriented Cyclical Interaction of Practice and Theory.

2. Forrester, *Truthful Action*, 43. Specifically Forrester states: "The balance or tension needs to be maintained for the sake of responsible and relevant theology, to save the Church from becoming a ghetto incapable of communicating with the culture and society in which it is embedded, and for a healthy and lively university which does not dodge or marginalise fundamental issues which are admittedly difficult to handle and almost impossible to resolve."

3. Browning, *Fundamental Practical Theology*, 4–7.

4. Anderson defines ecclesial praxis as "a *dynamic human process of critical reflection carried out*" (Anderson, *Shape of Practical Theology*, 51, emphasis in original). He states further, "In praxis, God's truth is revealed through the structures of reality by which God's actions and presence are disclosed to us through our own actions. It is not our human actions that constitute the praxis of God. Rather, God acts through our human actions to reveal the truth . . . The work of God in our midst discloses to us the word of God, even as the Word of God reveals its truth in producing God's work. God's Word of truth reaches its telos in healing, making whole, and restoring God's created purpose. This is the praxis of God's Word as truth" (ibid.).

According to two of the progenitors of modern practical theology, Don Browning and Ray Anderson, practical theology's "theological praxis" recognizes that, as a faith community's practice becomes ineffective, the church investigates its basis for action and must re-evaluate in order to formulate a new, effective action.[5] In theological praxis, the discovery activity is as much a part of theological practice as the ministry activity.[6] Furthermore, it is in the ministry activity that discovery becomes necessary leading to re-evaluation of the theological theory behind the action. This is action leading to the re-evaluation of design and back to action with the intention of accomplishing of the *telos*, also discovered or rediscovered in the process.[7]

Practical theology is a theology of action which "draws heavily on the paradigm of the social sciences" for its method along with biblical and theological considerations.[8] Browning promotes a "fundamental practical theology" asserting that all practice is ultimately theological, even if un-recognized as such.[9] In practical theology, the social sciences, ancient and

5. Specifically Browning states: "When a religious community hits a crisis in its prac-tices, it then begins reflecting (asking questions) about its meaningful or theory-laden practices. It may take time to describe these practices so it can better understand the questions precipitated by the crisis. Eventually, if it is serious, the community must reex-amine the sacred texts and events that constitute the source of the norms and ideals that guide its practice. It brings its questions to these normative texts and has a conversation between its questions and these texts . . . As its practices change its questions change, and the community will invariably see different meanings in its normative texts as its situ-ations and questions change" (Browning, *Fundamental Practical Theology*, 6). Similarly, Anderson, *Soul of Ministry*, 25ff. Elsewhere, Anderson states: "[Practical theology] is more than mere practice; it is a strategic perspective that links the hermeneutical with the empirical so as to achieve an integrative model that underlies the theological task as a whole" (*Shape of Practical Theology*, 26).

6. Anderson, *Soul of Ministry*, 27.

7. Ibid., 25–28.

8. Anderson, *Shape of Practical Theology*, 25. Heitink states, "practical theology deals with God's activity through the ministry of human beings" (Heitink, *Practical Theology*, 49).

9. Browning states: "We never really move from theory to practice even when it seems we do. Theory is always embedded in practice. When theory seems to stand alone it is only because we have abstracted it from its practical context. We have become men-tally blind to the practical activities that both precede and follow it . . . Once we grasp the practice-theory-practice structure of all theology, the gulf disappears between our high-level texts and courses and the practical activity of religious education, care, preaching, and worship" (Browning, *Practical Theology*, 9).

recent histories/traditions, systematized theological reasoning, and current practices inform the strategic questions of a living faith.[10]

A Scaffold: Shared Christian Praxis

As a means to employ such a practical theology, Christian educator Thomas Groome has developed a catechetical process called "shared Christian praxis," which is helpful to this investigation of contemporary congregational leadership and the changing world. This praxis-oriented methodology provides resources for investigating the theological, sociological, historical, and experimental considerations of this book. It expects that the reflection process itself initiates change, thus promoting a contextually relevant praxis. As this is the framework we will use for investigating pastoral leadership in transitional contexts, the few pages that follow offer a short overview of this shared Christian praxis.

A brief review of Brazilian educator Paulo Freire's work is helpful as background since Groome draws heavily from Freire's pedagogy. Freire focused on "help[ing] men (and nations) help themselves, to place them in consciously critical confrontation with their problems, to make them the agents of their own recuperation."[11] The primary methodology for this process is "conscientization" or making persons aware of their contextualized subjectivity.[12]

10. In application, those "theologies" become "fully or strategic practical theology" (Browning, *Practical Theology*, 7–9). Browning identifies four questions that goad the quest for a strategic practical theology: 1) descriptive theology asks, "How do we understand this concrete situation in which we must act?"; 2) historical theology asks, "What should be our praxis in this concrete situation?"; 3) systematic theology asks, "How do we critically defend the norms of our praxis in this concrete situation?"; and 4) strategic or fully practical theology asks, "What means, strategies, and rhetorics should we use in this concrete situation?" (ibid., 55–56).

11. Freire, *Education for Critical Consciousness*, 12. More than self-help, this process of engagement empowers people with responsibility for their lives; this is a process of "enabling the people to reflect on themselves, their responsibilities, and their role . . ." resulting in "an increased capacity for choice" (ibid., 12–13).

12. Ibid., 37–51; also see Freire, *Pedagogy of the Oppressed*, 79–86. Conscientization recognizes humans as "beings of 'praxis': of action and of reflection" and connects to Groome and other practical theologians who view lived theology as a critical process by which action and reflection are integrated as a whole, as a system. See Groome, *Sharing Faith*, 135–38; Anderson, *Shape of Practical Theology*; Bevans, *Models of Contextual Theology*, 70–87; Schreiter, *Constructing Local Theologies*, 91–93; Sedmak, *Doing Local Theology*.

Dialogue (being in conversation) best serves this intention when the "facilitator/teacher" presents the "class" with a practical, real-life, contextualized question for all to consider.[13] Unlike a "banking education" model where a teacher deposits knowledge into a student, thus "anesthetizing" and "inhibiting creative power," education for critical consciousness (conscietization) is a "problem-posing education."[14] From Freire's perspective, practical theology might be as Clemens Sedmak describes it as "an invitation to wake up: to be mindful and attentive."[15]

With Freire's pedagogy in mind, the heart of shared Christian praxis is "education for conation" or wisdom that fosters "ongoing *conversion*," when awareness of oneself in a context changes the context and shapes it by their presence with others.[16] The three descriptors of Groome's education

13. Freire, *Education for Critical Consciousness*, 40–41; Freire, *Pedagogy of the Oppressed*, 79–80. Note, "the teacher is no longer merely the-one-who-teaches, but one who is himself taught in dialogue with the students, who in turn while being taught also teach" (ibid., 80).

14. Ibid., 71–86ff. This is distinct from problem solving concepts. Problem posing does not preclude a positively focused approach. Problem-posing education has the following advantages: 1) it allows people to "develop their power to perceive *the way they exist* in the world . . ."; 2) it "affirms men and women as beings in the process of becoming" and thus education is "remade in the praxis"; 3) it is "revolutionary futurity" presenting the learners not as objects trapped in an uncontrollable world, but as subjects in a world they can influence and change. Ibid., 83–85, emphasis in original.

15. Sedmak, *Doing Local Theology*, 1.

16. Groome, *Sharing Faith*, 26ff., emphasis in original. Groome identifies education for conation as existing for the purpose of "the Reign of God," a "lived Christian faith," and for the "wholeness of human freedom that is fullness of life for all" (ibid., 14–25). Groome describes these three purposes as follows. 1) The reign of God as the "metapurpose of Christian religious education highlights the enterprise as an ontological one, demanding pedagogy that engages and forms people's very selves to be historical agents of God's reign" (17). 2) "[L]ived Christian faith is the action of agent-subjects who through an interdependent community of Christian faith engage in a threefold dynamic of historical activities: *believing, trusting,* and *doing* God's will" (18; italics in the text). 3) Finally, regarding the wholeness of human freedom, "*both the impetus for and the consequences of people living in Christian faith is the wholeness of human freedom that is fullness of life for all, here and hereafter*" (22; italics in the text). According to Groome, "[T]he whole ontic 'being' of agent-subjects actively engaged in partnership with others to consciously know, desire, choose, and responsibly do what is most humanizing and life-giving for all . . . [I]t is both consequence and source of who we are and what we do in time and place . . . [I]t is our style of 'being'" (30).

Groome defines "Remembrance of Being" as: "[A] way of knowing and/or a pedagogy must engage the whole "being" of participants as agent-subjects-in-relationship, enable them to bring to mind the consciousness that arises from their "being" with others in the world and to discern how they are both shaped by and are to be responsible shapers of

for conation, "shared," "Christian," and "praxis," offer important insights regarding his goals and methodology.

Principles and Process of Shared Christian Praxis

"Praxis" demonstrates a holistic approach to the practice-theory-practice investigative work described earlier.[17] Praxis is "active," including corporeal, mental, and volitional activities where the humans-in-relationship act in real time and place.[18] This is a "reflective" process helping people engage in analytical and social-critical consciousness that through conversation investigates the theoretical and formative meaning behind activities.[19] And, praxis is "creative." In action and reflection, human beings imagine and create something unique.[20] In keeping with the concerns of this book, this praxis-oriented approach models the skills needed to lead change as required by "adaptive" situations.[21]

"Christian" in this process speaks of the Christian Story and Vision.[22] The many stories within "the Story" and many visions within "the Vision" allow for diversity within the larger Christian community.[23] Story has various elements that connect well with "the renewing and creative process

their place and time together" (Groome, *Sharing Faith*, 34). Regarding ongoing conversion, see also Guder, *Continuing Conversion*, 71ff.

17. Groome states: "[Praxis is] the defining term of his pedagogical approach which refers to the consciousness and agency that arise from and are expressed in any and every aspect of people's 'being' as agent-subjects-in-relationship, whether realized in actions that are personal, interpersonal, sociopolitical, or cosmic" (Groome, *Sharing Faith*, 136).

18. Groome, *Sharing Faith*, 137.

19. Ibid.

20. Ibid., 137–38.

21. Heifetz, *Leadership without Easy Answers*, 72ff; Heifetz and Linsky, *Leadership on the Line*, 11ff.

22. Groome, *Sharing Faith*, 138–42.

23. Per Groome, "Story and Vision are metaphors that symbolize the whole historical reality of 'the Christian faith'" (ibid., 138). "Story symbolizes the living tradition of the Christian community before us and around us (the church) as it takes historical expression in a myriad of different forms . . . These forms include scriptures, traditions, and liturgies; creeds, dogmas, doctrines, and theologies; sacraments and rituals, symbols, myths, gestures, and religious language patterns; spiritualities, values, laws, and expected life-styles; songs and music, dance and drama; art, artifacts, and architecture; memories of holy people, the sanctification of time and celebration of holy times, the appreciation of holy places; community structures and forms of governance; and so on" (ibid., 139).

that invites discernment, choice, and decision" (i.e., events, characters, beliefs, values, emotions, tense).[24] Vision, according to Groome, has the reign on God in mind.[25] Neither Story nor Vision can be excluded; they are interconnected.[26]

Finally, "shared" promotes a communal, praxis-oriented, Christian, practical theology. Groome's *shared* pedagogy implies two things: 1) partnership, participation, and dialogue, and 2) the dialectical hermeneutics between "praxis" and "Christian."[27] First, people share in the learning process so that there is minimized teacher/student distinction; people collaborate and participate together in learning, even when a specific facilitator leads.[28] Against societal and current ecclesial forces pushing for individualized, competitive, clericalized, and authoritarian relationships, Christian identity is found through membership in an "inclusive discipleship of equals."[29] Second, a community works back and forth between current praxis and the Christian Story/Vision. In so doing, each interprets the other so that understanding expands and enhances critical reflection.[30]

24. Ibid.

25. Ibid. In Groome, "God's reign" is similar to others who reject Constantinian Christendom. Groome spends great effort clarifying this, illustrating his concern with how this concept has been misused in Christendom, and justifying its continued use in an appropriately biblical manner (ibid., 14–17). See also Brownson et al., *StormFront*, throughout, but especially 38–44; Grenz, *Theology*, especially 22–23; Guder, *Continuing Conversion*, throughout, but especially 44–48; Harvey, *Another City*, throughout, but especially 35ff.; Lohfink, *Jesus and Community*, throughout, but especially 26–29; Moltmann, *Trinity and the Kingdom*, throughout, but especially 191ff.; Stassen and Gushee, *Kingdom Ethics*, throughout, but especially 19–78.

26. Groome usually writes them together as "Story/Vision." Groome, *Sharing Faith*, 139. Three non-polemic dyads further clarify Groome's understanding of the Christian nature of his pedagogy: historical and practical, belonging and ownership, engaging and dialogical. Ibid., 140–42.

27. Ibid., 143–46.

28. Groome writes, "The word *shared* points to this approach as one of mutual partnership, active participation, and dialogue with oneself, with others, with God, and with Story/Vision of Christian faith" (ibid., 142, emphasis in the original). For comparison, see Freire, *Education for Critical Consciousness*, 40–41, 123ff; Freire, *Pedagogy of the Oppressed*, 80, 129. Groome further clarifies that the method for such partnership and participation is the dialogical work of a community reflecting as individuals, as a group, and with their context. Groome, *Sharing Faith*, 143–44.

29. Groome, *Sharing Faith*, 142. Here, Groome cites Schüssler Fiorenza, *In Memory of Her*, 154.

30. Groome, *Sharing Faith*, 145.

An Integrative Praxis-Based Methodology

Groome's shared Christian praxis has important connections to change as an educational methodology for "critical consciousness." He intentionally raises communal dialogue as a focal point for congregational life. The focusing activities and five movements, which are described in more detail in the appendix of this book, provide a helpful framework for this conversation.[31]

While the author-reader relationship prohibits the dialogue envisioned by Groome, the strength of his overall approach is reason for choosing it as the frame for this study. Some limits to this approach are worked out as part of a larger dialogue between academic and congregational communities. Browning, Anderson, Branson, Blackaby, and many others contribute to the overall work in ways that integrate into the goal of reorienting ourselves to God's action and our participation in that action with regards to leadership in Christ's church. Consider this book a practiced framework of Groome's focusing activities and five movements. This introduction serves as a "focusing activity" by identifying this investigation to be a study of leadership in liminal contexts.

31. See appendix A.

PART ONE

Naming and Reflecting on Forces that Shape Us

Chapter 1

"Change is Nature"

One of the "joys" of living with young children is their unique ability and desire to watch the same movie over and over again. When our daughter was a preschooler, one of her favorites was the Pixar classic *Ratatouille*, a film about Remy, a rat living in Paris who has a gift for cooking. For me, the most poignant scene of the movie comes during an interaction between Remy and his father, Django.

When Remy reveals that he has been working with a human, Django takes Remy to see the window of the famed French exterminator Aurouze, which features dead rats hanging in traps. Django shows Remy the traps explaining them as the consequence of being too comfortable with humans and pronounces, "This is the way things are. You can't change nature." Shaken but undaunted, Remy boldly proclaims: "No . . . No, Dad. Change is nature."[1]

"Change is nature." All around us the ground seems to be shifting. For instance, the instantaneous high-speed transmission of information made possible by the Internet and handheld devices, the economic impact of globalization, and the socio-political changes occurring as a result of these influences all have challenged what have been generally accepted foundations in Western, US culture. One place where this disorientation has been acutely experienced has been in churches and denominational structures. While change can create contexts for disorientation, it is the perception and experience of loss that creates resistance to change. To further aggravate things, the practices and methodologies historically employed to lead people through change exacerbates this disorientation. I suggest that there

1. *Ratatouille.*

3

are important questions we need to be asking that will inform how we live in and through disorientation.

Are we condemned only to endure this disorientation? Is our best option to try and recapture the past and relive glory days gone-by? How might our current practices of top-down, expertise-driven leadership make matters worse? What would it mean for congregations to encounter God and be shaped by the encounter in ways that are beyond our control? What would it mean for pastoral leaders to likewise be shaped as part of the congregation? What would happen for us and to us if we recognized God at work in our disorientation, seeing it as God's means for shaping us?

Captured and Colonized

Reading the Bible should sometimes make readers wonder, "How could they believe that?" There are certain stories and passages in Scripture that are particularly befuddling. This is certainly the case with many parts of the exodus story, but especially the beginning of Numbers 14. Prior to Numbers 14, the people that God rescued from Egypt complain openly on several occasions about being in the wilderness. As they complain, they longingly wish for those "good ole days" back in Egypt, where they remember meat pots, and free fish, and melons, cucumbers, leeks, onion, and garlic.[2] Thus by the time we get to Numbers 14, the people are in full rebellion.

Having made it through the wilderness to the borders of the promised land, God's people are now confronted with the reality that the land is occupied—and the occupants are giants. Rather than trusting God to lead them to their inheritance, they choose rebellion instead. As Numbers 14:1–4 states:

> That night all the people of the community raised their voices and wept aloud. All the Israelites grumbled against Moses and Aaron, and the whole assembly said to them, "If only we had died in Egypt! Or in this desert! Why is the LORD bringing us to this land only to let us fall by the sword? Our wives and children will be taken as plunder. Wouldn't it be better for us to go back to Egypt?" And they said to each other, "We should choose a leader and go back to Egypt."[3]

2. Exod 14: 12; 16: 2–3; Num 11: 4.
3. NIV.

It is hard to fathom. The people who groaned under slavery's burden and who cried out for help prompting God to respond now wanted to return to that slavery![4] God's people were talking about killing God's representative, Moses, and choosing a new leader to take them back to Egypt. How could they?

And yet we could ask the question differently. Why should they not want to go back? After all in light of their context, slavery offered a kind of comfort, a predictability and clarity, which was easy to understand and recognize. The wilderness was unpredictable, uncontrollable, and uncomfortable. Compared to their situation in the wilderness, slavery worked—except that it didn't. It was never God's intention that the plans for the redemption of humanity and all of creation would be lost in Egypt. God remembered accurately their true situation in slavery, looked past their discomfort in the wilderness, and envisioned a future that was being shaped in the process. And so he does for us as well.

History is filled with seasons of turmoil and tumult that from human perspective seem like tragedy. Alan Roxburgh and Fred Romanuk describe this upheaval as "discontinuous change" where change is "disruptive and unanticipated . . . challenging our assumptions" and where the skills we have learned are unhelpful.[5] This kind of change results in such upheaval and turmoil that there is "no getting back normal;" discontinuous change "transform a culture forever, tipping it into something new."[6] But while they may seem like tragedy, in God's work these might actually be seasons of shaping and reorientation toward a new future in keeping with God's preferred future for us.

Roxburgh identifies this process of transformation as "liminal transition."[7] Using the socio-anthropological framework of Victor Turner, Roxburgh identifies three stages of societal transition that describe the tumultuous situation of the Israelites leaving Egypt and perhaps describe the Western church's current situation. This process, which is described by the terms "separation," "liminal," and "reaggregation," helps to "describe how a group is transformed in its outward relationships to other groups and

4. Exod 2:23–24; 3:7.

5. Roxburgh and Romanuk, *Missional Leader*, 6–9, quote from pg. 7. They compare this to continuous change where what is happening is "expected, anticipated, and managed" (ibid.). In Heifetz and Linsky, *Leadership on the Line* these ideas are described using the terms "technical" and "adaptive" change.

6. Roxburgh and Romanuk, *Missional Leader*, 7.

7. Roxburgh, *Missionary Congregation*, 27.

institutions, and, equally important, in its own inner life."[8] I find the terms "orientation," "liminality," and "reorientation" helpful.

"Orientation" is the way things are in a socio-cultural context. It is the process of living with certain social norms and rules through which a people engage in relatively fixed rituals and roles and by which they engage established and accepted institutions. These norms and rules may be codified (made law) or may be simply understood by the members of the context. Often these norms and rules are so engrained that most people never realize their existence. In sociological terms, not following these social norms (whether codified or not) is understood as "deviance."

At the outset of "liminality," socio-cultural contexts begin to shift. The beginning of this shift is what Roxburgh refers to as "separation." He notes that "separation" is the removal of those socio-cultural norms and rules with their roles and relationships to institutions that leads to a "fundamental change in social location."[9] Separation in this sense leads to a marginalization and disestablishment. Roxburgh describes this marginalization and disestablishment as leaving us with frameworks that "seem disconnected from the emerging cultural context" where "our words are often received as a strange, foreign language."[10] This liminality is described by such words as "vulnerable," "anxious," "confusion," and "potential."[11]

The danger with liminality is that people have this unique knack for looking back to "Egypt" and to long for a return to those "better days" of slavery. This desire is a sure indicator of cultural captivity and colonization. And it brings to mind Romans 12:2, which is the context verse for this book's title, *Transforming Pastoral Leadership*.

In Romans 12:2, Paul challenges the Roman church, "Do not be conformed to this world, but be transformed by the renewing of your mind . . . ."[12] One interesting idea about this verse is that both the word συσχηματίζεσθε (translated "be conformed") and μεταμορφοῦσθε (translated "be transformed") are both passive voice words.[13] In Romans 12:2,

8. Ibid.

9. Ibid., 27–28; quote from 28.

10. Roxburgh, *Sky is Falling*, 20.

11. Roxburgh, *Missionary Congregation*, 29–30, 32.

12. NRSV.

13. To explain simply, active voice infers that the subject of a sentence performs the action: "I eat." The subject, "I" is doing the action, "eat." The passive infers the action is occurring upon the subject: "I am being eaten." Some unstated actor is performing the action on the subject.

things are happening to God's people. On the one hand we might be conformed and if so, then it is the world that is conforming us to look like it. The world, with its "patterns," "customs," and "behaviors" (phrases used by more modern translations),[14] is working to make us look like it. As an illustration, consider a Jell-O mold. Like Jell-O, people are poured into a container of culture and whatever the shape of the container is the shape they come out. For the Hebrews of the exodus, it was the cultural captivity of slavery. The work was so thorough that on the cusp of achieving their goal of realizing God's promise, they desired a return to slavery instead.

This cultural captivity is at work today as well. As seen in the next few chapters, church life has been powerfully shaped by patterns, customs, and behaviors of the world with regard to leadership structures and practices. For now these are simply named as "expertise-driven, pastor-centric leadership.

14. See the NIV and the NLT for example.

Chapter 2

Becoming the "Expert"

Historically, there are seasons of upheaval so massive that they change the fundamentals of how societies function. From a biblical account, we see such seasons in the stories of the exodus and exile. The Hebrew people are profoundly shaped in the context of God's activity during the decades of change and reorientation experienced in their rescue from Egypt and their exile in the East. Mark Lau Branson, Alan Roxburgh, and their colleagues at the Missional Network suggest that it is in precisely these kinds of contexts God's activity is most observable in part because of the disorientation experience.[1]

An ecological illustration I find helpful in describing this kind of change is that of the transition of a large fish tank from freshwater to saltwater. Freshwater is defined as water that contains less than .5g of the minerals classified as "salts" whereas saltwater has 35g of these same minerals per thousand grams of water.[2] Imagine these seasons of change as a large freshwater tank with an industrial sized canister of salt resting overhead. The freshwater tank and its inhabitants exist in a state of equilibrium. The salt container is then punctured allowing salt to begin infiltrating the norm of the freshwater tank. Over time the water's salinity will change to the point that the tank becomes a saltwater tank. In order for its inhabitants to survive, they must adapt or change. There is also the transition water that is not freshwater and not saltwater: brackish water. Brackish water is where freshwater and seawater meets in rivers and along coastlines. In our

1. For examples see: Roxburgh, *Missionary Congregation*; Branson, "Reflecting on the Gospel," and *Journal of Missional Practice.*

2. U.S. Office of Naval Research, "Ocean Water."

metaphor imagine brackish water as the liminal time between two epochs or eras.

This metaphor is a description of the state in which many in the West see the church. And more to the point, this metaphor helps us to understand the nature of pastoral leadership and the forces that have shaped much of our current state of transition. It is the assumption of this book that much of the dissonance facing pastoral leaders in the Western church today arises from the fact that after adapting centuries earlier to our freshwater context, many find themselves in a new state of brackish water that is becoming salty again.

Along with a changing external environment, pastoral leaders are also facing a changing internal environment. It may be an overstatement, but there seem to be few other professions where a person can be as highly trained as a pastoral leader and be maligned by her or his clients for being so well trained. There is an odd interplay of the expectation of expertise and the expectation that such training should not be trusted. Pastoral leaders are often expected to complete the Master of Divinity degree (one of the longest professional, post-baccalaureate programs in academia) in order to be worthy of hire. Yet, upon application of this training in many church contexts, the pastoral leader is often viewed as a threat to the "way we do things."[3]

Pastoral leaders often are seen as a threat because they often are a threat to the status quo. These men and women have spent years of training to consider carefully what and how the church should best represent God's mission in the world. They have received a particular skill set that often promises to assist them in "implementing" much needed change within the congregations they will serve. In the hiring process as in the educational processes, pastoral leaders are often expected to demonstrate certain skill sets that promote leadership as visionary and expertise.[4]

3. Jackson Carroll notes that conflict, which often causes pastors to doubt their calling, comes first around disputes over pastoral leadership, among other significant issues. He notes that these struggles are connected to changes in congregational life, and need not be negative, if "worked through constructively" (Carroll, *God's Potters*, 167–69). It is also important to note that Carroll's findings support both a double narrative that ministry is both a troubled profession and a deeply satisfying calling. Ibid., 185. These finding support the agenda of this chapter, that, as a profession, the pastorate is troubled.

4. Adair T. Lummis's work on identifying these skills is notable. In *Pulpit and Pew*, Lummis's research identifies the ideal leader as follows: "He or she would have the ability to envision theologically faithful patterns for their congregation's future and the entrepreneurial talents necessary to propose effective methods of realizing these patterns. In

Yet so often, these technical skills and preparation aimed at technical application leaves these women and men ill-prepared to address both the deepest kinds of change most churches are in need of experiencing as well as the conflict which results from resistance to adaptation. As pastoral leaders attempt adaptive kinds of change through technical leadership application, they often achieve disastrous results including diminished congregational vitality through loss of mission, disempowered laity, personal burnout and exhaustion, and professional disillusionment.

This is not to mean that technical leadership and expertise have no place in leadership.[5] After all, we certainly prefer to hear a sermon from someone who knows how to properly interpret and communicate the Scripture than someone who botches the message. Rather, this is a critique of misapplying expertise leadership in adaptive contexts where new and different perspectives are required of congregations. This misapplication concurs with a rationalized cultural overvaluation of knowledge, expert systems, and expertise.[6] Accordingly, this chapter examines how the Western church has come to define pastoral leadership as a specialized area of expertise for pastors, and exegetes and critiques expert systems as a product of rationalized modernity.[7] This allows us to acknowledge the limits of

---

addition such pastors would possess the charisma and people skills to mobilize congregational support for change, giving members voice in refining the vision and putting the plan into operation. Lay and regional leaders also want pastors who can preach wonderful sermons, conduct inspiring worship services, competently teach, care, counsel, and console. In choosing a new pastor, search committees differ in the abilities and characteristics to which they give priority, based on their past experiences with clergy and a host of other factors and influences" (Lummis, "What Do Lay People," 24).

5. See Heifetz and Linsky, *Leadership on the Line*, 14, 18, 110–13.

6. This work utilizes Giddens definitions of expert systems and expertise where expert systems are those mechanisms that disembed and organize professional skill and technical knowledge from localized social contexts and make it accessible across space and time. Giddens, *Consequences of Modernity*, 27–28. Expertise is the technical skill that comes through specialized training in and through the expert system, that certain individuals apply on behalf of laypersons of that particular system. Ibid., 27–28, 90, 144–45. Experts are persons trained in the expertise of a system and who serve as access points to expertise for laypersons of that particular system. Ibid., 27–28, 90. As an example: doctors (experts) are trained with specialized medical skills (expertise) acquired from the field of medicine (expert system) on behalf of patients (laypersons).

7. The critique of expert, technical leadership is part of a larger critique of clericalism, and its detrimental affects on churches and pastors. Hobbs, "Faith Twisted by Culture," 106–9; Guder, *Continuing Conversion*, throughout, but especially 120–41; Moltmann, *Trinity and the Kingdom*, 191ff.; Ogden, *Unfinished Business*; Roxburgh, "Missional Leadership," 190–98. See also, Hall and Elliot, "Pastors."

technical expertise and to discuss how mistrust of the pastor, as the perceived "expert system" bearer, allows people to avoid the work of adaptive change.[8]

The Historical and Cultural Context of Expertise

For modern persons, the existence of "expert systems" is a mundane reality. Most people experience these systems in a multiplicity of ways and never question their message, method, or meaning—until a system fails them.[9] Pastors are largely viewed as experts who employ the expertise of their particular expert system for the benefit of their constituents in the church.[10] However, in dealing with cultural issues of values, beliefs, and norms, technical expertise and expert systems inadequately address the kinds of change necessary for transformation in adaptive contexts. The work of Stephen Toulmin and Anthony Giddens as conversation partners are helpful due to the way Toulmin offers historical insight into the shaping of the forces under discussion and the way Giddens's framing of the outcome of that shaping seems to connect with my perception of ecclesial consequences. This is not to imply that there are not other exceptional critiques offered by others—notably Max Weber, Charles Taylor, George Ritzer, and Stanley Tambiah—but instead to identify the context in which these forces were shaped in order to develop a more appropriate understanding of our current experiences.

To understand the development of expert systems as a product of rationality, it is important to clarify the progression from humanism to the quest for universal certainty. Modernity is often portrayed as a product of seventeenth-century rationality and its champions Descartes, Galileo, and Newton. However, modernity occurs in two phases with the first having

---

8. Heifetz and Linsky point out that, "shouldering the adaptive work of others is risky . . . [W]hen you take on an issue, you *become* that issue in the eyes of many; it follows, then, that the way to get rid of the issue is to get rid of you" (Heifetz and Linsky, *Leadership on the Line,* 121, emphasis in original). They go on to clarify that, "To meet adaptive challenges, people must change their hearts as well as their behaviors . . . [S]olutions are achieved when the 'people with the problem' go through the process together to become 'the people with the solution.' The issues have to be internalized, owned, and ultimately resolved by relevant parties to achieve enduring progress" (127).

9. As an example in the medical field, see: Carey, "Medical Guesswork," 72ff.

10. See Hobbs, "Faith Twisted by Culture," 106–9; Roxburgh and Romanuk, *Missional Leader,* 11–13.

occurred in the sixteenth century with humanists Montaigne, Shakespeare, and others.[11]

Humanist Modernity

Toulmin contends that modernity's ascent occurred in two distinct phases with the first being defined as the "literary and humanistic phase" of the modern age.[12] In this initial phase practicality and flexibility shape the human understanding of the world.[13] Humanism valued the context, the concrete, the physical, and the time-specific realities of people permitting flexibility in understanding that allowed the humanists to acknowledge and accept uncertainty as part of being human.[14]

Apparent in this account of early modernity is that the uncertainty of the sixteenth century is held in tension with flexibility and stability. These thoughtful persons (Leonardo de Vinci, Michelangelo, Shakespeare, etc.) saw daily and practical significance in their work while remaining open to criticism and revision, all the while operating within the sphere of human existence and location: in time, place, and experience. As a result, tolerance and humble dialogue were valued.[15]

---

11. In this context, "humanism" is used within its historical confines, which includes the role of church and faith as instruments for understanding human agency and value. It is not to be confused with contemporary "secular humanism."

12. Toulmin, *Cosmopolis*, 23.

13. Ibid., 24. Toulmin declares, "Before 1600, theoretical inquiries were balanced against discussions of the concrete practical issues."

14. Toulmin states, "Montaigne claimed in the *Apology* that 'unless some one thing is found of which we are *completely* certain, we can be certain about nothing': he believed that there is no general truth about which certainty is possible, and concluded we can claim certainty about nothing" (ibid., 42).

15. Of Aquinas and Erasmus, Toulmin explains, "Neither of them claimed that human beings, however wise and inspired, could put matters of faith and doctrine beyond the scope of reconsideration and revision . . . Despite all its turmoil and religious divisions, the sixteenth century had been, by comparison, a time when the voice of sweet reasonableness made itself heard, and was widely valued. From 1610 on, and most of all after 1618, the argument became active, bloody, and strident. Everyone now talked at the top of his voice, and the humanists' quiet discussions of finitude, and the need for toleration, no longer won a hearing" (ibid., 79).

Modern Rationality: The Quest for Certainty

In contrast to the humanists of the sixteenth century, the transitional think-ers of the seventeenth century—Descartes, Galileo, and Newton—pressed an agenda aimed at developing *rational* absolutes in a quest for certainty.[16] The rationalist's retreat from the flexibility and humility described above occurs in four areas: oral to written, particular to universal, local to general, and timely to timeless.

First, regarding the retreat from rhetoric and oral tradition, sixteenth-century humanist scholars accepted that oral argumentation and logic were compatible in philosophy while the seventeenth-century rationalists shifted away from rhetoric and toward the written. The rationalists chose to preserve purported certainty in what can be re-read, without interpretive errors—unlike the spoken word—which in their view required interpreta-tion of verbal and non-verbal language.[17] Second, the rationalists moved from situational to universal concepts. While the humanists preferred theological and philosophical use of "case analyses" in dealing with ethical concerns (what is proper in a particular context an time), the rationalists shifted to emphasizing universal principles that purportedly transcended specificity (what is proper in all contexts and times).[18]

Third was a move from local to general. Renaissance humanists found ethnography, geography, anthropology, and history to be worthwhile fields of study as the local customs and practices of communities offered insight into the human experience.[19] However, the rationalists believed that "philosophical understanding never comes from accumulating experience of particular individuals and specific cases . . . [R]ationality impose[d] on

16. Toulmin contends that these are the minds of rationality and the "Quest for Cer-tainty" (ibid., 45–87).

17. Likewise, they wrongly assumed that the written eliminates emotionalism and social considerations allowing for evaluation of pure thought. Toulmin writes, "The research program of modern philosophy thus set aside all questions about argumenta-tion—among particular people in specific situations, dealing with concrete cases, where varied things were at state—in favor of *proofs* that could be set down in writing, and judged as written" (ibid., 31).

18. Ibid., 31–32. As Toulmin states, "After the 1650s, Henry More and the Cambridge Platonists made ethics a field for general abstract theory, divorced from concrete prob-lems of moral practice; and, since then, modern philosophers have generally assumed that—like God and Freedom, or Mind and Matter—the Good and Just conform to time-less and universal principles" (32).

19. Ibid., 32–33.

philosophy a need to seek out abstract, general ideas and principles, by which particulars can be connected together."[20]

Finally, issues of the medieval age focused on the specifics of particular moments in time.[21] This time-specific consciousness of the moment was lost to the rationalists. Removal of time made it possible for "transient human affairs" to take an inferior position for rationalism: "[From] Descartes' time on, attention was focused on timeless principles that hold good at all times equally: the permanent was in, the transitory was out."[22]

Abstract Systems as Disembedding Mechanisms

To achieve rational absolutes, certain disembedding mechanisms were required to decontextualize principles and skills steeped in time and place. "Disembedding mechanisms" refers to the process by which social relations and concepts are "lifted out of," or removed from "local contexts" and are "rearticulated across indefinite tracts of time-space."[23] This process can be described as a distinguishing mark of modern institutions that results in the "acceleration of the time-space distanciation which modernity introduces."[24] Hence, the rationalists' work is expressed by the creation of abstract systems that transcend time and space.

Disembedding occurs in part through abstract systems which are described by the two mechanisms "intrinsically involved" in modern social

20. According to the seventeenth-century philosophers, "abstract axioms were in, concrete diversity was out" (ibid., 33).

21. Toulmin states it this way, "All problems in practice of law and medicine are 'timely'. They refer to specific moments in time—now not later, today not yesterday. In them, 'time is of the essence'; and they are decided, in Aristotle's phrase, *pros ton kairon*, 'as the occasion requires'" (ibid., 33). This seems remarkably close to Jesus teaching that his followers should "not worry about tomorrow, for tomorrow will bring worries of its own. Today's trouble is enough for today" (Matt 6:34, NRSV).

22. The aim of Descartes and his followers "was to bring to light permanent structures underlying all the changeable phenomena of Nature" (Toulmin, *Cosmopolis*, 34).

23. Giddens, *Consequences of Modernity*, 18. This is not unlike Charles Taylor's disembedding of the individual, which he describes as part of the disenchantment of society. See Taylor, *A Secular Age*, 146–58. The distinction is that Taylor's agenda is focused on the person as actor where as in our current discussion we are concerned with the tools with which the actor acts: systems, knowledge, and application of systems and knowledge in vocation.

24. Giddens, *Consequences of Modernity*, 18.

institutions: *symbolic tokens* and *expert systems*.[25] The abstract nature of symbolic tokens and expert systems fits well within Ritzer's definition of "nothing:" "Nothing can be defined as a *'social form that is generally centrally conceived, controlled and comparatively devoid of distinct substantive content.'*[26] These abstract systems exist as the elimination of "distinct substantive content."[27] Symbolic tokens and expert systems are the application of the rationalists' universal, general, and timeless conceptualizations. To accomplish their purposes, "disembedding mechanisms, both symbolic tokens and expert systems, depend upon *trust*."[28]

Symbolic Tokens

Although not as applicable to our discussion, a brief overview of symbolic tokens is worthwhile. Symbolic tokens have no intrinsic value, but represent a determined value. Money is a good example. The bills and coins hold little intrinsic value, but symbolize confidence in the issuing government. While assets may back this value, these assets may or may not be sufficient to guarantee the value of the currency. Another example is credit. A credit card has no intrinsic value, however it symbolizes a person's, company's, or organization's promise to repay its borrowed value. It is possible to see here the importance of trust. Stable governments' currency holds its value. Unstable governments' currency is quickly devalued.[29]

25. Ibid., 22.

26. Ritzer, *McDonaldization of Society*, 167.

27. Again using money, in the early US each state issued its own currency backed by its own assets. Once the Federal Reserve banking system came into existence, notes became uniform, and for a time backed by hard assets (i.e., silver certificate). Despite economic crises, this has been the driving concept in Europe with the Euro currency. This unifying currency crosses nation-state boundaries in Europe generally devoid of French, Italian, German, or other national distinctiveness. Levin, *A Guide to the Euro*. However, this may be moot considering the use of credit worldwide. A European spends as freely with credit in Asia, North America, South America or Africa (where credit is accepted) as in their own city or town. See Anonymous, "The End of the Cash Era," 13; Anonymous, "A Cash Call," 71–73.

28. Giddens, *Consequences of Modernity*, 26, emphasis in original.

29. Ibid., 22–26; Giddens, *Modernity and Self-Identity*, 134. See also Ritzer's globalization of "nothing." Ritzer, *McDonaldization of Society*, 159–84; Ritzer, *Globalization of Nothing*.

Expert Systems

Of our primary concern, the development of expert systems created a process by which specialized technical and professional information and skill is gathered from localized contexts, organized in institutional structures, and disseminated across space and time. As a result this attempt at abstracting knowledge ironically creates a kind of unknowing that requires mediation. These generalized institutional structures and expert systems are heavily reliant on the trust of laypersons in experts as access points to the information the systems contain.

Reflexivity and Institutionalization of Knowledge

The disembedding of knowledge has resulted in a kind of reflexivity or self-reflection within rationalized modernity creating the necessity of the expert system as a means to handling this accumulation and disseminating it.[30] With the advent of technological advances such as the printing press, radio, television, and computer, the amount of information that can be acquired and disseminated has increased exponentially. Each new technology expands the process.[31] More importantly, with each advance, what is "known" supercedes that which came before, overwhelming human sensibilities:

> Modernity is constituted in and through reflexively applied knowledge, but the equation of knowledge with certitude has turned out to be misconceived. We are abroad in a world which is thoroughly constituted through reflexively applied knowledge, but where at the same time we can never be sure that any given element of that knowledge will not be revised . . . No knowledge under conditions of modernity is knowledge in the "old" sense, where "to know" is to be certain. This applies equally to the natural and the social sciences.[32]

30. Giddens explains: "In all cultures, social practices are routinely altered in the light of ongoing discoveries which feed into them. But only in the era of modernity is the revision of convention radicalized to apply (in principle) to all aspects of human life, including technological intervention into the material world" (ibid., 39).

31. The printing press increased the availability of the written word; the radio made worldwide events available by sound instantaneously; the television made those events immediately visible, the computer sped up the process of accumulating, correcting, and producing written information; and the internet made information instantaneously available nearly anywhere at nearly any time.

32. Ibid., 39–40.

With the accumulation of constantly fluctuating knowledge, the storage of increasing quantities of information requires the creation of institutions to house, maintain, and disseminate this knowledge, thus establishing expert systems. Robert Wuthnow states, "People typically do not invent or adopt new ideas without the assistance of some institution that has disseminated these ideas. The time and space between ideas and the social environment are thus mediated by institutions."[33] This institutionalization is critical in order to create the trust necessary for the system to work. However, because this trust is being placed in "nothing," the interface between the expert system and the recipient of the system's expertise becomes critical.

This expert, as the "access point," experiences the client's personal trust as described above. Expert systems make information and ideas general, universal and timeless (and mostly written) and only accessible and applicable by appropriately trained persons.[34] Once gathered knowledge could be systemized and institutionalized then it could be disseminated so that all had access to the same information and the same standard of information as absolute.

33. Wuthnow, *Meaning and Moral Order*, 265. Wuthnow contends that for a system of knowledge to become institutionalized it must meet four criteria: autonomy, social resources, communication and organization, and legitimacy. "First, they require a sufficient degree of *autonomy* (differentiation) from other organizations to be able to apply resources to the attainment of certain ends. Second, *social resources* must be available for the staffing of creative (productive) and administrative roles and for the payment of others costs incurred in developing and disseminating cultural forms. Third, an internal systems of *communication and organization* must be present in order for the various activities involved in producing cultural forms to be coordinated. And finally, a degree of *legitimacy* is required in order to sustain favorable relations with centers of power, the state, potential clients or recruits, and other significant collectives in the broader environment. When these conditions have been satisfied, a cultural form has become institutionalized" (ibid., 265).

34. This is what Giddens refers to when he states, "By expert systems I mean systems of technical accomplishment or professional expertise that organize large areas of the material and social environment in which we live today" (*Consequences of Modernity*, 27). This organization or systemization is a process that disembeds information from context, hence "providing 'guarantees' of expectations across distanciated time-space" (ibid., 28).

Trust and Access Points

Trust may be understood as "a form of 'faith,' in which the confidence vested in probable outcomes expresses a commitment to something rather than just a cognitive understanding."[35] From another perspective, Francis Fukuyama defines trust as "the expectation that arises within a community of regular, honest, and cooperative behavior, based on commonly shared norms, on the part of other members of the community."[36] From trust develops the context for "social capital."[37] While social capital can be achieved without trust, it would be problematic in a relational, ecclesial context.[38] Thus, regarding trust, social capital "is an instantiated informal norm that promotes cooperation between two or more individuals."[39] This trust remains essential to the success of disembedding abstract systems.

35. Ibid., 27. "Trust exists . . . when we 'believe in' someone or some principle . . . " (ibid.). Giddens balks at the use of "faith" in this context arguing that "trust is not the same as faith in the reliability of a person or systems; it is what is derived from that faith . . . All trust is in a certain sense blind trust!" (ibid., 33).

36. Fukuyama, *Trust,* 26. He goes on to explain that these norms can be: "deep 'value' questions like the nature of God or justice, but they can also encompass secular norms like professional standards and codes of behavior. That is, we trust a doctor not to do us deliberate injury because we expect him or her to live by the Hippocratic oath and the standards of the medical profession."

37. "Social capital is a capability that arises from the prevalence of trust in a society or in certain parts of it . . . Social capital differs from other forms of human capital insofar as it is usually created and transmitted through cultural mechanisms like religion, tradition, or historical habit. Economists typically argue that the formation of social groups can be explained as the result of voluntary contract between individuals who have made the rational calculation that cooperation is in their long-term self-interests. By this account, trust is not necessary for cooperation: enlightened self-interest, together with legal mechanisms like contracts, can compensate for an absence of trust and allow strangers jointly to create an organization that will work for a common purpose" (ibid., 26).

38. To this end, Fukuyama clarifies that: "[W]hile contract and self-interest are important sources of association, the most effective organizations are based on communities of shared ethical values. These communities do not require extensive contract and legal regulation of their relations because prior moral consensus gives members of the group a basis for trust" (ibid, 26).

39. Fukuyama, "Social Capital," 3. Further, Fukuyama states, "By this definition, trust, networks, civil society, and the like, which have been associated with social capital, are all epiphenomenal, arising because of social capital but not constituting social capital itself." From Giddens: "Trust is different from 'weak inductive knowledge,' but the faith it involves does not always presume a conscious act of commitment. In conditions of modernity, attitudes of trust toward abstract systems are usually routinely incorporated into the continuity of day-to-day activities and are to a large extent enforced by the intrinsic circumstances of daily life. Thus trust is much less of a 'leap to commitment' than

Discussing the role of trust in abstract systems (i.e., token symbols and expert systems), Giddens determines that "trust is only demanded where there is ignorance—either of knowledge claims of technical experts or of the thoughts and intentions of intimates upon whom a person relies."[40] There are two particular kinds of trust: trust in systems and trust in persons.

Trust in systems is faith, which "is sustained in the workings of knowledge of which the lay person is largely ignorant."[41] This is the expert's trust of the system. "Trust in persons," states Giddens, "involves facework commitments, in which indicators of integrity of others (within given arenas of action) are sought."[42] This becomes especially clear as Giddens develops the issue of ontological trust, which he identifies as the basic human trust or reliance upon another for ones own well-being. Drawing on Erik Erickson's work, Giddens underscores the importance of the social context as the arena in which trust must occur.[43] Security and a sense of self reside with those in whom we trust. In other words, people need people in order to be people. Therefore, it is indispensable for laypersons that expert systems have "trustworthy" representatives. This is the layperson's trust in the expert.

The disembedding of knowledge and systems requires a reembedding of trust into certain localized individuals, which Giddens calls "facework commitments." Facework commitments are "trust relations which are sustained by or expressed in social connections established in circumstances of copresence."[44] In relation to expert systems, this is trust in persons versus the "faceless commitments" of trust in the abstract systems.[45] There is an assumption that the system is "near infallible" by the nature of its accumulated knowledge and is therefore trustworthy. The social nature of human beings (a theological point emphasized later in chapter 6) requires a personal encounter and the expectation that the persons representing these systems are doubly trustworthy: 1) because of their expertise, and

a tacit acceptance of circumstances in which other alternatives are largely foreclosed" (Giddens, *Consequences of Modernity*, 90).

40. Giddens, *Consequences of Modernity*, 89.

41. Ibid., 88.

42. Ibid.

43. Ibid., 92–100. He states in *Modernity and Self-Identity*, "Attitudes of trust, in relation to specific situations, persons or systems, and on a more genralised level, are directly connected to the psychological *security* of individuals and groups" (19).

44. Giddens, *Consequences of Modernity,* 80.

45. Ibid., 84.

2) because of a commitment perceived as "personal" by the recipient of their expertise. Giddens describes this as "encounters with representatives of abstract systems" which "take on the characteristics of trustworthiness associated with friendship and intimacy."[46]

This facework-oriented trust counterbalances the trust in faceless commitment required for trust in systems of knowledge. Likewise, trust in systems is amplified because of the trust in the individual representative. Giddens further clarifies:

> At access points the facework commitments which tie lay actors into trust relations ordinarily involve displays of manifest trust-worthiness and integrity, coupled with an attitude of 'business-as-usual,' or unflappability . . . There is no skill so carefully honed and no form of expert knowledge so comprehensive that elements of hazard or luck do not come into play . . . [F]acework commit-ments are generally important as a mode of generating continu-ing trustworthiness . . . Reembedding here represents a means of anchoring trust in the trustworthiness and integrity of colleagues.[47]

While believing that the system has the information and therefore the power to help, a person's real trust is in the personal representatives of the system. The success or failure of the system affects the perceived trustwor-thiness of the "personal" representative. Its failure destroys this person's credibility. It might also be true that personal failure of the representative may negatively affect the perception of the system, but not necessarily so.

It is arguable that when the system's representative fails, it is possible there was a misapplication of the expertise or a miscalculation by the rep-resentative. For instance, a patient's family sues a doctor when a patient dies from a difficult to diagnose illness. Their complaint is that the doctor misdiagnosed the illness and therefore was negligent with the knowledge at his or her disposal. While the access point is being blamed for the death of the patient, the system (in this case the medical system) can be exoner-ated, in theory. What is unclear is to what degree the system produced the environment in which the access point (expert) failed. Did the doctor, who received a standardized education, act as the system had trained him or her

46. Ibid, 85. Giddens clarifies by stating, "Cognitive frames of meaning will not gen-erate that faith [in the coherence of everyday life] without a corresponding level of un-derlying emotional commitment—whose origins, I shall argue, are largely unconscious. Trust, hope and courage are all relevant to such commitment" (Giddens, *Modernity and Self-Identity*, 38).

47. Giddens, *Consequences of Modernity*, 85–87.

to do so, or did the doctor fail to utilize the system by which she or he was trained? This question is possible because of the institutionalization of the expert system, which is why the reflexive nature of rationalized modernity has such importance. In the failure of an access point (expert), it is not uncommon for the procedures of that system to be reevaluated and studied to determine if such failures can be prevented in the future.

Thus, reflexivity of knowledge creates a particular tension at the points of interface, where the system and its representatives connect with the parties receiving service. This might be the doctor, banker, teacher/professor, or pastor. What inevitably happens is that the system, despite its expertise, will fail or fall short of the expectations of those it serves. Knowledge disseminated will be determined inadequate, creating a disenfranchised beneficiary. However, because the context has changed—freshwater fish living in a saltwater tank—it becomes easier to blame the expert than to distrust the expert system.

Consequences of the "Quest for Certainty"

While it is neither possible nor entirely desirable to eliminate the results of the rationalists' "Quest for Certainty," there are consequences and limitations that should be acknowledged and mitigated. Despite the best intentions of rationalized systems, these processes, realized in institutional bureaucracy, are actually detrimental to human life, creating "settings in which people cannot always behave as human beings—where people are dehumanized."[48] Two of these detrimental effects are the disembedding and dehumanization of experts, and cognitive distrust on the part of experts and laypersons alike.

---

48. The full quote from Ritzer states, "Despite the advantages it offers, bureaucracy suffers from the *irrationality of rationality* . . . In other words, they are settings in which people cannot always behave as human beings—where people are dehumanized" (*McDonaldization of Society*, 27). He further clarifies that, "Human beings, equipped with a wide array of skills and abilities, are asked to perform a limited number of highly simplified tasks over and over. Instead of expressing their human abilities on the job, people are forced to deny their humanity and act like robots" (ibid., 34). Ritzer identifies four manifestations of this process: efficiency (choosing the optimum means to a given end), calculability (increasing quantity), predictability (guaranteed results by systematization), and control (through non-human technology). Ibid. 43–133.

Disembedding and Dehumanization of Experts

Whatever the good-intentions, these rational processes effectively rob human beings of their humanity. As John Drane states, "But more often than not, the thoroughgoing way in which rationalization has been pursued seems to carry along with it other aspects that are less than satisfying, precisely because they are mechanical, and therefore dehumanizing."[49] It is notable for our purpose that social relations are reordered by the disembedding of the access points (experts) from the social systems in which they function.

In the "hidden curriculum" of formal education, children learn through "general social attitudes, an aura of respect for technical knowledge of all kinds."[50] However, despite this respect, those who possess such knowledge at high levels can be treated as disembedded objects, "outsiders" who are often stereotyped and the recipients of hostility and fear.[51] This is partly because the rationalized modern world has disembedded experts from *kinship-relations* and placed them in *contractual relationship*, which lie outside comfortable ranges of ontological security.

Thus, while trust in persons is required as part of the layperson's access to the expert system, the potential pain and loss of betrayal fills laypersons with such angst and fear that they find it easier to hold experts at a distance either as heroes or clods, as objects of expectation rather than as fellow subjects in relationship.[52] In this sense, Giddens describes the modern social world as a "world of strangers" where persons live at the intersection of "intimacy and impersonality."[53] Experts, often themselves under mandates of professional distance, become necessary so far as they bring a particular set of skills to a relationship and are able to fulfill others' expectations with those skills.[54] However, as objects of expectation, experts are particularly vulnerable to isolation.

---

49. Drane, *McDonaldization of the Church*, 32–33.
50. Giddens, *Consequences of Modernity,* 89.
51. Ibid., 89–92
52. Ibid., 92–111; 142–44.
53. Ibid., 142ff.
54. Harvey, *Another City*, 120–21.

Cognitive Mistrust

Reflexivity has much to do with the speed at which information travels. Giddens states that, "the reflexivity of modern social life consists in the fact that social practices are constantly examined and reformed in the light of incoming information about those very practices, thus constitutively altering their character."[55] This leads to a sense of relativism such as James W. Sire states, "By the 1990s everyone in the Western world and much of the East came to see that confidence in human reason is almost dead . . . Knowing itself comes under fire, especially the notion that there are any truths of correspondence. Conceptual relativism . . . now serves not just religious experiences but all aspect of reality."[56] What we knew yesterday is changed in the reading of the morning paper today.[57] In rationality, what confidence can we have in anything we think we know?

Expert systems, while functionally necessary, have become suspect and concertedly deteriorated, including those related to ecclesial expert systems. Because expert systems cannot do all that is expected of them, experts, as persons whom laypersons' trust, are particularly vulnerable to issues of focused distrust at key moments of a system's failure to meet lay expectations. This distrust has profound consequences for the life of the church.

55. Giddens, *Consequences of Modernity*, 38.

56. Sire, *Universe Next Door*, 178.

57. One example might be the nature of dieting. For decades people have been told that a balanced diet was the healthiest diet. Now with the advent of Weight Watchers, Atkins, South Beach, Jenny Craig and many more, people receive constantly changing information—all of it "backed" by scientific data—concerning what is the healthy way to eat. This changing information causes many to wonder if anyone really knows what is the best way to eat. Add to this a growing understanding of genetics and it now seems that there is not one good way to eat, but perhaps 7 billion appropriate ways to eat healthily (each according to his or her own needs).

Giddens writes in *Modernity and Self-Identity*, "The more or less constant, profound and rapid momentum of change characteristic of modern institutions, coupled with structured reflexivity, mean [sic] that on the level of everyday practice as well as philosophical interpretation, nothing can be taken for granted. What is acceptable/ appropriate/recommended behaviour today may be seen differently tomorrow in the light of altered circumstances or incoming knowledge-claims" (Giddens, *Modernity and Self-Identity*, 133–34).

Chapter 3

Cultural Conformity: Expertise and the Church

Like medicine and law, ecclesial expert systems have been shaped by rationalized modernity. The movement from the local and specific to the general and universal created the environment wherein the knowledge and skills found in expert systems have been moved from locally controlled settings in congregations to the academy. In the pre-modern era, the study of Christian theology, while mainly carried on in the monastery, had as its purpose "the beatific vision, fellowship with God, wisdom and, at a more mundane level, the equipping of clergy and the people of God for their tasks."[1] The latter reflects specific, local contexts wherein people were prepared to work where they lived.[2] Centralization of teaching and dogma arose in the Roman Catholic Church as a means of protecting the church "against the corrupting consequences" of Protestant "heresies" and the French Revolution.[3] The rise of the modern university in Germany led to the formation of theology as a formal academic study.[4] This reveals a

---

1. Forrester, *Truthful Action*, 33.

2. As Toulmin states, "Historically, the Western Church was a transnational institution and it dealt realistically with people from Scotland to Sicily, from Poland to Portugal. Moral issues had pluralism built in from the start; the wisest resolution came from steering an equitable course between the demands that arose in practice, in specific cases" (Toulmin, *Cosmopolis*, 136).

3. Ibid.

4. Forrester writes, "In this tradition [University of Berlin, 1809] the university is properly concerned only with *Wissenschaft*, a scientific commitment to relate everything to universal rational principals. Theology had to justify its place in such a university . . ." (Forrester, *Truthful Action*, 35).

disembedding of theological education from local and specific contexts to the university with its scientific process and universal concepts.

Disembedding: Institutionalization and Academia

One result of modern rationality on the church is that ecclesial systems as recognized in institutional/denominational churches—Roman Catholicism to Southern Baptists, Anglican to Assemblies of God—have disembedded ecclesial expert system from the immediate life of the church through the establishment and control of seminaries. In these schools, certain "important" skills are bestowed upon select individuals who often have had to meet certain standards of "calling" and denominational recognition. Attainment of these skills, ascertained by the completion of the Master of Divinity degree, initiates a person into the professionalized class of clergy. For those unable or unwilling to pursue these specialized academic skills, denominational professionals offer "remedial" courses in workshops and training sessions to help the clergy achieve the "special training" needed to be successful church leaders. These specially-trained persons are presumed to have the knowledge, skills, and resources to lead churches according to modern standards: efficient, calculable, predictable, and controllable.[5]

Ray Anderson writes a determined and demanding memo to theological educators in which he argues, "Christian tradition is misunderstood and misused if it becomes institutionalized and loses its cumulative and liberating function within the praxis of the Spirit."[6] Damning is his indictment of academic institutions for theological instruction that have little if any relevance to the churches they are meant to serve. Emphasizing orthodoxy above orthopraxis has encouraged the disembedding of theology as academic theology and left ecclesial mission underserved.[7] This demonstrates the impact of ecclesial systems in rationalized modernity where universal principles—disembedded from time and space—can be transmitted by non-practitioners. The academy generally teaches those who care for the church how to care for the church without dealing with specifics of time, location, or culture.[8]

5. Ritzer, *McDonaldization of Society*; Drane, *McDonaldization of the Church*.

6. Anderson, *Shape of Practical Theology*, 320.

7. Ibid., 321.

8. Farley, *Theologia*; Muller, *Study of Theology*; and Banks, *Reenvisioning Theological Education*.

All of this leads to a professionalization of the pastorate. The academy promotes highly trained professionals as necessary for the church's future. Arlene R. Inouye writes, "The current form of training Christian leaders, especially pastors, grew out of the modern era and the image of pastor as professional. Crudely put, the function of formal training has been to prepare people to serve in a religious institution."[9] In our current brackishness, many of us in academia have noted with concern the rise of pastoral training programs within local church contexts. In many ways this is reflective of both the mistrust of expert systems (particularly academia) and the desire to create experts trained with a particular understanding of expertise. These appear to be attempts at recreating universalized structures and processes embedded in localized contexts. Toward what end is not entirely clear.[10]

It is important to state outright that less education is not the answer. The changing academic landscape, specifically the advent of online education, may offer certain kinds of relief but not without producing its own kinds of difficulties. It may be that it is not only the structure of academia that must change, but the structure of the church. Changes in the structure of academia will continue to drive the ecclesial structures, which they were meant to serve. It seems there is need for better balance and interplay between the two structures toward a mutually informed shaping. These are important questions raised about the way academia acts as a tool to disembed knowledge with certain consequences for pastors, churches, and society.

Modern Ecclesiological Consequences

There are certainly many factors leading to what might be described as a eroding of the church's standing in the West. Clergy scandals, competition for the laity's attention, and a general loss of biblical literacy are examples of some of these. Therefore, avoiding the implication that there is only one

9. Inouye, "Revisioning the American Evangelical Church," 179. Also Banks, *Reenvisioning Theological Education*, 208–22; Drane, *McDonaldization of the Church*; Wagner, *Escape from Church, Inc.*; Ogden, *Unfinished Business*; Roxburgh, "Missional Leadership"; Kitchens, *Postmodern Parish*, especially 85–99.

10. An additional question worth considering elsewhere is the nature of disembedding from the academy to the internet. The institutional function of disseminating information bestowed to the academy has been subverted and become even more universalized leaving many to wonder what exactly is the role of the university or seminary.

source for the many difficulties facing churches and pastoral leaders, these difficulties are amplified by our experience in the freshwater tank of modernity and the current brackish water in which we now swim.

Despite the importance of theological preparation through the academy, there are also negative consequences for ecclesial expert systems. This is particularly true in contexts where traditional leadership preparation and acquired skills are insufficient to leading congregations through adaptive change. Drane sums up the situation in ecclesial structures this way: "Many churches and their leaders have lost a sense of confidence in the ability of the system . . . ."[11] I would suggest that while there may be many consequences, here are four exemplary of the Western church's reliance on radicalized ecclesial expert systems: 1) a disengaged laity; 2) isolated pastors; 3) disillusionment; and, 4) the undermining of mission.[12]

A Disengaged Laity

Increasingly, pastors perceive that they alone do the work of the church rather than equipping others for the work (Eph 4:12). However, the system has eliminated the laity from the equation. This occurs as the result of a self-perpetuating process of systemic control. The system funnels expertise into the "expert" by training the pastor to be leader of the church; this creates lay dependency upon the pastor for vision, initiative, and preparation in order to perceive and pursue the church's mission; this mission is conceived through the expert system's design; the expert system's design is best interpreted by experts trained in the language and processes of the system.[13] "Deskilling" occurs because of specialization, which naturally occurs when expertise is funneled from the expert system into an individual (in this case, a pastor).[14] The "superstar" mentality emphasizes that clergy

11. Drane, *McDonaldization of the Church*, 6. This quote concludes, ". . . to address their own deepest needs." It is not the suggestion of this study that the church exists for this purpose. The church, as witness to God's reign will sometimes meet needs, but mostly it is to live in testimony of God's advance in the world, even if that requires giving up our own needs. The point here is that the system fails to operate as it was designed and therefore, creates distrust as exacerbated by the liminality of the current age.

12. It is fair to question the degree to which these are symptoms of the systemic environment or caused by the systemic environment. Others are free to argue this point or to more fully research the question. Whether causal or not, they do seem to be inextricably linked.

13. Drane, *McDonaldization of the Church*, 101–2.

14. Giddens notes, "Abstract systems deskill—not only in the workplace, but in all the

are trained to do specialized work, which includes motivating laypersons to achieve the pastor's vision of the church.[15]

The lay responsibility is resourcing (particularly time and money) a "successful" vision's end. Many laypersons choose to leave, feeling disgruntled because of the pastor's failure to meet their expectations. For those who remain, they receive in exchange a weekly spiritual "recharge." Few seem to have any real awareness of God's missional presence in the world; even fewer seem to realize their role as witnesses of the kingdom's work.

Pastoral Isolation

Loneliness is the natural conclusion of these patterns where pastors are identified as "leaders of the flock but alone in the crowd."[16] As with all experts, because of their "leadership role," pastors are trained to maintain a "professional distance" from the flock they lead. The intense loneliness stems from a pressure "to present an image of perfection in order to better represent the church or the gospel, though no one can fulfill that ideal."[17] Patti Simmons writes:

> Clergy face daunting expectations. They must fill countless roles-
> spiritual leader, psychologist, counselor, business manager, human
> resource specialist, to name a few-and those roles expand so rap-
> idly that a sense of futility sets in as the gap between what they
> were prepared for in seminary and what they encounter on a daily
> basis steadily widens. In addition to feeling unprepared, clergy feel
> alone.[18]

Therefore, as the expert interface, the pastor becomes disembedded from the congregation. The social consequences are certainly demanding as described by Ogden: "I fear that many participants in the church view their pastors as specialists in the things of God, so they need not be bothered with that realm [temporal]. As a result, clergy are held in both respect and contempt."[19] The disconnect described here isolates pastoral leaders, while

---

sectors of social life that they touch" (Giddens, *Modernity and Self-Identity*, 137).

15. Ogden, *Unfinished Business*, 92–93.

16. Hall and Elliot, "Pastors."

17. Ibid.

18. Simmons, "Supporting Pastoral Excellence," 186.

19. Ogden, *Unfinished Business*, 89.

the mundane work of maintaining the institutional church drains what spiritual life they have left.[20]

Disillusionment

Pastors, as theologically trained experts (systematic theology; biblical languages—Greek, Hebrew, and Aramaic; hermeneutics and exegesis; church history; church leadership and administration; church growth; pastoral counseling; discipleship; etc.), are perceived as the expert interface with the expert system undergirding the church's culturally contrived current reality. The layperson in the modern church expects the pastor to accomplish all of these tasks and more. However, in an adaptive change context where the church functions as a "vendor of religious goods and services," technical skill will fail to meet the congregation's expectations. More importantly, the pastor should not make it his or her job to meet these expectations because the expectations themselves are often in need of conversion.[21]

Attempts and failure to meet these perceived needs invalidates the expert system that is "organized religion" (i.e., the church). This has led to a general disillusionment with the church as "organized religion," which has promised to fulfill felt needs as part of a church growth model, to the point that many leave the system to find spiritual fulfillment elsewhere.[22] At this

20. Alan Roxburgh and Mike Regel discuss the effects of rationalized modernity's disembedding process on the church: "Disembedding is not a by-product of modernity; it is the core agenda. One irony is that the methodologies and systems developing to counteract this disembedding are drawn from modernity. That is why for example we have seen the emergence in this century of pastoral leaders (i.e., an attempt to redefine the traditional model of pastor into modernity categories) as efficient managers trained to solve problems. This paradigm of leadership not only deepens the church's loss of identity, but also shapes leaders who look for solutions primarily from the new-and-the-next. These leaders are essentially cut off from any meaningful engagement with the Christian story's response to modernity. One suspects that the current turn among leaders to issues and styles of spirituality is an expression of the growing unease with techniques and management models that have pervaded the church for most of this century" (Roxburgh and Regel, *Crossing the Bridge*, 40).

21. Guder, *Continuing Conversion*, 150ff.

22. Drane describes the scene this way: "I have mentioned those who leave the Church. Though I described them as giving up on faith, things are not usually that straightforward. Not only do such people rarely abandon faith altogether, they also frequently claim that leaving the Church is actually a way of maintaining their faith. Increasing numbers of people today regard the spiritual search as something that is not necessarily supported or enhanced by involvement in the life of organized religious institutions" (Drane, *McDonaldization of the Church*, 5).

point pastors trained in the abstract systems of the institutional structures miss integration with their congregations and fail to provide the kind of adaptive leadership necessary. Thus, the pastor is particularly susceptible to being both the focus of this disillusionment as well as becoming irreparably disillusioned by means of being the interface with the system.[23]

The Undermining of Mission

The church is called into the world by the power of the Spirit to bear witness of Christ's ongoing mission for the Father.[24] However, radicalized ecclesial expert systems have focused on human control and management of this mission to the detriment of Christian witness.[25] After the Protestant Reformation, there was only "modest interest" in missionary activity. When interest was finally shown, "'Missions' became a program of the church."[26] By programming missions, the church manufactures, distributes, and controls the instruments of salvation including the message and the methods.[27] In so doing, the church attempts to appropriate the work of Christ—the "author and perfecter of faith."[28] Controllability and management of mission diminish the affective nature of God's work in human lives, attempting to make it dependent upon our efforts rather that upon God's.

Further, as the church ceases its witness to Christ's activity, it attempts to replace Christ and establishes itself as the source and place of salvation.[29] Hence, the current status of the church as a "vendor of religious services" becomes apparent.[30] This kind of mission is no mission at all. The critical issue may be that the institutional church in the West ceased living for Christ's sake and began living for its own self-preservation. As Jesus warned, "For those who want to save their life will lose it, and those who lose their life

---

23. Heifetz and Linsky, *Leadership on the Line*, 32–37.

24. Anderson, *Shape of Practical Theology*, 40–46.

25. Drane states, "Mission is another key area of Christian activity that cries out to be released from the influences of McDonaldization" (*McDonaldization of the Church*, 198). Banks contends that theological education trains pastors as missional persons first and academicians last. Banks, *Reenvisioning Theological Education*, 129–86.

26. Dietterich, "What Time Is It?," 3–4.

27. Guder, *Continuing Conversion*, 97–119.

28. Heb 12:2, NASB.

29. Guder, *Continuing Conversion*, 135–41.

30. Hunsberger, "Sizing Up the Shape of the Church," 133–44, especially 138–42.

for my sake will find it. For what will it profit them if they gain the whole world but forfeit their life? Or what will they give in return for their life?"[31]

Christian communities, especially local churches, have always faced opportunities and challenges resulting from societal shifts and changes. In the age of modernity,[32] the dominant default method for responding to these changes has been to defer to and rely upon expert, professional leadership. Modern churches—particularly in the West—have generally accepted this perspective under the influence of cultural perspective on leadership, which views the pastor as the expert or professional leader of the church.[33] More recently, questions about the modern approach to church leadership have come from a variety of arenas.

One critique is that this form of leadership actually "deskills" the church. This lay deskilling is largely the result of an expert system designed by professionals to be operated only by persons with specialized training in the language and processes of the system.[34] As a result, congregations defer to pastors for answers to the questions facing the church. So long as these answers lie within the system and the pastor's expertise, this works well enough.[35] However, when the context changes, when the old ways no longer work, and when the world changes the rules, this expertise no longer is helpful. At this point, trust in the expert fails and an assumption is made that this person is to blame.[36] This leads to a related critique that pastors are isolated by the nature of their role. It has been accepted that loneliness is a normal consequence of leadership.[37]

As the church faces change (either from without or from within), churches which feel ill-prepared to handle this change expect pastors who are equally ill-prepared to "fix" problems that have no ready answers. These pastors are increasingly isolated and are often the brunt of congregational frustration. Ultimately participation in the mission of God suffers. In short,

31. Matt 16:25–26, NRSV.

32. Modernity here is used in reference to a "rationalist" approach to understanding the world as it is in Toulmin, *Cosmopolis*, 9.

33. Roxburgh, "Missional Leadership", 194–98. This point is also made by others: Drane, *McDonaldization of the Church*, 101–2; Ogden, *Unfinished Business*, 89–93.

34. "Deskilling" is the language of Giddens, *Consequences of Modernity*, 144.

35. This kind of leadership is best described as "technical leadership" by Heifetz and Linsky, *Leadership on the Line*. This is not saying that such leadership is presumptively best, only that it can work and work well under certain conditions and toward certain ends. Evaluations as to the legitimacy of the conditions and ends is worth consideration.

36. Giddens, *Consequences of Moderntiy*, 91.

37. Hall and Elliot, "Pastors."

the modern agenda has not always been helpful in understanding pastoral leadership, especially during times of intense congregational and social change. One of the ways to address this difficulty is through the rediscovery of lost meaning with regard to the dominant Christian metaphor for congregational leadership, notably the metaphor of "pastor."

Others have done exceptional work on metaphors for congregational leadership. For example, Scott Cormode's "Multi-Layered Leadership: The Christian Leader as Builder, Shepherd, and Gardner" investigates the interplay of three important metaphors at work in the church today: the visionary/CEO, the pastoral care facilitator, and the meaning-maker.[38] While Cormode successfully and helpfully investigates the application of these metaphors, I am after something related, but different—I am after the meta-metaphor's meaning.

To illustrate, note that all three of Cormode's typologies of leadership share a similar biblical heritage—the person whose leadership is described by these typologies is titled the "pastor."[39] This is appropriate because nearly all Christian-communities utilize this designation in reference to a singular leader or group of primary expert and professional leaders within a congregation. It is this usage of the biblical metaphor in reference to the expert designee, despite the typology of leadership she or he practices, with which this work is concerned.

This is a concern for two reasons. First, widespread misuse has led to an abuse of its meaning. For instance, consider the keynote speaker at a denominational pastor's conference tell his listeners that they are essential to the flock because without them, their flocks will wander off a cliff. Second— this is a confession of bias—despite numerous Christian statements regarding the priesthood of all believers, especially among Protestants,[40] there is

---

38. Cormode, "Multi-Layered Leadership," 69–104. Cormode demonstrates effectively that these three metaphors are not three separate ways of leading, but rather are three interconnected means of leading within any particular context.

39. Ibid., 74, 77, 88.

40. This concept is not unique to Protestant theology nor is it widely agreed upon within Protestant theology as to what exactly the "priesthood of all believers" means. Vatican II's statement on the integration of priesthoods into the one priesthood of Christ is a helpful point of contact for Protestants and Catholics, though care must be taken not to read it through the eyes of Luther, Calvin, Zwingli, Roger Williams or Menno Simons. Specifically *Lumen Gentium* states: "Christ the Lord, High Priest taken from among men (100) made the new people "a kingdom and priests to God the Father" (101). The baptized, by regeneration and the anointing of the Holy Spirit, are consecrated as a spiritual house and a holy priesthood, in order that through all those works which are

still a failure to recognize the pastoral role of persons in our congregations who never carry an official title nor receive ecclesial sanctioning.

While the story of modernity has had much to say regarding the role of pastors as expert, professional leaders, the Gospel of God offers an alternate narrative, especially in light of adaptive situations.[41] However, this requires us to once again access our history and reclaim our heritage. Accessing the Christian story means that we engage in more than storytelling; it is a search for meaning about how to live as responsible witnesses of God's reign.[42] This search for meaning demands consideration of those dangerous memories[43] which challenge conventional, authoritative stances—specifically that the pastor is the "ruler" of the church.[44]

those of the Christian man they may offer spiritual sacrifices and proclaim the power of Him who has called them out of darkness into His marvelous light (102) . . . Though they differ from one another . . . the common priesthood of the faithful and the ministerial or hierarchical priesthood are nonetheless interrelated: each of them in its own special way is a participation in the one priesthood of Christ (2*)" (Vatican Council, *Dogmatic Constitution*, 2:10).

41. This is Mark Lau Branson's language. See Branson, "Reflecting on the Gospel."

42. Groome, *Sharing Faith*, 215ff. Specifically Groome states, "Christian Vision, of course, does not provide a blueprint for life or easy answers to the problems and complexities people must face. But it tenders truths by which to make meaning, ethical principles to guide decision making, and virtues to live by; it offers images of promise and hope to sustain people and of responsibility and possibility to empower historical agency towards God's reign . . . The Vision should reflect God's promises of shalom and wholeness, yet empower people in their historical responsibility to work in partnership for the realization of what God wills—peace and justice, love and freedom, wholeness and fullness of life for all . . . Educators are to teach the Vision of Christian faith as something *immediate* and *historical*, in that it calls people to do God's will on earth now as if God's reign is at hand, and as something *new* and *ultimate*, in that it always calls people beyond their present horizons of praxis in faith until they finally rest in God" (ibid., 216–17, emphasis in original). This relates to Ray Anderson's "interpretive paradigms" and "historical consciousness" (see Anderson, *Shape of Practical Theology*, 26–31).

43. Groome states, "[A hermeneutic of suspicion] attempts to recognize and refuse what is destructive in texts of tradition and it searches for their 'dangerous' or 'subversive' memories, often forgotten or excluded by dominant hermeneutics . . . Texts of Christian Story/Vision always have dangerous memories that call ourselves and our world into question, that can empower people in ongoing conversation and social transformation toward God's reign" (Groome, *Sharing Faith*, 233). This follows Metz: "definite memory breaks through the magic circle of the prevailing consciousness . . . Christian faith can and must, in my opinion, be seen in this way as a subversive memory . . . The criterion of its authentic Christianity is the liberating and redeeming danger with which it introduces the remembered freedom of Jesus into modern society and the forms of consciousness and praxis in that society" (Metz, *Faith in History and Society*, 90).

44. This was the pronouncement of one of the twentieth century's most noted

Southern Baptist pastors, W. A. Criswell, whose influence and that of his "students" has arguably crossed a multiplicity of evangelical denominations. See Norsworthy, "Rationalism and Reaction," 88.

PART TWO

Remembering a New Way

Chapter 4

Our Leader Metaphor Revisited: Old Testament

In one of my favorite movies, *The Princess Bride*, there is a scene in which one of the characters, Vizzini, exclaims for about the third time, "Inconceivable!" Recognizing that Vizzini keeps using this word for events that keep happening, one of his comrades in crime, Inigo Montoya, replies, "You keep using that word. I do not think it means what you think it means."[1] I have long wondered if in the modern church, we have continued to use the word "pastor" but it does not mean what we think it means. So what if "pastor" does not mean what we have made it to mean? This chapter and the next investigate the "dangerous memories" and biblical themes surrounding the "pastor" metaphor as they relate to questions of community and communal leadership as found in the Old and New Testaments. From these findings, it is possible to describe a Christian perspective of missional leadership that informs and is informed by the praxes of leadership communities.[2]

---

1. *Princess Bride.*

2. This is not an all-encompassing assessment of authority and power from a biblical perspective. There are numerous biblical passages not considered here that do consider these issues as well. These questions are left to another person's work. In this book the interest is in how the shepherd metaphor works in relationship to conversations regarding power and leadership since it is used so widely. Clearly, this work does not claim to be the final word on this question. Here the book looks anew at this particular metaphor with a hope toward recapturing some of those forgotten and dangerous considerations that can and should speak into congregational leadership praxis.

The Metaphor of Pastor as Shepherd

Investigating the metaphorical meaning of "pastor" is complicated by several factors. First, the New Testament metaphor developed from Old Testament concepts with ancient cultural meaning significantly obscured in contemporary usage.[3] Second, New Testament scholars are equally perplexed by the function or role of pastor in relation to that of overseer or bishop and disagree concerning whether or not a pastoral office was intended by New Testament writers.[4] Third, investigating the pastoral role according to New Testament themes is complicated by the fact that "pastor," the dominant office title for most Protestants (particularly Evangelicals), is rarely used in most English translations.[5] While I do not fully resolve these thorny issues, I do make suggestions concerning how particular resolutions impact the issues related to this study. Further, by investigating the terminology and meaning of the shepherd metaphor, I attempt to recapture certain theological elements regarding "pastoral" leadership that benefit churches in adaptive situations. To accomplish this purpose, I begin by exploring patterns of usage in the Old Testament.[6]

Old Testament Considerations on Power and Authority in Leadership

This work is not an all-encompassing investigation of power and authority. That said, there is still a particular approach to those matters that informs

---

3. Along this thought, see Köstenberger, "Jesus the Good Shepherd," 67–96; Laniak, *Shepherds*, 37, 42ff; Chae, *Jesus*, 19–94.

4. See Knight, "Two Offices" 1–12; Hoehner, *Ephesians*, 544; Jeremias, "ποιμήν," 497–98.

5. This work will primarily use the NASB and NRSV translations for comparison and contrast: the NASB considered more theologically "conservative" and the NRSV considered more theologically "liberal," though such distinctions are often hard to justify. The NASB and the NRSV each use "pastors" only once (Eph 4:11). The KJV uses pastor in place of shepherd nine times in the Old Testament and once in the New Testament (Eph 4:11). These Old Testament usages are largely a misrendering of the term, and are corrected in the New King James Version, which follows the NASB and NRSV renderings.

6. Branson's insight is helpful here: "Word counts cannot dictate theology; however, observations inform priorities and relationships" (Branson, *Intercultural Church Life*, 66). This follows Barr's argument against overemphasizing word meaning at the expense of word usage. See Barr, *Semantics of Biblical Language*, throughout, but see 233–34 for an example of his argument.

our understanding of the biblical texts that will be explored in relationship to the pastoral metaphor. As an introduction to one kind of lens by which to approach the conversation of pastoral leadership and the pastoral metaphor, it is important to unpack several of more commonly used Old Testament narratives regarding leadership in pastoral contexts.

Moses as Shepherd-Leader of Israel

One of the most common Old Testament narratives appropriated in pastoral leadership conversations is that of Moses. The general approach to this narrative is that Moses was the shepherd-leader of Israel who rescues God's people from slavery. That he was ordained by God to give direction and vision to the rescue and that he was a transcendent and heroic leader. These are powerful stories that promote strong leadership. However, many tellings of these narratives and more importantly, most application of these narratives to pastoral leadership misrepresent the biblical text. I suggest two specific corrections to the reading of these narratives, which help to bring the larger shepherd narrative into clearer focus. The first has to do with the Moses' role leading the Israelites.

Moses: A Follower in the Flock

Moses undisputedly occupies the prime and unequivocal position as the human leader of the Israelites in the exodus. As such there is a natural tendency to refer to Moses as the Shepherd of Israel during the exodus. There are reasons why it might be natural to presume such a title for Moses. There is Moses' profession in the wilderness out of which YHWH calls him to go to Pharaoh. Moses as a shepherd of sheep was certainly accustomed to leading the flock and caring for the sheep. Or perhaps it was the way the role of Moses gets reinterpreted through later lenses.[7] However the idea of Moses as shepherd of Israel is a difficult one to reconcile with the text. What is missed in the reading of the text is how Moses leads; he leads by following.

In Exodus 13:17–22 we are introduced to YHWH the leader and Shepherd of Israel who leads Israel from slavery by pillar of cloud and pillar of fire. Throughout the exodus narrative, YHWH fulfills the shepherd's role

---

7. For instance see: Isa 63:11; Ps 77:20; Freedman and Simon, "Exodus Rabbah," 2.

of leading, protecting, assuring, correcting, and healing his flock (i.e., Exod 13:21–22; 14:19–20, 23–25; 15:25–27; 16:4–5, 11–16; 17:5–7; 40:34–38; Deut 7:17–24). Moses, as a primary member of the flock designated with being the human role model and leader within the flock pointed to and focused the community's attention on following YHWH who was present with them. In his final address, Moses defers to YHWH as the leader of Israel.[8] To misread this as Moses' heroic leadership is to misunderstand Moses' own testimony of God's activity.

A word is necessary here as a deferral to New Testament theology. Moses clearly held a singularly important role in the exodus and was used by YHWH to teach and imprint God's people with the teaching of the law. Not unlike the prophets of later periods, the resting of the Spirit upon individuals makes them able to do the work of God as his spokespersons and guides for the people. As indicated above, this was God's design for his work prior to the coming of the Spirit upon all people. Prior to the incarnation and the advent of the Holy Spirit, God works by his Spirit's work through the select few. A new method emerges post-Pentecost.

The second correction to the Moses narrative has to do with regard to Moses' authority and the application of that authority in response to dissent. Moses is often portrayed as a strong leader demanding to be followed without question, exacting severe consequences for disobedience. However, the biblical text again offers a contrary perspective. When confronted with rebellion, Moses recognized that it was against YHWH and not against him (Num 14; Deut 31:26–27). As a result, Moses chooses to allow YHWH to contend with his people. This passive response to "rebellion" recognizes God's primacy over his flock that fails to assume Moses' ongoing role as the leader of God's people.

Kings as Shepherd-Leaders of Israel

A second narrative set that needs to be reconsidered is that of the Kings of Israel/Judah as shepherd-leaders of Israel. The narrative tends to be used to exemplify kingly leadership as a model for how pastoral leadership functions in the church. I remember a pastoral mentor who mostly in jest used to say, "It is good to be King." While for my mentor this claim was humorous, this philosophy is no joking matter for many pastoral leaders.

8. This is presumed to be the historical narrative of Deut 1:6—4:40. Merrill, *Deuteronomy*, 40; Rofé, *Deuteronomy*, 19; Robson, "Literary Composition," 39.

Too many take W. A. Criswell at his word when Criswell boldly stated, "The pastor is the ruler of the church."[9] Since the Old Testament offers us the most prolific insight into God's perspective on kings, a short overview of that perspective is important.

Deuteronomy 17 offers a view into God's thoughts on kings for his people.[10] In Deuteronomy 17, the possibility of kingly leadership is raised as a possibility initiated not by God's directive, but as an allowance of the people's desires. The phrase "and you will say, 'I will set a king over me like all the other nations'" makes it clear that kingly leadership is initiated not by YHWH, but by Israel. At best, the kingship is God's permissive allowance for Israel's weakness and childish need to "be like everyone else."[11] Whatever the reason for YHWH's permission, it is also clear that kingship is dealt with here "in fairly lukewarm terms, viewing it (pejoratively) as an imitation of the nations, limiting it, and warning about its injustices."[12]

This offers a background (or insertion into the Law) that gives further clarity to Samuel's response to Israel's request in 1 Samuel 8 where YHWH identifies Israel's desire for a king as a rejection of his divine rule. (". . . they have rejected me from being king over them" 1 Sam 8:7). YHWH's response also recognizes this rejection as a continuation of Israel's rejection of YHWH's leadership from the exodus ("Just as they have done to me, from the day I brought them up out of Egypt to this day, forsaking me and serving other gods, so also they are doing to you" 1 Sam 8:8.). To follow this idea through, could it be that pastoral leadership that follows a kingly paradigm are actually indication of a rejection of God's leadership in our churches?

This is largely what makes the Davidic reign unique in the life of Israel. David serves as the great king of Israel who recognizes YHWH is

9. See Norsworthy, "Rationalism and Reaction," 88.

10. It is worth noting that there is considerable disagreement among scholars as to whether Deuteronomy and this section in particular is attributed to Mosaic authorship (or that time frame) or a much later document (possibly post-exilic) that is an attempt to reframe the experiences of Israel/Judah. This disagreement is noted not so much as to take a side or to advocate a position, but to recognize that such questions might influence degrees to which Deuteronomy might or might not have influenced the Hebrew understanding of kingship. As an example, see Miller, *Deuteronomy*, 5–16 and Merrill, *Deuteronomy*, 22–27 for differing perspectives on these authorship and time frame issues.

11. As Telford Work notes, "This passage does not recommend a king (cf. 1 Sam 8) . . . It implies a divine tolerance for a range of culturally sensitive institutional polities under the rule of Law" (Work, *Deuteronomy*, 171). See also, Nelson, *Deuteronomy*, 222.

12. Rofé, *Deuteronomy*, 8.

his Shepherd (Ps 23). In his imperfection and brokenness he submits to the leadership of YHWH (Pss 32, 51). This is a reflection of the trajectory of Deuteronomy 17, which identifies kings as "exemplary citizens" living under the Law and not lifting himself above his fellow citizens.[13] As Miller states, "The fundamental task of the leader of the people, therefore, is to exemplify and demonstrate true obedience to the Lord for the sake of the well-being of both the dynasty and the kingdom. King and subject share a common goal: to learn to fear the Lord (v. 19)."[14]

This is nowhere more clearly understood than by the kings' responses to the dissent of prophets and the kings' behavior among and toward fellow citizens. As the exemplar king who recognizes YHWH's place as Shepherd over his people, David responds in repentance and brokenness when confronted by Nathan (2 Sam 12) and Gad (2 Sam 24). He dances with abandon, in an "unkingly" manner before the Ark of the Covenant (2 Sam 6). He takes instruction from Zadok (1 Chron 24:3), Abigail (1 Sam 25), and Joab (2 Sam 19:5–8). He purchases what he needs to offer sacrifice (2 Sam 24:18–25). He is contrasted with the kings who follow him in Judah and Israel and reject the prophetic word, abandon the ways of YHWH, refuse instruction, and take wantonly what they want from the people they serve. And ultimately, David will be found to have fallen short of the ideal, so that only in his descendant who will reign forever—the shoot of Jesse—can the ideal be realized (Isa 11).

These alternate readings challenge presumptuous incomplete readings that supplant the place of YHWH as Israel's Shepherd. Reorienting Moses, David, the kings of Judah/Israel, and the role of the prophets helps us to identify a counter-narrative to the language of leadership expertise, authority, and power prevalent in our culture, including the church. We discover the place of leaders within the flock as being those among us to help us recognize and follow the One who is our Shepherd. As we shall see, this is the dominant nature of the shepherding metaphor patterns in the Old Testament.

---

13. For instance, Johnston notes that the king is to "focus on 'this law'; having his own copy, reading it daily, and adhering to it steadfastly. An integral part of this discipline is not exalting himself above other members of the community', a significant limitation of the power of kingship implied by the comparison with surrounding nations" (Johnston, "Civil Leadership in Deuteronomy," 148).

14. Miller, *Deuteronomy*, 149.

Old Testament Patterns of Usage for "Shepherd"

The "shepherd"/"shepherding" metaphor is rooted in the OT. There are three primary usages of רעה when translated by the verbs "shepherding," "tending," "herding" or by the nouns "shepherd," "shepherdess," or "herdsman": 1) herders of livestock; 2) YHWH as Shepherd of Israel; 3) a person or group as leaders/rulers.[15] The following are brief overviews of these usages.

Herders

Simply stated, the first usage describes people who herd livestock (sheep, goats, etc.).[16] This usage occurs predominantly within the Pentateuch, and mostly in Genesis.[17] Its usage establishes patterns of comprehension for the other two usages. Herders were responsible for the flock's well-being.[18] This included feeding, leading to pasture, tending, and protecting.[19] Although "feeding" and "leading to pasture" appear as two separate functions, they are related. While occasionally a shepherd might feed the flock "intensively" by giving it grain, more commonly the shepherd's responsibility was to lead the flock to a variety of vegetation and water, feeding it "extensively."[20] Sheep and livestock could eat without assistance, when the environment allowed.[21]

---

15. Generally occurs as רָעָה (verb) and רֹעֶה (m. noun), רֹעָה (f. noun). Other similarly associated meanings derived from רָעָה include: "to pasture," "to guide," and "to feed." Words often have a wide of semantic range, hence, רָעָה has two other meanings linked with it: "to associate with" and "to take pleasure in" or "desire." See Brown, *Hebrew and English Lexicon*, 944–46.

16. Translated as "tend," "herd," "pasture," "herdsman," "herders," "shepherd," or "shepherding:" Gen 4:2; 13:7, 8, 26:20; 29:3; 37:2; 46:32, 34, 47:3; 48:15, also, Exod 2:17, 19; Lev 27:32; Num 14:33. English interpreters use the nouns "herdersmen," "shepherds," "shepherdesses" and the verbs "herd," "tend," "pasture," and "shepherd" to describe the persons and their activities.

17. This usage occurs in about 30 percent of the 86 verses when רָעָה is translated "shepherd."

18. Sources consulted for this section include: Borowski, *Every Living Thing*; Galtay and Johnson, *World of Pastoralism*; Huntzinger, "The End of Exile"; Dirksen, "Shepherding the Herds."

19. Laniak, *Shepherds*, 53–57.

20. Ibid., 51, 54.

21. Giles and Gefu, "Nomads, Ranchers, and the State," 100–105.

Although the dominant understanding is that shepherds lead from "before" the flock, it is notable that both David and Amos are taken from "following the flock."[22] Shepherds moved "before," "within," and "behind" the flock, depending on the need.[23] Wherever the shepherd was in relation to the flock, there are two methods of maintaining flock cohesion that are particularly intriguing for this study: the use of voice commands to keep strays from wandering and the use of bells worn by animals chosen because they willingly and lovingly follow the shepherd. This idea of the bell-sheep, a method still practiced by the herding peoples in the Middle East today, offers us a unique perspective into the pastoral role, which we will pick up more fully later.[24]

From whatever position the shepherd chose to "guide" the flock, it is clear that his or her presence comforted the flock as they grazed and slept because of the shepherd's care. Shepherds tended and protected the flock. Tending meant caring for the lame and sick.[25] Shepherds likewise used the staff and other weapons to protect the flock from predators and thieves.[26]

Socioculturally, many cultures reviled shepherds making it far from being a noble profession. Hence, when Joseph's family joins him in Egypt, they are warned that shepherds are "abhorrent" or "loathsome" to Egyptians (Gen 46:34). Eventually, even in Israel, herding becomes a despised

---

22. In Hebrew, "מֵאַחַר הַצֹּאן" 2 Sam 7:8; 1 Chron 17:7; Amos 7:15. Laniak contends that these mean "driving" in each instance. Laniak, *Shepherds*, 54; see also Huntzinger, "End of Exile," 59 n. 10. However, the location of the herder is not clear in the biblical text. He contrasts this with "leading" which he contends is done from the front; again unclear in the biblical text. It is more likely that the shepherd or herder led through presence within the flock (perhaps more toward the back of the flock) and hence could better see and call to a straying animal. Leading from the "front" would make this more difficult. A particularly striking anthropological study of the Bedouin demonstrates that in some instances the sheep followed the shepherd's donkey, while the shepherd walked behind the sheep. See Dirksen, "Shepherding the Herds." Photographic evidence from the Bedouin and other shepherding peoples show the shepherd in the midst of the flock and rarely in the front. See also Paul, *Amos*, 247–48, 249.

23. Laniak contends that sheep followed the shepherd, but occasionally are led ("driven") from behind to prevent grazing in agricultural fields. Laniak, *Shepherds*, 54 n. 40; also Huntzinger, "End of Exile," 59.

24. Dirksen notes the Bedouin use bells in this manner. Dirksen, "Shepherding the Herds."

25. Huntzinger, "End of Exile," 59; Borowski, *Every Living Thing*, 49; Taylor, *Tend My Sheep*, 9.

26. Borowski, *Every Living Thing*, 49; Laniak, *Shepherds*, 56.

trade, associated with dishonesty and ruthlessness. This pattern persists into the New Testament.[27]

YHWH as Israel's Shepherd

A second usage of "shepherd" imagery in the Old Testament references YHWH as Israel's Shepherd.[28] This usage first occurs in the Patriarch narratives where YHWH is shepherd to Jacob and his clan (Gen 48:15; 49:24).[29]

---

27. Huntzinger's research indicates that much of the social status change for shepherds in pre-exilic Israel occurred "when land and livestock holdings came under the control of a small number of wealthy owners." This promoted a professional class of hired laborers who managed the sheep. These laborers were purported to have sold animals to travelers in order to supplement their income while claiming the missing animals were killed by wild animals or stolen by thieves. Over time, this and other similar biases created a general disdain for shepherds. Since shepherd were presumed dishonest, religious and social leaders limited the civil and religious rights of shepherds including prohibiting them from testifying in trials, barring their participation in temple rituals, and encouraging a general prejudice against the profession. As a result, Huntzinger states: "The use of shepherd imagery to refer to Israel's leadership may be understood as exotic. It cannot be assumed, therefore, that all the biblical writers who made use of the shepherd/sheep imagery had expert knowledge of shepherds or sheep . . . [I]t is to be expected that *care was exercised in the use of the vocabulary and images drawn from this field in the service of the metaphor.* The use of the terms related to sheep farming in the prophetic and synoptic literature simply attest to the significance of the imagery in the shared culture of the people" (Huntzinger, "End of Exile," 66–69, quote from 68–69, emphasis in original).

28. This usage occurs in about 20 percent of the verses where רעה is translated "shepherd." See: Gen 48:15; 49:24; Pss 23; 28:9; 74:1; 77: 20; 78:52–55; 79:13; 80:1; 95:7; Isa 40:10–11; 49:9–13; Jer 23:2; 31:10; 50:19; Ezek 34:31; Mic 2:12–13; 4:6–8; 7:14–15. Chae, *Jesus*, 25. The Israelites where not the first to use "shepherd" in reference to deity; it was common terminology for surrounding cultures. See Huntzinger, "End of Exile," 69–78; Laniak, *Shepherds*, 59–58–61, 67–69, 72–74.

Huntzinger's observation is important here: "The description of God as a shepherd and the people as sheep is just one of many figures found in the Old Testament. The fact that a variety of figures are used to depict God and people in Scripture indicates the complex nature of the divine/human relationship and the fact that not any one figure exhaustively describes it . . . Biblical metaphor is . . . an effort to say something meaningful about him in view of the knowledge and experience possessed by the community. A meaningful reference to God need not be unrevisable or exhaustive in its description of him. In fact, the variety of metaphors used for describing God in Scripture argues for a realistic perspective of God in that not any one image is regarded as adequate in itself to speak of him. When God is depicted as a shepherd rather than as some other kind of worker in certain texts it is because this particular metaphorical depiction is meaningful" (Huntzinger, "End of Exile," 89).

29. Chae, *Jesus*, 25–26; Huntzinger, "End of Exile," 78.

It occurs in the Psalms, notably in Psalm 23, but also carrying the images in others (i.e., Pss 28, 80, and 121).[30] During the monarchial narratives, YHWH is established as Israel's Shepherd and the monarch as YHWH's undershepherd.[31]

However, shepherd imagery is decidedly used of YHWH throughout the exodus and exilic narratives[32]—the two most liminal periods of Old Testament history.[33] Hence, the metaphor's use regarding God occurs at particular "times of upheaval and dislocation among the people."[34] In the exodus narratives, YHWH is the prime shepherd while in the exilic narratives, YHWH and his Davidic appointee are co-shepherds.[35] Ezekiel and Zechariah develop the description of this appointee in the context of an eschatological view of God's redemptive activity.[36] This usage becomes associated with Messiah in the prophetic tradition.[37]

These narratives make apparent that "YHWH as shepherd" is a central theme to understanding God's leadership, rule, and care for God's people. Notably, YHWH is only identified with a singular "flock" and never the plural "flocks." As Israel's Shepherd, YHWH's presence is in midst of the flock, before the flock, and behind the flock as necessary.[38] That YHWH is Israel's

30. Huntzinger, "End of Exile," 80–81.

31. Chae, *Jesus*, 26–27. See also Laniak, *Shepherds*, 108–14.

32. Chae, *Jesus*, 26.

33. J. Jeremias states: "It is to be noted that the references are spread evenly over the whole of the O.T. It is true that in Exodus-Deuteronomy shepherd terms are used in the exodus stories ('to lead,' 'to guide,' 'to go before,'), but in general it is hard to determine whether there is any conscious feeling for the shepherd metaphor. More commonly, and with details which show how vital the concept is, the figure of speech is found in the Psalter and in the consoling prophecy of the Exile" (Jeremias, "ποιμήν," 487). With appreciation to Chae for this citation; Chae, *Jesus*, 26.

34. Huntzinger, "End of Exile," 81.

35. Chae, *Jesus*, 26.

36. Ibid., 38–94. Chae states: "One of the key outcomes of YHWH's eschatological shepherding will be the renewed obedience of the flock to YHWH's laws and decrees. To secure this, YHWH will set up one shepherd like David over the restored people. This is the consequence of the restorative act of YHWH, the true shepherd of Israel" (ibid., 92).

37. Huntzinger, "End of Exile," 82.

38. All three positions are demonstrated in the exodus narrative. As the people journeyed, they followed YHWH's pillar of cloud/fire that went before them (Exod 13:21–22). When the Israelites are pursued by Pharaoh's army, YHWH's pillar of cloud/fire is positioned behind Israel between them and the Egyptians in a defensive posture (Exod 14:19–20, 24). In the evenings and the Sabbath the tabernacle (the place of YHWH's presence) is placed in the middle of the camp with all the tribes surrounding it (Exod

Shepherd ruler, provider, and caretaker makes Israel's rejection of YHWH more shocking (1 Sam 8:4–22).[39] God's dire warnings against earthly rulers create a context by which to compare the good rule of YHWH with the evil rule of the hirelings.[40] Ultimately, YHWH removes these Jewish rulers and ruling instead through Gentile kings.[41] Throughout, YHWH is shepherd and keeper of the flock, determining their rebuke and redemption.

Human Leadership

The third Old Testament usage of "shepherd" references the earthly rulers of Israel, both political and religious.[42] Although implied regarding Moses and later Joshua,[43] it becomes normative in the Davidic narrative.[44] Those who ruled after David would likewise be associated as undershepherd-kings, but with the caveat of being measured against David, the "man after God's own heart" (1 Sam 13:14; cf. Acts 13:22, NASB). Those who acted in faithfulness to YHWH are associated with good shepherds; those who

---

40:34–38; Num 2: 2ff.).

39. Laniak writes: "Israel received its desired king, but only on the condition that it understand his role as derivative from and dependent upon the rule of YHWH, the flock's true Owner. Kings, beginning with Saul, were to be measured in term of their responsiveness to the words of that Owner, words mediated regularly through his messengers the prophets" (*Shepherds*, 102).

40. See particularly Ezek 34 and Zech 10–11.

41. Interestingly, Cyrus, King of Persia, is called "shepherd," one of the only times Gentile rulers are referenced thusly. Chae states that, "the case of Cyrus may characterize YHWH's free and sovereign exercise of his shepherd rulership" (Chae, *Jesus*, 25 n. 34).

42. This usage occurs nearly half of the times when רעה is translated "shepherd." See regarding Israelite rulers: Num 27:17; 1 Sam 21:8; 2 Sam 5:2; 7:7–8; 1 Kgs 2:17; Ps 78:70–72; Isa 56:11; Jer 2:8; 3:15; 10:21; 22:22; 23:1–4; 25:34–36; 50:6; Ezek 34:2–10; Zech 10:3; 11:5–8. See regarding Gentile rulers: Isa 44:28; Jer 6:3; 12:10; 25:34–36; 49:19; 50:44; Nah 3:18. Chae, *Jesus*, 25. See also, Duguid, *Ezekiel*.

43. Laniak, *Shepherds*, 77–93. As indicated above, this is to be understood as having characteristics of shepherding, not as being the shepherd, thus supplanting YHWH's place as Israel's Shepherd.

44. Huntzinger, "End of Exile," 78–80. Huntzinger notes that David was "shepherd-king of the people. God is the owner of the flock, but David is given charge of the flock. This delegation of power is distinctive to the image of shepherd-king in Israel and underscores the fact that God is ultimately shepherd of his people" (ibid., 79). Further, he sites 2 Sam 7:5–10 as support for David's role as undershepherd. Ibid., 80. See also Laniak, *Shepherds*, 248–49. As indicated earlier in this chapter, his example is the means by which David most acts in a shepherding manner, perhaps giving insight into 1 Pet 5:3.

acted unfaithfully with wicked shepherds.[45] However, it is notable that no-where in the Old Testament are ruling Jewish kings called "shepherd."[46]

By Ezekiel and Zechariah's day, political and religious leaders had co-opted the "shepherd" with disregard for YHWH's rule. Throughout the prophets, rulers who called themselves shepherds are decried as faithless, wicked, and thieving, caring for themselves rather than the flock under their care (see Ezek 34:1–10; Zech 10:3; 11:4–17).[47] Zechariah's oracle is particularly damning as he considers them hirelings, who run when the flock needs them the most.[48] Exilic usages of the shepherd metaphor in relation to earthly rulers express the very worst of those who use, abuse, and abandon the flock. In the end, YHWH determines to destroy these and to establish God's final shepherd in the Davidic Messiah.[49] This Shepherd will be present with God's people, leading them in faithfulness to God's rule, and caring for God's flock by restoring to them "shalom."[50]

This recalls an important pneumatological perspective: in the Old Testament, YHWH's pleasure and approval are associated with the rest-ing of God's Spirit upon God's own servants: Joseph, Moses, the judges, David, the prophets, etc. The terms "Spirit of God" and "Spirit of YHWH" are associated with those who are faithful undershepherds, fulfilling God's own desires. In Ezekiel, YHWH's removal of glory from the temple and ultimately from God's people represents YHWH's rejection of the cultic and political leadership of the day that had so destructively led Judah away from following God.[51] Those who served faithfully (albeit imperfectly) are associated with God's presence in the Spirit.[52] Those who serve unfaith-fully are associated with the Spirit's absence.[53] Thus, the coming of YHWH's Messianic shepherd will have God's Spirit residing upon him (Isa 11:2; 42:1; 61:1–2, Mic 5:4) as foreshadowing for the outpouring of YHWH's Spirit on

45. Huntzinger, "End of Exile," 80

46. Chae, *Jesus*, 26; Turner, "History of Religions Background," 38.

47. Laniak, *Shepherds*, 151–53, 162–68.

48. Ibid., 167–68.

49. Chae, *Jesus*, 93–94.

50. Ibid., 93–94.

51. Duguid, *Ezekiel*, 124, 131.

52. Laniak, *Shepherds*, 248. Note also Num 11:24–30: God sends the Spirit upon the 70 elders.

53. Note the dichotomy of Saul and David (1 Sam 11:6; 16:14; 16:13; Ps 51:11).

all God's people (Num 11:29; Isa 32:15; 44:3; Ezek 37;[54] 39:29; Joel 2:28–29; Zech 12:10).

Summary Thoughts–Old Testament Shepherding Imagery

Leadership and authority associated with the shepherd metaphor in the Old Testament ultimately resides with YHWH. The use of this image in the Old Testament is particularly prominent during seasons of adaptive/discontinuous change as evidenced by its dominant usage in the exodus and exilic narratives. The establishment of human authorities is a response to human frailties and is viewed by YHWH as rejection of God's own rule. While God grants this human request for a "king," the metaphor of shepherd is applied here with an undershepherd application, as YHWH is owner and final authority over the flock. Ironically, while herders have become socially despised by the time of the Old Testament's close, the leaders of Israel are despised by YHWH.

Despite later co-opting of the term "shepherd" by political and religious leaders, all human authority is ultimately determined as legitimate or illegitimate based on its faithfulness in relation to God with the Holy Spirit as indicator of God's presence and approval. This seems to reflect that in the context of herding, shepherds sometimes choose other sheep to help steer the herd (the Bedouin "bell" sheep), sheep which are chosen based on their love for and loyalty to the shepherd and obedience to God's voiced commands (Law).[55] Otherwise, human leaders as "shepherds" overwhelmingly are perceived as faithless, resulting in YHWH's determination to destroy the faithless shepherds and to establish a final Davidic Shepherd whose reign will be faithful and unending. This Shepherd will usher in a new era as expressed by the Spirit's residing in and on God's people.

54. Duguid, *Ezekiel*, 104–5.

55. See note 24 above.

Chapter 5

Our Leader Metaphor Revisited: New Testament

By the New Testament, shepherd imagery is widely accepted as part of the continuing heritage of the Jewish people. Particularly, Ezekiel and Zechariah's eschatological vision of the One promised shepherd in the line of David has formed messianic expectations.[1] In the New Testament, "shepherd" is the general translation of the noun ποιμήν and the act of "shepherding" or "tending" is a translation of the verb ποιμαίνω.[2] ποιμήν and ποιμαίνω are semantically used in a variety of ways.[3] I pursue these usages in a moment,

1. At the OT's close, the Davidic shepherd image is just coming into focus. During the intertestamental period, this image is influenced by Greek conquest (particularly the rule of Antiochus Epiphanes), a brief Maccabean revolt, and the eventual Roman domination. Interest in the one Davidic shepherd/messiah wanes with the advent of the Greek rule of Alexander and grows with the rise of the Hasmonean dynasty, which "revived messianism, spawned by the Maccabean revolt (163 B.C.)" (Chae, *Jesus*, 160–72, quote from 95). Ultimately, with the failed Maccabean revolt and the Roman conquest, many Jewish apocalyptic communities embraced a militaristic view of independence under the renewed Davidic kingdom. Laniak, *Shepherds*, 171–72. See also, Huntzinger, "End of Exile," 158–71.

2. ποιμαίνω is infrequently translated "rule," which will be discussed later in this chapter. The word more commonly translated "rule" in ecclesial contexts is ποΐστημι. See Lincoln, *Ephesians*, 251.

3. ποιμήν (noun) occurs 18 times in the New Testament (Matt–3, Mark–2, Luke–4, John–6, Eph–1, Heb.–1, 1 Pet.–1). ποιμαίνω (verb) occurs 11 times in the New Testament (Matt–1, Luke–1, John–1, Acts–1, 1 Cor–1, 1 Pet–1, Jude–1, Rev–4). Kubo, *Reader's Greek-English Lexicon*. Because errors in Kubo (for instance, Kubo lists 13 occurrences of ποιμήν in Matt; should be 3), Bauer's *Greek-English Lexicon* was cross-referenced, confirming number and usage. In these introductory paragraphs on New Testament usages of ποιμήν and ποιμαίνω, insights are drawn extensively from Bauer, *Greek-English*, 683–84; also of ἀρχιποίμην, ibid., 113.

but first a word about the New Testament considerations on authority and leadership, and the New Testament linguistic context.

New Testament Considerations on Power and Authority in Leadership

As with the Old Testament narratives, the New Testament narratives contain within them certain misconceptions and lost meanings that, when reframed, better inform an understanding of the shepherding metaphor in the New Testament. As previously indicated, this is not an all-encompassing discussion of power and authority. Instead, it is an attempt to clarify how misuses of the metaphor might conform more to patterns of the world than to the biblical narrative.

The Specter of Caesar

Much has been written regarding the political nature of Jesus' claims and then those of his followers as perceived by the Romans.[4] That the phrase "King of kings and Lord of lords" is associated with Jesus in the Western context is a sure sign of the victory of Christ over the Imperial cult of Rome and other competitors of the first three centuries.[5] It is important for our purposes to recognize the way in which "king" and "kingdom" language functions in relation to the New Testament context in order to under-

4. See for instance Carter, *Matthew and Empire*.

5. Osborne, *Revelation*, 686. That Caesar Augustus was recognized as a King of kings might be best seen in the biblical text with regards to Herod's response to the magi. As vassal king of the Jews in the service of the Roman emperor, Herod was tasked with promoting the Roman agenda set out for him by Caesar. The arrival of wise men from the East, likely Parthia-Rome's competitor for regional dominance, puts Herod in a difficult position with Caesar. Their pronouncement of a new king is intolerable as it falls outside of the Roman authority, and threatens the existing power structure with Herod's neck squarely on the block along with all who have capitulated to this structure to maintain their own power (i.e., the High Priest and Jewish Temple cult). Carter, *Matthew and Empire*, 11–17, 62–63. See also, Evans, "King Jesus," 120–25.

As fallout of the civil war with Mark Anthony and Cleopatra, Augustus will have Cleopatra and Julius' son, Caesarion, executed because Anthony's pronouncement that Cleopatra VII was "Queen of Kings" and Caesarion "King of kings" (Aune, "Influence, 22). It is also notable that the language "King of Kings" was used more explicitly in other empires including Egypt, Assyria, Babylon, Persia, and Parthia. Aune, *Revelation*, 953–55; Koester, *Revelation*, 759; Herms, *Apocalypse*, 202.

stand why its appropriation in terms of pastoral power and authority are misguided.

In the context of the Greco-Roman world, Zeus/Jupiter, the supreme god of the Roman world held the title of "King of kings."[6] Under Augustus and then throughout the first three centuries of the Roman Imperium, the term "son of god" and other variations on the theme are used of the Caesars. The implication is clear: Zeus is divine King of kings and his son the earthly embodiment of that rule. The response to deify dead Caesars and later living ones is the logical conclusion of the arc. It is also significant that the ruler of Rome's chief rival in the region, Parthia, more explicitly used the designation in reference to imperial reign in Parthia.[7]

Whether directly subsuming the title of Caesar or making a point of taking that of Caesar's rivals in the region, the use of "King of kings" and "Lord of lords" in association with Jesus the Anointed One (i.e., Heb.: "Messiah;" Grk.: "Christ") makes a clear distinction that Jesus alone rules.[8] By comparison, "[The Roman emperor's] absolute reign was pretense in light of the absolute sovereignty of the Lamb, the true "Lord of lords."[9] This becomes important in light of Jesus' commands about power and lording.

Power and Lording

As recorded in Matthew 20:20–28,[10] Jesus is asked by James' and John's mother that Jesus allow her sons to sit at the right and left of his throne when Jesus becomes King. After challenging them with the bitter cup of Jesus' mission, deferring to the Father's authority, and recognizing the indignation of the other ten, Jesus takes this as opportunity to teach his closest followers about power and authority: "You know that the rulers of the Gentiles lord it over them, and their great men exercise authority over them. It is not this way among you, but whoever wishes to become great

6. Koester, *Revelation*, 759.

7. Aune, *Revelation*, 954–55.

8. The use of the phrase so broadly used in the ancient Near East is intended to put all on notice that Jesus alone rules. With regard to Caesar specifically, Osborne notes, "the Lamb, not the Antichrist . . . is Lord of lords and King of kings" (Osborne, *Revelation*, 623). It is noteworthy that the use of the phrase "King of Kings" to describe Caesarion was sufficient to have him executed by Augustus. Caesar allows no rivals. Aune, *Revelation*, 945.

9. Osborne, *Revelation*, 623.

10. Cf. Mark 10:35–45.

among you shall be your servant, and whoever wishes to be first among you shall be your slave; just as the Son of Man did not come to be served, but to serve, and to give his life a ransom for many."[11] The contrast is clear: Jesus' followers serve; the Gentile rulers (Caesar, his ruling elite and patrons) lord and enslave. These two kingdoms are distinct and different. And the means by which people in leadership lead determines which kingdom he or she serves.

The suggestion and ongoing misperception that pastoral leaders "rule the church" is a dangerous narrative to pursue because in so doing pastoral leaders 1) determine by their leadership that the kingdom of Caesar is preferable to the kingdom of Christ, and 2) place themselves in a place of rivalry with the only One who is able to claim kingly authority, namely Jesus, the King of kings and Lord of lords. This is not to say that leadership has no function. Returning briefly to the Old Testament, the kings were intended to be exemplary citizens of YHWH's kingdom. Peter picks up this discussion on power and lording in 1 Peter 5 in the context of "shepherding"[12] elders are reminded to give oversight and leadership "not yet as lording it over those allotted to your charge, but proving to be *examples* to the flock."[13] Paul likewise picks up the theme of exemplary leadership in 1 Corinthians where Paul states, "Follow my example, as I follow the example of Christ."[14] These themes then reshape application of New Testament usage of the Shepherd metaphor.

New Testament Patterns of Usage for "Shepherd"

First, ποιμήν (the noun form of the word) is used literally of herders only in the birth narrative of Luke 2. Otherwise, it occurs as simile in numerous places: crowds who are lost "like sheep without a shepherd" (Matt 9:36; Mark 6:34), of Christ as a shepherd who separates the "sheep from the

---

11. Matt 20:25–28; NASB.

12. This usage will be discussed more fully later in this chapter.

13. 1 Pet 5:3, emphasis added; NASB.

14. 1 Cor 11:1; NIV.

goats" (Matt 25:32),[15] Jesus the "Good Shepherd" of John 10.[16] Likewise, Matthew and Mark recognize Jesus as Zechariah's stricken shepherd and the disciples as a scattered flock (Matt 26:31; Mark 14:27; cf. Zech 13:7).[17]

A second usage as a noun is figurative of church leadership. Interestingly, this usage only occurs four times in the noun form.[18] Three of these four times it refers to Christ as "shepherd" of the church—twice in emphasized fashion ("great Shepherd of the flock," Heb 13:20; "Chief Shepherd," 1 Pet 5:4).[19] The fourth time it occurs regarding church leadership is in Eph 4:11 where it is usually translated "pastor" in reference to church leaders.[20]

In this same figurative context regarding church leadership, the verb ποιμαίνω is used equally for human leadership in the church and Christ's leadership over the church. Regarding human leadership, ποιμαίνω is translated as "tend"[21] and "shepherd."[22] Regarding Christ's leadership,

15. Luke uses ποιμαίνω when Jesus speaks in simile of a servant "tending the sheep" (Luke 17:7, NRSV) before coming in to serve the tables. Similarly, Paul uses ποιμαίνω while discussing his right to earn a living: "Who at any time pays the expenses for doing military service? Who plants a vineyard and does not eat any of its fruit? Or who *tends* a flock and does not get any of its milk?" (1 Cor 9:7, NRSV; emphasis added). Otherwise, ποιμαίνω occurs referencing church leadership.

16. Allegorical shepherd imagery also occurs in the parable of the lost sheep: "So he told them this parable: 'Which one of you, having a hundred sheep and losing one of them, does not leave the ninety-nine in the wilderness and go after the one that is lost until he finds it? When he has found it, he lays it on his shoulders and rejoices. And when he comes home, he calls together his friends and neighbors, saying to them, "Rejoice with me, for I have found my sheep that was lost." Just so, I tell you, there will be more joy in heaven over one sinner who repents than over ninety-nine righteous persons who need no repentance'" (Luke 15:3–7, NRSV; cf. Matt 18:12–13). Note: ποιμήν and ποιμαίνω are not used in this context.

17. Matthew likewise cites Mic 5:2 referencing the ruler who comes from Bethlehem "to shepherd [ποιμαίνω] my people Israel" (Matt 2:6, NRSV).

18. Including ἀρχιποίμην (1 Pet 5:4).

19. Heb 13:20: "τὸν ποιμένα τῶν προβάτων τὸν μέγαν." The third reference is in 1 Pet 2:25 where Christ is described as the "shepherd and guardian of your souls" (NRSV): "τὸν ποιμένα καὶ ἐπίσκοπον τῶν ψυχῶν ὑμῶν." Note: Jesus addresses his followers as his "little flock" in Luke 12:32.

20. ποιμένας (nom. masc. pl.) is listed as one of Christ's gifts (with apostles, prophets, evangelists, and teachers) to the church to "to equip the saints for the work of ministry, for building up the body of Christ, until all of us come to the unity of the faith and of the knowledge of the Son of God, to maturity, to the measure of the full stature of Christ" (Eph 4:12–13, NRSV).

21. John 21:1 in NRSV, NASB; 1 Pet 5:2 in NASB.

22. Acts 20:28 in NRSV, NASB; 1 Pet 5:2 in NRSV.

ποιμαίνω occurs in two books: Matt 2:6[23] and Revelation. The Revelation usages are interesting because three of the four usages referencing Christ are exclusively translated "rule."[24] ποιμαίνω is never translated by the NRSV nor the NASB as "rule" for non-Christ persons in the New Testament.[25]

Other New Testament images develop around shepherding imagery that use neither ποιμήν nor ποιμαίνω, but clearly reference these concepts. These images and semantic patterns reflect Old Testament influences and themes that continue to inform New Testament conceptualizations. Three similar patterns of usages occur: herders of sheep, Jesus—YHWH incarnate as Davidic/Messianic Shepherd, and church leaders in under-shepherd leadership roles.

Sheep Herders

As stated above, Luke's Gospel is the only New Testament document recording the presence of shepherds (Luke 2). New Testament scholarship confirms continuation of Old Testament beliefs that herders are scoundrels and thieves.[26] This may have been in part because of their transient nature.[27] As important, the shepherds' occupation kept them from ceremonial cleanliness. It is ironic that those keeping the flocks for the cult sacrifice were themselves unable to participate in such sacrifice. That these are recipients of the nativity announcement has widely been regarded as expressing God's inclination toward society's outcasts.[28]

23. ποιμαίνω here is a Greek translation of רָעָה. An alternate translation here is "rule" (NRSV). Garland notes that Matthew conflates Mic 5:2 and 2 Sam 5:2 (1 Chron 11:2) which "contains God's promise to David, 'you shall shepherd my people Israel' (see 9:36; 10:6; 15:24)" (Garland, *Reading Matthew*, 29).

24. Rev 2:27; 12:5; and 19:15 (NRSV, NASB). Translated "shepherd" only in Rev 7:17 (NRSV, NASB).

25. ἀρχή normally references human rulers; usage #3 in Bauer, *Greek-English Lexicon*, 112. Likewise, see ἄρχων (ibid., 113–14) and the verb ἄρχω (ibid., 113). Also, see note 2 regarding ποῖστημι.

26. Huntzinger, "End of Exile," 66–69.

27. As Turner suggests: "one may consider the shepherd as a *liminal* figure, oscillating between two worlds, between the isolation of the wilderness and the hustle and bustle of the settled communities" (Turner, "History of Religions Background," 40; emphasis in original).

28. See Hendricksen, *Gospel according to Luke*, 149; Barclay, *Gospel of Luke*, 22–23; Tolbert, "Luke," 29. Contra: Bock, *Luke 1:1—9:50*, 213–14.

Jesus—YHWH Incarnate the Messianic Shepherd

As described above, Ezekiel and Zechariah, among others, proclaimed an eschatological hope for Israel's redemption through a promised messianic shepherd from David's line. Within this context, Jesus—YHWH incarnate—enters history. It is the central Christian position that Jesus is the God/Man, fully divine and fully human—God in flesh. Turner's observation of the liminal nature of shepherding makes shepherd an apt metaphor for Jesus as the "mediator between the divine sphere and the luxurious, seductive sphere of civilised existence."[29] Further, this theological position is formed by Jesus' claims to be God. Jesus' declaration to be the Good Shepherd of Israel is one of those claims, identifying himself as YHWH, Shepherd of Israel.

It should be no surprise that Jesus associated himself with the weak, meek, and socially outcast. The metaphorical use of shepherd plays into this construct. As the shepherd who goes after the one lost sheep (Matt 18:12–13; Luke 15:3–7), Jesus clarifies that his mission is to "seek out and to save the lost" (Luke 19:10, NRSV; cf. Matt 15:24; 18:11–13).[30] Thus, Jesus recaptures the Old Testament shepherd imagery and reshapes it in light of religious collusion with the powers and principalities of Rome.[31] The gospels clearly identify Jesus as the promised shepherd and focus the imagery on Jesus as YHWH's eschatological messiah, while reclaiming the metaphor from militaristic overtones that developed over time, but especially in the intertestamental period.[32]

One other note before investigating specific usages: just as the Old Testament messages link the eschatological Shepherd with the Holy Spirit, the New Testament also emphasizes the link between Jesus and the Holy Spirit. The two Gospel birth narratives both record the Spirit's involvement in Jesus' conception (Matt 1:18, 20; Luke 1:35). The Spirit descends upon Jesus at his baptism along with the heavenly voice of affirmation (Matt 3:16; Mark 1:10; Luke 3:22; John 1:32; cf. Matt 12:18; Isa 42:1). John the Baptizer portrays Jesus as one who will immerse his followers into the Spirit (Matt 3:11; Luke 3:16; John 1:33). Further, Jesus promises the coming of the Spirit upon his followers at his return to the Father (Mark 13:11; Luke 11:13;

29. Turner, "History of Religions Background," 40.

30. As Huntzinger reminds, this is not the only image Jesus and his followers employ to describe Jesus's ministry. Huntzinger, "End of Exile," 172–74.

31. Ibid., 172–78.

32. See Chae, *Jesus*, 159, 169. See also France, *Gospel of Mark*, 261.

12:12; John 14:25–27; 16:7–15; John 20:22; Acts 1:8). The presence of the Spirit in Jesus further identifies him as the promised shepherd of YHWH's flock. That Jesus promised (and provided) the Spirit's presence in all of his flock speaks to important realities for his flock's ability to hear and respond to his abiding presence with significant implications for "undershepherds."

The Synoptics

The Synoptic Gospels most commonly use the shepherding motif referring to Jesus as the promised Davidic shepherd of the prophets. In Matt 9:35–38 and Mark 6:34, Jesus is moved to compassion because he sees the people are "harassed and helpless" (Matt 9:36) like "sheep without a shepherd." David E. Garland comments on the desperate missional nature of the situation, remarking that "if Israel, who was supposed to be a light to the nations, is lost, as Jesus divulges in 10:6 (see 15:24), how great must be the darkness for the nations?"[33] This "shepherdless" image recalls Ezek 34 and Zech 9–11 where the prophets describe the abandoned and plundered flock awaiting "YHWH—the ultimate shepherd of Israel—[who] promises to come and shepherd his flock by himself, thereby seeking the lost, healing the sick, and strengthening the weak."[34] Demonstrating Jesus as YHWH incarnate (the promised shepherd), Matt 9:35–36 presents the exact picture presented in Ezek 34:16.[35] To an uncared for and untended flock, Jesus intervenes and becomes their shepherd (Luke 12:32).[36]

The Synoptics identify Jesus as a shepherd seeking his lost sheep (Matt 10:6, 16; 15:24).[37] Exilic themes of lostness and wandering are brought into relation with the shepherd who provides rest (Matt 11:28; cf. Ps 23:1–3a). Jesus fulfills his role as shepherd by restoring the flock to a place of wholeness. In so doing, he identifies himself as YHWH in flesh,[38] putting himself

33. Garland, *Reading Matthew*, 109.

34. Chae, *Jesus*, 209.

35. Ibid.

36. France, *Gospel of Mark*, 265; Lane, *Gospel according to Mark*, 225–26; Chae, *Jesus*, 208–12. Specifically with regard to Jesus as healer (bringer of "shalom"), see ibid., 279–326.

37. France, *Gospel of Mark*, 212–19. Garland demonstrates that while the primary mission at this moment in Matthew is to the "lost sheep of Israel," mission to the Gentiles is "anticipated everywhere in the Gospel ([10:18] 24:14; 26:13; 28:19)" (Garland, *Reading Matthew*, 112).

38. Per Chae: "By assuming YHWH's role, Jesus gathers YHWH's flock as promised

further at odds with the religious leaders who viewed him as an idolater and heretic. That Jesus was Messiah is undoubted in Matthew's perspective as he attributes to Jesus the prophecy of one who would "rule" (ποιμαίνω) coming from Bethlehem (Matt 2:6; cf. Mic 5:2; 2 Sam 5:2).

Jesus utilized the shepherd imagery in Matt 25, describing himself as the eschatological shepherd-judge who separates the sheep from the goats,[39] dispensing justice to the good and the evil.[40] Here Jesus associates with the poor, weak, and least as their king and defender.[41] However, the shepherd king is also the stricken king (Matt 26:30–35; Mark 14: 26–31). Before he judges, Jesus must die and the flock be scattered. Then, he is raised as everlasting ruler and shepherd judge who gathers his community.[42] Appropriating Zechariah's prophecies, Jesus demonstrates that he is the promised shepherd, not only in strength, but also in weakness, giving his life for his flock.[43]

John 10

In John 10, Jesus gives an extended illustration of his divine mission through the metaphor of the Good Shepherd.[44] He recounts the contrast between the Good Shepherd and hirelings and wicked shepherds (Ezek 34; Zech 9–11).[45] By giving his life, Jesus demonstrates the depth of his devotion as the flock's shepherd.[46] Contrastingly, the thieves and wicked shepherds use

in the Old Testament Davidic Shepherd tradition" (Chae, *Jesus*, 218). Jesus thereby claims in action and word an Old Testament role reserved for YHWH.

39. Garland, *Reading Matthew*, 242.

40. Chae, *Jesus*, 219–32; Laniak, *Shepherds*, 191–92.

41. Huntzinger, "End of Exile," 233; Laniak, *Shepherds*, 192.

42. Chae, *Jesus*, 327–71.

43. Laniak, *Shepherds*, 179–81; Chae, *Jesus*, 327–71. Chae demonstrates that the resurrection of Christ is the reversal of Zech prophecy regarding scattering. Jesus the resurrected Shepherd gathers and sends as divine Lord over all nations, that YHWH's promise to Abraham might be fulfilled. Ibid., 347–59.

44. Laniak suggests a more appropriate title might be the "Model Shepherd." In addition to semantic rationale (particularly the usage of "καλὸς"), Laniak notes that Jesus is calling his followers to live a life that reflects his own, even to the point of death. Laniak, *Shepherds*, 211–12.

45. Ibid., 210.

46. Notice that Jesus is identified not only as shepherd (ποιμήν) but also as sacrificial lamb (ὁ ἀμνὸς τοῦ θεοῦ; John 1: 29, 35, cf. Rev 7:17). This reversal occurs only in John's writing. Ibid, 218–20.

the flock for their own purposes—a commentary on the religio-political context of Jesus' day.[47]

In addition to emphasizing his intention to die for his flock, Jesus emphasizes his knowledge of the flock and their mutual knowledge of him.[48] The flock hears his voice and knows it, responding to his calling. They know him because he gives his life for them according to the Father's will. His devotion and love are manifested in this act, unlike the hireling who runs from danger.[49] In a final missional note, Jesus explains that the Good Shepherd expands the flock, adding to his fold those outside (i.e., Gentiles).[50]

The gospels utilize shepherding imagery in a variety of ways, most frequently portraying Jesus as the shepherd of the flock, fulfilling Ezekiel and Zechariah's prophecies.[51] Jesus' self-proclamation to be shepherd is indicative of his claim to be YHWH incarnate.[52] These understandings influenced Peter and others in their later writings.[53]

General Epistles

While the shepherd image is not the only, nor even the primary metaphor used in 1 Peter,[54] 1 Peter is one of three places outside the Gospels where the image occurs in reference to Jesus. Written during a time of intense persecution, 1 Peter reminds its readers of Jesus, their suffering shepherd, as a means of comfort in their own suffering.[55] As "aliens" and "strangers" (1:1; 2:11), these followers are like "wandering sheep" (2:25),[56] in the presence

47. Ibid., 213.

48. Ibid., 216–18; Turner, "History of Religions Background," 41–43; Painter, "Tradition, History and Interpretation," 65.

49. Haenchen, *John 2*, 48. As a result of his resurrection, those entrusted to his care are unable to be snatched away.

50. Beasley-Murray, *John*, 171; Haenchen, *John 2*, 48–49. Contra: Painter, "Tradition, History and Interpretation," 65–66.

51. See, Martin, *Metaphor and Composition*, 258–60.

52. See Achtemeier, *1 Peter*, 204.

53. Michaels, *1 Peter*, 151.

54. Troy Martin notes that the theme of diaspora is the "controlling metaphor" of 1 Peter and as such, recalls the exodus and exilic wanderings. Martin, *Metaphor and Composition*, 144–61. See also, Laniak, *Shepherds*, 226–29.

55. Laniak, *Shepherds*, 229–31; Elliot, *1 Peter*, throughout, but especially 520–39.

56. Elliot states this image is a conflation of Isa 53:6 and Ezek 34:4–11, 16. Elliot, *1 Peter*, 537–38.

of the devouring lion—the Devil (5:8), metaphors used in literary contexts where Jesus is identified as shepherd of the flock (2:25, 5:4).[57] As shepherd, Jesus leads the wanderers, protecting them from being devoured in a threatening and dangerous (liminal) world.[58] Jesus' primacy as shepherd is amplified in 1 Peter by the modifier ἀρχι (also in Hebrews by μέγαν).[59] Whatever role others have *within* the flock, their role exists under Jesus' rule *over* the flock.[60]

Revelation

Finally, in Revelation John returns to the metaphor of shepherd to describe Jesus. In a construct unique to John, Jesus is described as the lamb who is the shepherd (Rev 7:17).[61] This "lamb" has "shepherded" a flock from every people ("ἐκ παντὸσ ἔθνους"; Rev 7:9) to his throne fulfilling the missional work of bringing "others" into his flock (cf. John 10:16). In this particular shepherd motif, Jesus is a loving, guiding shepherd who cares for those who have suffered and been martyred for following the lamb (Rev 6:9–11; 7:14–16; cf. 1 Pet 2:19–25; 5:10–11). However, in the remaining usages of ποιμαίνω the lamb "rules" over the nations as judge and king against a "preying" enemy (Rev 2:27 (cf. Ps 2:9); 12:5; 19:15).[62] Amplifying this image, Christ rules with an iron rod, an Old Testament symbol of absolute power found in all three New Testament contexts where ποιμαίνω is thusly used.[63] It bears repeating that ποιμαίνω is never used in the New Testament as "rule" referring to human governance (ecclesial or otherwise).

57. Laniak, *Shepherds*, 229–34.

58. This recalls the YHWH shepherd metaphor of the Old Testament. Martin, *Metaphor and Composition*, 263. Michaels associates ποιμήν and ἐπίσκοπος under the shepherding motif. Michaels, *1 Peter*, 151–52.

59. In Heb 13:20 Jesus is the "great Shepherd of the sheep" (τὸν ποιμένα τῶν προβάτων τὸν μέγαν). In 5:4, Peter uses the unique construct ἀρχιποίμην in referencing Jesus as the Chief Shepherd indicating his primacy as owner of the flock as well as his role as keeper. Achtemeier, *1 Peter*, 329.

60. The Hebrew's writer uses shepherd only in 13:20, but as Bruce states, "it is a title which comprehends the other roles which are assigned to Him" (Bruce, *Epistle to the Hebrews*, 410–11).

61. Mounce, *Book of Revelation*, 175–76.

62. Ibid., 176 n. 32.

63. Mounce states that ruling with an iron rod in this context "means to destroy rather than to govern in a stern fashion. The shepherd not only leads his flock to pasture but defends the sheep from marauding beasts. His rod is a weapon of retaliation. The

Shepherd Elders in the Church

A third usage of the shepherd motif relates to Christ's "undershepherds." This usage is rare, yet it is the most common title for the congregational leadership office ("pastor") in the church. The following contexts demonstrate this usage.

John 21:15ff.

At the conclusion of John's Gospel, Jesus reinstates and commissions Peter using shepherding imagery.[64] John 21:15–17 contains three distinct commands given in response to Peter's declaration of love: "feed my lambs," "tend my lambs," "feed my sheep."[65] The imagery here is clear: Jesus, the Good and Chief Shepherd, charges Peter to care for those for whom Jesus has cared. Often lost here is that Jesus does not relinquish ownership of the flock nor does he offer Peter unlimited control of the flock.[66] Also, Jesus does not give Peter authority to "rule" over the flock, but to "feed" and "tend" the flock from within it.[67] Feeding and tending are matters of care and love not domination and power.[68] Further, Jesus' charge to Peter does not imply Jesus' absence, which would ignore the pneumatologically mediated presence of Christ in his followers (Acts 2). Rather, caring for others is Peter's demonstration of love for his Shepherd.[69] Recall the image of the Bedouin bell sheep chosen to keep flock cohesion because of their love for the shepherd in their midst. Peter's role is to follow his Shepherd, hearing the voice of Jesus and then passionately clanging his bell so that the flock might likewise follow the Shepherd. This devotion is Peter's witness to God's reign and Christ's "divine mission."[70] Such devotion would be necessary in the days between Jesus' ascension and the anticipated coming of the

Messiah's rod is a rod of iron; that is, it is strong and unyielding in its mission of judgment" (ibid., 347).

64. Haenchen, *John 2*, 226.

65. John 21:15, "βόσκε τὰ ἀρνία μου." John 21:16, "ποίμαινε τὰ πρόβατά μου." John 21:17, "βόσκε τὰ πρόβατά μου."

66. Brown, *Gospel according to John*, 1115–17. See also Köstenberger, *John*, 596.

67. Brown, *Gospel according to John*, 1116.

68. Borchert, *John 12–21*, 336.

69. Laniak, *Shepherds*, 222.

70. Borchert, *John 12–21*, 337. D. Moody Smith Jr. notes that Jesus' questioning of Peter was a test of Peter's loyalty, perhaps for Peter's sake. Smith, *John 4*, 396–97.

promised Spirit, when these Jewish believers would experience significant discontinuous change that required a new adaptive manner of obedience to God.

Acts 20:28–31

In Luke's account of Paul's journeys, Paul's usage of the shepherd imagery is unusual as he rarely references this image in his writings. Consistent with biblical narrative, Paul emphasizes that the flock is God's, purchased with divine blood.[71] A peculiarity in this passage is reference to the selection of these leaders by the Holy Spirit. This suggests communal recognition of the Spirit's rule over the congregation and the leaders' sensitivity to the Spirit's presence.[72]

Referencing the activity of the "elders" (20:17) who are "overseers" (20:28) of the flock they "shepherd" (20:28; NRSV, NASB), Paul draws together all three of the dominant terms used to describe ecclesial leadership.[73] This seems to equate the three roles in the congregation, causing some to question whether three distinct offices existed in the New Testament church.[74] Despite differing terminology, the same expectation of meekness, gentleness, and love apply to leaders throughout the New Testament. The use of the plural (common in Luke) indicates a plurality of leadership, avoiding "individualism, monarchial authoritarianism or simple economic necessity turn[ing] the pastoral role into a 'one-man show' . . . ."[75]

Paul's charge to "keep watch over yourself" as well as over "the flock" indicates a commonality between shepherding elders and the flock. They cannot claim authoritative superiority, since they also need watching, presumably by the other shepherding elders.[76] Finally, it is significant that Paul's charge comes to the Ephesian leaders at a time of liminality. Paul's departure with no expected return, the imminent presence of "savage wolves," attempts at distorting the truth—these expectations point to immense

71. Bruce, *Acts*, 392–93; Dunn, *Acts of the Apostles*, 272–73. Gaveneta, *Acts*, 287–88.

72. Polhill, *Acts*, 426–27. See also, Bruce, *Acts*, 392; Gaveneta, *Acts*, 287–88.

73. πρεσβυτέρους (vs. 17, noun translated as "elders"); ἐπισκόπους (vs. 28, noun translated as "overseers," later "bishop"); ποιμαίνειν (vs. 28, verb translated as "shepherd").

74. Perhaps "pastor," "elder," and "overseer" are different perspectives on the same church leadership role. Larkin, *Acts*, 298.

75. Larkin, *Acts*, 297.

76. Ibid.; Polhill, *Acts*, 426.

difficulties and change. The shepherding elders are responsible for guiding the flock through these difficult times. Fittingly, Paul's final words are "remembering the words of Jesus . . ." (20:35). A fellow sheep in Christ's flock, Paul sounded the way to following Jesus' call (1 Cor 4:16; 11:1; 1 Thess 1:6).

Ephesians 4:11

Significantly, Paul's letter to the Ephesians is the only other place where he uses ποιμήν. Paul views the placement of "pastors" (along with apostles, prophets, evangelists, and teachers)[77] into the Ephesians' context as Christ's gifts to his church (Eph 4:11). Christ utilizes individuals from within the community to empower the flock for the community's work (Eph 4:12).[78] The question of office is much debated; however, Hoehner is adamant that these describe "function with no hint of reference to an office."[79] There is further indication that this usage signifies an overlap in meaning between elder, overseer, and pastor without design toward authoritarian rule.[80] Like the Acts 20 passage, a plurality of leadership is assumed with equal accesses to God's grace afforded to all the community.[81]

1 Peter 5:1–4

In 1 Pet 5:1–4, the author utilizes several important constructions that aid understanding for the role of pastoral persons.[82] First is the unique use of

77. Much has been written regarding the association of ποιμήν and διδάσκαλος. This author sides with Lincoln who sees these as two roles in the congregation with closely related functions. Lincoln, *Ephesians*, 250. Also Hoehner, *Ephesians*, 545.

78. Simpson rightly contends that Christ has not left the church orphaned, but rules over his church guiding its way by his design. Simpson, "Ephesians," 94.

79. Hoehner, *Ephesians*, 544. Lincoln, *Ephesians*, 250–51, 252. Contra: Klein, "Ephesians," 118–19.

80. Lincoln, *Ephesians*, 251; Perkins, *Ephesians* 100.

81. "The New Testament affords no hint of a priestly caste, 'commanding all the approaches of the soul to Him', usurpers of the title they clutch at; but the universal priesthood of believers, each occupying his proper place in the body of Christ, has its clear authorization. In the theocracy of grace there is in fact no laity" (Simpson, "Ephesians," 95). See also Garland, "A Life Worthy of the Calling," 523.

82. Notice the similar commingling of terms as in Act 20:28 with "elder," "overseer" (oversight), and "shepherd" (tend) used inter-relatedly. Laniak, *Shepherds*, 232–33; Elliot, *1 Peter*, 822; Jobes, *1 Peter*, 302–04. It is impossible to read this passage and not recall John 21:15–18. Michaels, *1 Peter*, 282; Elliot, *1 Peter*, 823; Jobes, *1 Peter*, 304.

ἀρχιποίμενος in the context of instructing the undershepherds.[83] Referring to the elders as his "fellow elders,"[84] Peter notes from a position of mutuality that they are all accountable to Christ for care of Christ's flock. Never are persons with pastoral responsibilities given freedom to do as they wish (cf. Ezek 34; Zech 9–11).[85] They are entrusted with the task of following the Chief Shepherd and leading the others to do likewise.[86]

Second, this passage reflects a κύριος/ποιμήν dichotomy. In a recitation of the words of Jesus (Matt 20:25ff.; Mark 10:42; Luke 22:24–27; cf. Ezek 34:4), Peter reminds the elders that they are to "tend" God's flock, leading by example, not "lording" over them.[87] Shepherd elders care, not by harsh demanding/driving leadership, but by example because there is only one Lord (κύριος), the Chief Shepherd—Jesus.[88]

Third, Peter notes that these elders are "among" (NRSV, NASB) the flock ("οὖν ἐν ὑμῖν" vs. 1; "τὸ ἐν ὑμῖν" v. 2).[89] Peter reminds elders and non-elders that shepherd elders are also sheep embedded in Christ's flock.[90] While their calling gives them responsibility within the context, it is so because of their embeddeding within the flock.[91] Again, the Bedouin bell sheep are exemplary: shepherd elders lead by example from within the flock

83. Achtemeier, *1 Peter*, 329.

84. Marshall, *1 Peter*, 160–61; Davids, *First Epistle of Peter*, 176.

85. Elliot rejects a formalized understanding of offices in this context. "The elders do not occupy positions in a hierarchialized organizational structure, of which there is no hint in 1 Peter. It is thus inappropriate and anachronistic to speak of them as 'officials' or 'office-holders'" (Elliot, *1 Peter*, 815).

86. Davids, *First Epistle of Peter*, 180–82.

87. This is part of a series used to describe Godly leadership, each offset by μὴ or μηδὲ and ἀλλὰ: "*not* under compulsion, *but* willingly . . . *not* for sordid gain, *but* eagerly . . ." (NRSV; emphasis added) "*not* as lording . . . *but* be examples" (NASB; emphasis added). Laniak, *Shepherds*, 233; Marshall, *1 Peter*, 163; Elliot, *1 Peter*, 832; Achtemeier, *1 Peter*, 326–27; Davids, *First Epistle of Peter*, 178–80.

88. Laniak, *Shepherds*, 234; Martin, *Metaphor and Composition*, 260–61; Davids, *First Epistle of Peter*, 180–81. Achtemeier notes that Jesus' life is the "supreme instance of one who provided the example for Christian conduct . . ." (Achtemeier, *1 Peter*, 328).

89. Michaels, *1 Peter*, 283.

90. Laniak, *Shepherds*, 234 n. 43; Jobes, *1 Peter*, 308. Achtemeier states: "Christians are not the subjects of the elders, as is the case in the secular realm with leaders and subjects, but rather all Christians belong to God, and so the presbyters must carry out their duties as servants of God, not as lords of the Christians under their care. Arrogance toward other Christians and arbitrary exercise of power have no place in the leadership of the church . . ." (Achtemeier, *1 Peter*, 329).

91. Elliot, *1 Peter*, 831.

as they passionately follow the Chief Shepherd, with their lives "clanging" for others to follow as well.[92] This is especially important during times of adaptation, difficult and changing times of opposition, when the desire to renounce the gospel of God is most appealing. For Peter's readers, persecution most certainly would have tempted many to abandon following Jesus. Living among a marginal people in the context of social change, shepherd elders were to live lives that inspired the flock to hear and follow Christ despite the pain such devotion would require.

Summary Thoughts—New Testament Shepherding Imagery

Like the Old Testament, the New Testament utilizes shepherding imagery in two primary ways: Jesus as the Great Chief Shepherd of his people and of undershepherds who serve Christ's flock through the Spirit's prompting. Jesus' claim to be the shepherd of God's people is a claim to be God incarnate. The presence of the Spirit in his life and work and his promise to send the Spirit to his followers seals his claim. For followers of Christ, the Spirit leads the congregation to recognize some as guides for the flock. These shepherd elders oversee the flock's well-being, understanding that they serve at the Spirit's will within a specific embedded context.

These shepherd elders lead by their exemplary lives, following the Great Shepherd and inviting others to join them in witnessing God's activity in the world. Shepherd elders serve mutually with others, each set aside by a congregation who recognize the Spirit's consecration of these individuals. Regarding the question of office, it seems that New Testament writers did not intend an office when speaking of "pastors." There is also no sense that shepherd elders functioned in perpetuity, which is more similar to the Old Testament Levitical priesthood than the New Testament priesthood of all believers over whom Christ is the High Priest. Rather than establishing a hierarchical, rigid structure, Christ in his Spirit rules the church with fluidity.

---

92. "Elders are therefore to exercise their authority by showing through their conduct how Christians are to live their own lives" (Achtemeier, *1 Peter*, 328).

Implications of Biblical Imagery

From this investigation into the biblical imagery, there are several important implications for our understanding of the metaphor and its practical application to the life of God's people. First, God reserves sole claim as shepherd of God's people. Only one "rules" the church—Jesus Christ, through the presence of the Spirit, on behalf of the Father. While God utilizes "undershepherds," it is always with the caveat that they answer to God for their role. Second, the Old Testament and New Testament both emphasize the Spirit's presence in the lives of leaders. The New Testament amplifies this by the Spirit's presence in all believers, thus assigning "undershepherds" as guides for helping God's people discern the Spirit's promptings. This does not ignore the guidelines of the New Testament (particularly Paul) that church leaders be filled with the Spirit. Rather it illustrates that they must have a unique, even an uncommonly special sensitivity to the Spirit that that makes them more able to guide the flock to hear and follow the Shepherd and to participate in his work.

Third, for pastoral leaders, this means empowering others to hear and respond to God's promptings as they move onto God's agenda and become witnesses of God's missional activity in the world. This requires helping the church to discover, empower, and release other shepherd elders. Finally, pastoral leaders must be embedded participants in the congregation. These primarily lead by example. Shepherd elders are sheep in the flock helping others follow the shepherd. This becomes particularly important when the "old ways" no longer seem to fit the new experiences. The flock must seek the Shepherd more earnestly to be certain that it is his voice they are hearing (John 10:3, 5, 16) and not just purveyors of passing new trends or comfortable old patterns.

For pastoral persons, this will create enormous change in how they fulfill their calling. It will mean understanding the word "pastor" to mean something different than they have previously understood it to mean. It will likely require sacrificing old paradigms and comfortable seats of authority. However, in return pastoral persons may find that their once lonely vocation is now a wonderfully interconnected and dynamically relational calling *within* a people of whom they are a part. Pastoral leaders are not permitted to avoid the challenges of change. Instead we are encouraged to hear the voice of our Shepherd and to joyfully chase after him, our bells clanging away that others might find him as well.

This reconsideration of the biblical metaphor of shepherd drives the church toward new considerations related to structure and roles. As this occurs, it is increasingly important that the church redefine those structures and roles accordingly, reinterpreting the metaphors used to describe the church's leadership. As it does, the church will find itself being drawn into a greater dynamic relationship with the God whom it seeks to emulate. It is within this relationship that answers to the church's challenges become apparent as God reveals them to God's people.

Chapter 6

Entering the Trinitarian Life

Throughout the first seven centuries of the church history, Christians struggled to make sense of God's revelation as witnessed and recorded in Scripture. In particular, these early church fathers and mothers wrestled with the monotheistic claims of Scripture that seemed to clash with the revelation of God in Christ, the God-Man. Out of these struggles developed the doctrine of the Trinity with its language of "persons" and "essence." But with the advent of modernity and rationality, the Trinity with all of its mystery became something of an embarrassment to the Christian church. Take for instance Immanuel Kant's infamous statement: "The doctrine of the Trinity, taken literally, has *no practical relevance at all*, even if we think we understand it; and it is even more clearly irrelevant if we realize that it transcends all our concepts . . . Whether we are to worship three or ten persons in the Deity makes no difference."[1] In this and many other ways, a core doctrine of the Christian faith was marginalized. While many denominations assented to belief in a Trinity, few actually pursued its implications throughout modernity.

In the twentieth century, at the dawn of "postmodernity," Christian theology has experienced a renewed interest in the Trinity and has been reenergized by Trinitarian theology's concept of relationality.[2] Relational or social Trinitarian thought emphasizes the threeness of God as the starting place for understanding God.[3] By conceiving of God "who is both one

1. Kant, *Religion and Rational Theology*, 264; emphases added.

2. Grenz, *Rediscovering the Trinity*, 117. Cunningham, *These Three are One*, 26.

3. See further Grenz, *Theology*, 53–97. Chapter 2, "The Triune God" and chapter 3, "The Relational God" demonstrate and describe the Tri-unity of God as it relates to God's

and three" and "whose being consists in a relationality that derives from the otherness-in-relation of Father, Son and Spirit,"[4] social Trinitarian theologians develop a perspective that identifies the interconnectedness of personhood between the Father, Son, and Spirit as essential for understanding God's fullness.[5] Some of contemporary theology's most important theologians argue that such Trinitarian thinking has implications for the church and its mission in the world.

Many are considering anew how this kind of theological reflection and systematic consideration informs the church and society concerning faithful Christian living.[6] These implications stem from belief that the nature and character of God has meaning for those created in God's image. Just what is that meaning and to what extent it applies is part of the discussion. Miroslav Volf contends that it is "odd to claim that there are no analogues to God in creation" all the while maintaining "that human beings are created in the image of God . . . [B]etween 'copying God in all respects' . . . and 'not copying God at all' . . . lies the widely open space of human responsibility which consists of 'copying God in *some* respects.'"[7]

Theologians pursuing a social Trinitarianism are relating Trinitarian thought to issues of anthropology, ecclesiology, missiology, ecology, leadership, gender, and other "variegated dimensions."[8] As they pursue these agendas, they faithfully draw out the implications of such thinking.[9] For a

---

inner-life as Father, Son, and Holy Spirit.

4. Gunton, *One, the Three and the Many*, 7.

5. Ibid., 214. See also such diverse and impressive thinkers as Zizioulas, *Being as Communion*, 40–49, 83–89; Moltmann, *Trinity and the Kingdom*, 162–70, 172; Pannenberg, *Systematic Theology*, 1:322–25; Jenson, *Systematic Theology*, 1:75–161. These contend that in relationality the Father, Son, and Spirit are the one God.

6. See McDougall, "The Return of Trinitarian Praxis?," 177. Drolly, Cunningham calls renewed interest in Trinitarian thought, "not so much like a renaissance as a bandwagon" (Cunningham, *These Three are One*, 19). My appreciation to my colleague William Whitney for bringing this statement to my attention.

7. Volf, "'Trinity is Our Social Program,'" 404, 405; emphasis in original.

8. Grenz, *Rediscovering the Trinity*, 3.

9. Leonardo Boff states, "as long as the present social inequalities remain, faith in the Trinity will mean criticism of all injustices and a source of inspiration for basic changes" (Boff, *Trinity and Society*, 13). He later correlates Trinitarian theology and economic, political, and ecclesial institutions. Ibid., 148–54. Similarly, Moltmann writes that the triune God, living in community and fellowship, "community, fellowship, issues an invitation to his community and makes himself the model for a just and livable community in the world of nature and human beings" (Moltmann, *History and the Triune God*, xii–xiii). One result of this multiplicity of application is that significant portions of

highly individualized Western culture, Trinitarian thinking is relevant to all areas of human relationality.[10] Social Trinitarianism maintains that what is mined from understanding God as Father, Son, and Holy Spirit in relation with one another bears directly upon societal existence.[11] With this in mind, I pursue several important Trinitarian themes. These are not the only themes arising from social Trinitarianism, but they are important ones in discussing ecclesial and missional issues.

Perichoresis and Diversity

Traditional Christian theological method begins with the one God and then is forced by the Incarnation to discuss how that one God is also three.[12] Contrastingly, social Trinitarian theologians begin with such questions as "What Divine Unity?"[13] Underlying these questions are historical debates related to questions of person and substance. Jürgen Moltmann writes that "if the concept of person comes to be understood in trinitarian terms— that is, in terms of relation and historically—then the Persons do not only subsist in the common divine substance; they also exist in their relations to the other Persons."[14] Understanding a biblical theology of God requires beginning with the Trinity and then working toward unity. The answer to unity is *perichoresis*.[15]

this chapter have been previously published not only in relationship to leadership as it is here, but also in relationship to ethnic relationships and—in a revised and condensed version—in relationship to the work of disability ministry. For this author, this theological orientation has been an essential element of developing an ethic of Kingdom praxis: Kinnison, "The Social Trinity and the Southwest," 261–81; Lane and Kinnison, *Welcoming Children with Special Needs.*

10. Per Cunningham: "If the claim that 'these three are one' applies not only to God but, *mutatis mutandis*, to the created order as well, then it has dramatic implications for the kinds of lives we are called to live . . . The doctrine of the Trinity is a challenge to the modern cult of the individual; it teaches us to think in terms of complex webs of mutuality and participation" (Cunningham, *These Three are One*, 8). Gunton sees ethical implications for social/urban life extending to how Trinitarian thought speaks to issues like the love of driving cars (Gunton, *One, the Three and the Many*, 177–78) and sexual morality (Gunton, *Father, Son and Holy Spirit*, 223–24).

11. See further Volf, "'Trinity is Our Social Program.'"

12. Grenz, *Rediscovering the Trinity*, 11–32. Generally, *perichoresis* is the basis for understanding other themes. See Moltmann, *History and the Triune God*, 86–87.

13. Moltmann, *Trinity and the Kingdom*, 148; chapter 5 section heading.

14. Ibid., 174.

15. Moltmann argues that if biblical witness is the "point of departure, then we shall

Perichoresis is a rich Greek term first used in Christian theology by Pseudo-Cyril[16] and later used by John of Damascus to speak of Trinitarian relationality.[17] Simply stated, *perichoresis* is "the mutual indwelling and coinherence of the persons of the Trinity . . . ."[18] While the Latin church translated *perichoresis* as *"circumcessio"* and *"circumincessio,"*[19] *circumcessio* carries the more "dynamic connotations" of the original term *perichoresis* emphasizing the reciprocal nature of the term.[20] Highly individualized and isolating modern terminology used to describe *perichoresis* ("coinherence" and "interpenetration"), hinders contemporary understandings of the term.[21] However, differentiated personhood appeals to Boff, Moltmann, and others who begin with the Tri-unity. In *perichoresis*, differentiation is *toward* not *from* others.[22] Boff and Moltmann describe perichoretic indwelling of the three persons as the sharing of essence that is the one God.[23] In discussing *perichoresis*, Moltmann clarifies that distinctions and differences among the three persons of the Trinity become the source of

---

have to start from the three Persons [because] of the history of Christ. If philosophical logic is made the starting point, then the enquirer proceeds from the One God" (ibid., 149).

16. Volf, *After Our Likeness*, 208. Likewise, Fiddes, *Participating in God*, 71.

17. Collins, *Trinitarian Theology*, 210. Collins gives an excellent overview of the term worth reviewing; ibid., 209–15. See also Volf, *After Our Likeness*, 208–10; Letham, *Holy Trinity*, 240–42; Torrance, *Christian Doctrine*, 168–202; Fiddes, *Participating in God*, 71–89.

18. Gunton, *Father, Son and the Holy Spirit*, 44; also see Cunningham, *These Three are One*, 180–81; Collins, *Trinitarian*, 209–10.

19. Collins, *Trinitarian*, 209.

20. Ibid., 209–10.

21. Cunningham, *These Three are One*, 180–81.

22. Per Boff: In *perichoresis*, persons "emerge as three Subjects who engage in mutual dialogue, love one another and are intimately related. Each person is *for* the others, *with* the others and *in* the others. The everlasting love that pervades them and forms them unites them in a current of life so infinite and complex as to constitute the unity between them . . . They are not the embodiments of One (nature or substance or absolute Spirit or Subject) but three Subjects in eternal (and therefore essential) communion, always united and interpenetrating one another" (Boff, *Trinity and Society*, 138–39).

23. Regarding *perichoresis*, Moltmann state: "An eternal life process takes place in the triune God through the exchange of energies. The Father exists in the Son, the Son in the Father, and both of them in the Spirit, just as the Spirit exists in both the Father and the Son. By virtue of their eternal love they live in one another to such an extent, and dwell in one another to such and extent, that they are one" (Moltmann, *Trinity and the Kingdom*, 174–75).

their unity.[24] Similarly, it is Gunton's understanding that *perichoresis* "is the foe, not the agent, of homogeneity."[25] This demonstrates that in the distinctions of persons—Father, Son, and Holy Spirit—variety finds constitution through inter-relatedness.[26]

Emphasis on Trinitarian relationality raises the charge of tritheism, a charge that Letham, Molnar, and others throw at social Trinitarian theologians rather freely.[27] *Perichoresis* is the answer to such charges. Moltmann writes, "Their relations within the Trinity and the trinitarian *perichoresis* are complementary: the perichoretic unity does not do away with the distinct relations . . . The perichoretic concept of trinitarian unity gets over the dangers of tritheism and modalism equally."[28] Boff describes a Christian understanding of God as recognizing "distinctions without multiplying God and falling into tritheism or polytheism."[29] To a fragmented and disconnected world, Gunton suggests that in understanding *perichoresis*, creation can hope for an integrated existence:

> . . . a God conceived trinitarianly, a God who contains within himself a form of plurality in relation and creates a world which reflects the richness of his being, can surely enable us to better conceive something of the unity in variety of human culture . . . [I]f the triune God is the source of all being, meaning and truth, we should be able to develop a theology of the unity of culture without depriving each of its dimensions of its distinctive approach and validity.[30]

---

24. Ibid., 175. Specifically Moltmann states, "The unity of the trinitarian Persons lies in the circulation of the divine life which they fulfill in their relations to one another. This means that the unity of the triune God cannot and must not be seen in a general concept of divine substance. That would abolish personal differences. But if the contrary is true—if the very difference of the three Persons lies in their relational, perichoretically consummated life process—then the Persons cannot and must not be reduced to three modes of being of one and the same divine subject. The Persons themselves constitute both their differences and their unity" (ibid.); see also Moltmann, *History and the Triune God*, xii.

25. Gunton, *One, the Three and the Many*, 172.

26. Ibid.

27. Letham, *Holy Trinity*, 307–9, 377; Molnar, *Divine Freedom*, 97, 232–33.

28. Moltmann, *History and the Triune God*, 86. He further contends that *perichoresis* is relationally, complementary, and equally expressed among the three persons. Ibid.

29. Boff, *Trinity and Society*, 139.

30. Gunton, *One, the Three and the Many*, 177.

In the *perichoretic* understanding of God, the fragmentation produced by modernity is critiqued by a God who is uniquely three and distinctly one.[31] Wholeness and distinction resonate as themes held in tension by Trinitarian theologians. *Perichoresis* makes the holding of such themes possible.[32]

Mutuality

A particular effect of *perichoresis* is mutuality.[33] The distinction of mutuality within *perichoresis* is the nature by which each Trinitarian person *willingly* and fully gives of themselves and receives fully to themselves the others without dissolving the distinction of personhood.[34] The relational quality of mutuality is captured nicely by Millard Erickson, who states that while in human relationship there is often separation and distance created by fear of rejection, in the Trinity there is no option of separation: "They are eternally and permanently one with the others."[35]

Pannenberg regards this mutuality as essential to understanding the intratrinitarian relations between Father and Son as it relates to handing over of power, rule and lordship:

31. Ibid., 173ff.

32. See Torrance, *Christian Doctrine*, 173–80. "Wholeness" and "distinction" are titles used in conjunction with Torrance's discussion of *perichoresis*. Letham is also noteworthy here. Under sub-heading "Unity in Diversity and Diversity in Unity," Letham points to the peculiarity of the Christian witness of the Trinity, without discussing *perichoresis*. He then critiques culture accordingly. See chapters "Islam: Unity without Diversity" and "Postmodernity: Diversity without Unity" (Letham, *Holy Trinity*, 439–57).

33. Moltmann states that the "*perichoretic* doctrine" is the norm for understanding the "levels of relationship in *perichoresis* and mutuality within the Trinity. Moltmann, *History and the Triune God*, 132.

34. This distinction is important as many of the theologians mentioned here use similar terminology regarding *perichoresis*, but speaking of "mutual" indwelling. See Moltmann, *History and the Triune God*, 84–87. While related, this work is more interested in mutual giving and receiving at this point. Volf notices this point while contending for ecclesial mutual giving and receiving. For Volf, Trinitarian "reciprocal *interiority*" and "mutual permeation," are precisely the nature by which the church should attempt "interecclesial correspondence to the Trinity . . . in 'being from others' and 'seeking to be toward all others'" (Volf, *After Our Likeness*, 208, 209. Quote from 208). See also Volf, "'Trinity is Our Social Program,'" 409ff.

35. Erickson, *God in Three Persons*, 226.

> In the handing over of lordship from the Father to the Son, and
> its handing back from the Son to the Father, we see a mutuality
> in their relationship . . . By handing over lordship to the Son the
> Father makes his kingship dependent on whether the Son glorifies
> him and fulfils his lordship by fulfilling his mission . . . [H]is [the
> Father's] kingdom and his own deity are now dependent on the
> Son.[36]

Additionally, the relations of the Trinitarian persons makes them mutually constitutive. The Father is not Father without the Son, nor the Son a Son without a Father.[37] As Letham appraises Pannenberg's theology, "The Father's deity is dependent on the Son, and so all three persons are fully reciprocally related, although in different ways."[38] Pannenberg thus asserts that within the Godhead, this mutuality prevents any one person, particularly the Father, from being the source of deity. Rather, "the relations between the persons are constitutive not merely for their distinctions but also their deity."[39] Jenson makes origin a mutual experience arguing that the Father's speaking of the Word is an act that calls for a response in the same way in which the breathing of the Spirit is the Father's entry into the Spirit's "communal freedom." Each act has a reciprocal and mutually required act.[40] The danger in this language is that it implies an ontological hierarchy that is at least philosophically tenuous if not also theologically undesirable.[41]

Leonardo Boff makes a particularly intriguing application of the principle of mutuality by suggesting that in the mutual relationships held within the Triune Godhead, everything is triadic.[42] Mutuality is best defined by

36. Pannenberg, *Systematic Theology*, 1:308–19, quote 1:312–13. Also regarding the Spirit, ibid., 1:315–18.

37. Ibid., 1:311–12. A weakness of Pannenberg's argumentation here relates to the personhood of the Spirit. Pannenberg seems to concur with the Augustinian idea that the Spirit is the bond between the Father and the Son. Ibid., 1:316–17. While this certainly goes toward my point of mutuality, it seems to greatly lessen the Spirit's personhood as being only constituted by nature of the Father and Son's relationship rather than as a "living realization of a separate center of action" (ibid., 1:319).

38. Letham, *Holy Trinity*, 317.

39. Pannenberg, *Systematic Theology*, 1:322–24, quote from 323.

40. Jenson, *Systematic Theology*, 1:119. This view is similarly held by Zizioulas; see Zizioulas, *Being as Communion*, 40–49.

41. In Boff and others, the question of ontological equality is reconcilable with language other than that of procession. Further investigation is needed on the critiques over whether such language later in this chapter.

42. Boff, *Trinity and Society*, 146. Intriguing is how Boff reverses the *Filioque*

Boff as "relationship[s] . . . of reciprocal participation . . . of correlation and communion . . . Each person receives everything from the others and at the same time gives everything to the others."[43] This view allows Boff to overcome the language of procession and speak in terms of "communication and communion."[44] Moltmann likewise sees a mutuality that overcomes procession language. Contending that each person "receives the fullness of eternal life from the other," Moltmann agrees with Hegel that each Trinitarian person "comes to himself by expressing and expending himself in others." This occurs through "self-surrendering love"[45] and has the effect not only of eliminating subordinationism,[46] but also is the means by which "they bring one another mutually to manifestation in the divine glory . . . The Persons of the Trinity make one another shine through that glory, mutually and together."[47] Gunton is particularly helpful here.[48] He holds that the "*reciprocal* eternal relatedness" of the Father, Son, and Spirit "constitute one another's being" in a way that protects a "particular kind of relational

---

argument, suggesting a *Patreque* and *Spirituque*: "Consequently, we should say that the Father reveals himself through the Son and the Holy Spirit . . . The Father reveals the Son as his Word with the participation of the Spirit, who is always the Spirit of the Son and the Father. The Son is 'begotten' by the Father in the Holy Spirit . . . [T]he Father 'begets' the Son virginally in the maternal-virginal womb of the Holy Spirit. In trinitarian terms: the Father 'begets' the Son *Spirituque*, that is, in communion with the Holy Spirit . . . [T]he Son reveals the Father in the light of the Holy Spirit . . . The Son is also revealed to the Holy Spirit as co-related to the Father since the Father will be eternally the Father of the Son. He also reveals to the Spirit the unfathomable mystery of the Father in his overflowing outpouring of love and self-bestowal. The Spirit . . . 'proceeds' from the Father and rests on the Son, being thus *ex Patre Filioque*" (ibid., 146–47).

43. Ibid., 147.

44. Ibid.

45. Moltmann, *Trinity and the Kingdom*, 173–74; quotes from 174.

46. Ibid., 175.

47. Ibid., 176. See also Moltmann, *Church in the Power of the Spirit*, 58–59. Moltmann suggests that "mutuality and community [within the Triune Godhead] proceeds from the Holy Spirit" as a sort of third movement in the unity of the Godhead. He begins with the Father as the means by which the "'monarchial' unity of the Godhead" is formed and then secondly suggests that the Son is the center around which the Godhead is concentrated. The Spirit is the divine luminary of Trinitarian unity. Moltmann, *Trinity and the Kingdom*, 177–78. However unintentionally, he still holds a functional hierarchy within the Trinity, a position he feverishly attempts to overcome. Ibid., 191–222.

48. Gunton, *One, the Three and the Many*, 163ff. This discussion of mutuality comes under the heading of "*Perichoresis*" in chapt. 6, subhead. 3 demonstrating the closeness between *perichoresis* and mutuality.

diversity."[49] The focus on reciprocal relatedness allows for an understanding of mutuality that is important to later concepts. In social Trinitarian thought, no one person is served by the others or is servant to the others by compulsion. Each serves the others freely and mutually.[50] In this respect, it is possible to see the absence of a hierarchical relationality.

Egalitarianism

Cunningham declares that "one of the central claims of classical trinitarianism is that the Three are radically equal to one another; none is in a position of superiority over the others."[51] However, the limitation of language makes it difficult to draw out a consistent theology of God's relational reality.[52] While most social-Trinitarian theologians advocate for essential or ontological equality, some theologians, including Zizioulas, Pannenberg, Gunton, Jenson, and Fiddes, suggest or outright argue for functional subordination of the Son and Spirit to the Father.[53] For these, the Father is the Monarch deity in relation with the Son and the Spirit.[54] Gunton, while holding to a primacy of the Father,[55] moves from language of procession or source (Father as "mon-arche") to language of interrelation and

---

49. Ibid., 164; emphasis added.

50. Not all social Trinitarians hold this perspective. However, Zizioulas and others who hold to a primacy view of the Father contend that mutuality is a part of the interrelatedness of the Trinity. These place mutuality as a sub-theme of love.

51. Cunningham, *These Three are One*, 111–14. Contra see Horrell, "Toward A Biblical Model," 399–421.

52. Cunningham, *These Three are One*, 111–14.

53. See Zizioulas, *Being as Communion*, 39–49, specifically 44ff.; Pannenberg, *Systematic Theology*, 1:322–27; Gunton, *Father, Son and the Holy Spirit*, 73–74; Jenson, *Systematic Theology*, 1:115–24, 156; Fiddes, *Participating in God*, 79, 89–96.

54. Pannenberg sees monarchy/lordship as a mutual expression of deity. Pannenberg, *Systematic Theology*, 1:308–19. Also, Torrance's position is that the monarchy is found in all of the Trinity as a result. Per Letham, *Holy Trinity*, 377. See Torrance, *Christian Doctrine*, 180–85.

55. Gunton, *Triune Creator*, 157–62, especially 159. Gunton seems to embrace modalistic tendencies, promoting the "two hands of God" concept as a Trinitarian view of the creation. Unfortunately, the mutual agency of the three persons is lost. See also Gunton, *Promise of Trinitarian Theology*, 166–70.

community.[56] He recognizes a distinction between the Father's economic priority and ontological equality.[57]

Moltmann contends for radical egalitarianism, but seems compelled to advocate the primacy of the Father as the source of deity.[58] Holding that the Father is the "starting point" or "origin of the Godhead," Moltmann also insists that *perichoresis* banishes "all subordinationism in the doctrine of the Trinity."[59] The "monarchy of the Father" establishes the Trinity, but has "no validity within the eternal circulation of the divine life and none in the perichoretic unity of the Trinity. Here the three Persons are equal . . . ."[60] This seems inconsistent to say the least.[61]

Volf takes a similar approach to Trinitarian egalitarianism[62] to advocate egalitarian ecclesial structures.[63] Against "hierarchical constructions of the Trinitarian relations," Volf is adamant that "hierarchy is not necessary to guard either the divine unity or the distinctions between divine persons" finding such arguments "unintelligible" for a "community of perfect love between persons who share all divine attributes."[64] However, while con-

56. Gunton, *One, the Three and the Many*, 163–64, 214ff. See also Gunton, *Father, Son and the Holy Spirit*, 72–73.

57. Gunton, *Promise of Trinitarian Theology*, 166, 167. My appreciation again to William Whitney who brought this reference to my attention.

58. See note 47.

59. Moltmann, *Trinity and the Kingdom*, 175–76.

60. Ibid., 176, 177.

61. Moltmann's arguments seem contradictory at this point. How is the Father source without being ontologically superior to those who have come from Him? If the monarchy of the Father constitutes the Trinity, how can the Triune God exist without the Father's prior existence in eternity past?

62. Volf cites Moltmann throughout, but especially relating to egalitarian understandings. See Volf, *After Our Likeness*, 216–17, 236.

63. Volf, *After Our Likeness*. Part II is a "free church" response to the hierarchical structures proposed in the Trinitarian theologies of Roman Catholic Joseph Ratzinger (now Pope Benedict XVI) and Greek Orthodox Metropolitan John Zizioulas. Volf's thesis is that "an appropriate understanding of the Trinity suggests a more nuanced and promising model of the relationship between person and community in the Church" (ibid., xi). Volf presents an egalitarian ecclesiology resulting from his investigation into Trinitarian themes: throughout, but especially chapter 4 "Structures of the Church" (221–57).

64. Volf, "Social Program," 407. Volf's critique of hierarchy becomes quite impassioned: "They [hierarchical constructions of the Trinity] seem to be less inspired by a vision of the Triune God than driven either by a nostalgia for a 'world on the wane' or by fears of chaos that may invade human communities if hierarchies are leveled, their

tending, "Persons and community are equiprimal in the Trinity,"[65] Volf also preserves the primacy of the Father as the source of deity.[66] What is troublesome is the direct application of economic Trinitarian language of procession as a means to explaining the immanent Trinitarian inner-life, a point Ogbonnaya is able to avoid.[67]

A. Okechukwu Ogbonnaya inserts an important distinction between temporal submission and ontological equity into the discussion, a point Gunton, Fiddes, and others infer. Reinterpreting Tertullian back into an African context, Ogbonnaya argues that Tertullian holds to ontological equality but a temporal and historical subordination.[68] Similar thinking enables Fiddes to state the essential nature of fatherhood and sonship in the divine relationship is a historically bound relationship seen in the historical Jesus.[69] Hence, filial subordination to the Father is historically mediated, but not ontologically necessary. But what about the Spirit? Leonardo Boff's insights are helpful.

Boff's initial move of distinguishing between the experience of God, the expression of response (doxological faith in God's revelation), and the explication of that experience (formulation and formalization of theological explanation) allows him to move within tradition without abandoning it.[70] This creates freedom for Boff to promote not only *Filioque*, but also

---

surface biblical justification notwithstanding" (ibid., 407–8).

65. Ibid., 409.

66. Volf, *After Our Likeness*, 217. Volf promotes Trinitarian equality regarding the question of source, stating, "with regard to the immanent Trinity, salvation history thus allows us to infer the fundamental equality of the divine persons in their mutual determination and their mutual interpenetration."

67. The counter argument of course is how else do we know the immanent Trinity other than by the economic Trinity. Perhaps we cannot. However, something distinct and unique, even for God occurs in the incarnation. The "God become flesh" moment is distinct and therefore to sustain a primal placement for the Father based on how the God/man responds seems untenable. Jesus' response to the Father was as exemplary of his human response to the creator as it was relational as God to God. See Erickson, *God in Three Persons*, 223. Thus, Ogbonnaya's argument for a distinction between the temporal and the ontological accounts for this difference preserving both the humanity and the deity of Jesus the Son. This is not to suggest that Ogbonnaya's whole approach is to be embraced. Ogbonnaya, *Communitarian Divinity*.

68. Ogbonnaya, *Communitarian Divinity*, throughout, but especially 85–86.

69. Fiddes, *Participating in God*, 89–90.

70. Boff, *Trinity and Society*, 1–2ff.

Spirituque and *Patreque*[71] as an outflow of the *perichoretic* Tri-unity.[72] His insistence that all three Persons are co-eternal, having "*their* origin from all eternity" creates a "relationship of reciprocal participation rather than hypostatic derivation, or correlation and communion rather than production and procession."[73] The "complete circulation of life and a perfect coequality between persons" is possible because of *perichoresis*.[74] Therefore, Trinitarian relations are "the source of the utopia of equality—with due respect for differences—full communion and just relationships in society and in history."[75]

Openness to Other

Another significant consideration of the social Trinitarian theologians correlates to how relational existence demands openness to the other. Essential to a *perichoretic* understanding are the two-fold realization of diversity and of openness to other within the Trinity. Moltmann focuses on this idea by emphasizing the distinctness of each of the three.[76] Central to his understanding of *perichoresis* is the idea that within the Godhead's indwelling of one another the three in no way lose their distinctiveness.[77] Pannenberg

71. See note 42 above.

72. "[E]ach Person receives everything from the others and at the same time gives everything to the others" (Boff, *Trinity and Society*, 146–47).

73. Ibid., 146, emphasis added. "Mutual origination" and "origination" within the eternal Godhead has significant difficulties not discussed here, but worthy of considerable investigation.

74. Ibid., 93. Boff states: "This formulation [of *perichoretical* relationships] avoids the danger of subordinationist hierarchization in God (first the Father, then the Son, then the Holy Spirit) or of unequal subordination: the Father has everything, receives nothing from the others; the Son receives only from the Father, while the Holy Spirit receives from the Father and the Son, or only from the Father through the Son. It also avoids theogonism or modalism . . ." (146). Likewise, for Torrance, this *perichoretical* understanding "ruled out of consideration any conception of trinitarian relations arising out of a prior unity, and any conception of a unity deriving from the underived Person of the Father" (Torrance, *Christian Doctrine*, 179–80, citation from 179).

75. Boff, *Trinity and Society*, 93.

76. Moltmann, *History and the Triune God*, 87. Moltmann, *Trinity and the Kingdom*, 105ff. Moltmann, *Church in the Power of the Spirit*, 52–60. In fact, this may be such a focus that he leaves himself open to charges of tri-theism. For example see Neuhaus, "Moltmann vs. Monotheism," 239–43. Moltmann overcomes this charge through *perichoresis*.

77. Moltmann, *Trinity and the Kingdom*, 150, 175. See also Pannenberg, *Systematic Theology*, 1:273.

demonstrates that in contrast to losing distinctiveness, the Three exist as "separate centers of action" and that "each of the three persons relates to the others as others and distinguishes itself from them."[78]

This is Volf's assertion with his "mine/not mine" dialectic.[79] In order for the Son as Son to love the Father and the Spirit, he must not erase his own boundaries, thus avoiding self-negation.[80] At the same time, boundaries are not for keeping others out, which Volf, reflecting on Zizioulas, notes is a kind of self-negation.[81] This openness to other, found within the Godhead, is the essence of existence according to Zizioulas. Without relationship, there is no personhood.[82] In personhood is the uniqueness of identity.[83] Rather than losing distinctiveness, Moltmann argues that the perichoretic love for other within the Triune God actually is the means by which God opens God's self to the other.[84] Furthermore, love and relationship with the other within the Trinitarian inner-life opens God to loving relationships with the other outside of the Trinitarian life—the creation. Why create? Grenz suggests that:

> [T]he world exists as the product of the outflow of the divine love, the eternal [triune] relationship . . . Thus, as a product of God's essence (which is love) and as God's counterpart, the world exists in order to participate in the life of the social Trinity. We may summarize God's intention for the world by employing the term "community." Just as the triune God is the eternal fellowship of the trinitarian members, so also God's purpose for creation is that the world participate in "community."[85]

While God experiences the self-love of "kind" for "kind" in the Father's, Son's, and Spirit's love for each other, the ability for self-love opens

78. Pannenberg, *Systematic Theology*, 1:319–20

79. Volf, "'Trinity is Our Social Program,'" 410.

80. Ibid.

81. Ibid., 410–11. See also Zizioulas, *Being as Communion*, 48–49.

82. Zizioulas, *Being as Communion*, 46–48.

83. Ibid., 47–48. See also Fiddes, *Participating in God*, 81–89.

84. Moltmann, *Trinity and the Kingdom*, 158. He states: "We have understood the unity of the divine trinitarian history as the open, unifying at-oneness of the three divine Persons in their relationships to one another . . . For this trinitarian history is nothing other than the eternal perichoresis of Father, Son and Holy Spirit in their dispensation of salvation, which is to say in their opening of themselves for the reception and unification of the whole creation" (ibid., 157).

85. Grenz, *Theology for the Community of God*, 112.

God to loving non-self other.[86] Per Boff: "[B]y their own inner dynamic, the three divine Persons spill over outwards, creating other different things and beings (the cosmos and humankind) for them to be receptacles of communicative love and the boundless ocean of trinitarian life."[87]

Love

As indicated above, belief that love for one another binds the three divine Persons heavily influences social Trinitarian themes. Love constitutes the *perichoretic* divine community as a mutual, equal, and open community. Pannenberg notes that love is the "unity of the divine being of the Father, Son and Spirit."[88] Love manifests in reciprocal relations for those bound together in love. It has power by means of giving selfhood to those who give of themselves to others.[89] In *perichoresis*, divine relations are "not merely logical but existential," where by "mutuality of their ec-static indwelling the life of the divine Spirit fulfils itself as love."[90] Love is the source of mutual-

86. Moltmann, *Trinity and the Kingdom*, 106. See also Moltmann, *Church in the Power of the Spirit*, 50–65.

87. Boff, *Trinity and Society*, 147. Regarding creating Trinity, see Gunton, *Triune Creator*.

88. Pannenberg, *Systematic Theology*, 1:422–48, quote, 425. He further writes, "They [the Trinity] do not merely have love as a common quality or mind; they are love in the 'unity of free persons' that can never be separated." He makes a careful distinction stating that "if, however, the one loves self in the other instead of loving the other as other, then love falls short of full self-giving which is the condition that the one who loves be given self afresh in the responsive love of the one who is loved" (ibid., 426).

89. Ibid.

90. Ibid., 428. This leads Pannenberg to a difficult conclusion: love as the Spirit of God. He correlates the statements "God is Spirit" and "God is love" as the "same unity of essence by which Father, Son and Spirit are united in the fellowship of the one God" (ibid., 427). It is unclear if Pannenberg refers to the third Trinitarian Person—the Holy Spirit—or to divine essence permeating all three. Ibid., 427–32. Pannenberg states: "On the one side the Spirit and love constitute the common essence of deity, and on the other they come forth as a separate hypostasis in the Holy Spirit" (429). This implies that the Spirit—third Person or permeating essence—is the Godhead's source: "Both Father and Spirit in their different ways represent the Godhead as a whole" (429). He continues, stating that, "this is least true of the Son, because he partakes of eternal deity only through his relation to the Father and as filled by the Spirit of the Father." This is an ontologically problematic statement that contradicts his earlier statement: "Love is no more a separate subject than the Spirit apart from the three persons" (428). Similarly, see Grenz, *Theology*, 489. For a critique of Pannenberg's "monarchy of the Spirit" as source of Godhead, see Min, "The Dialectic of Divine Love," 262–64.

ity, unity, and God's openness to the world.[91] Boff echoes similar themes, identifying love with the ontological essence of the triune Godhead.[92] Love makes *perichoresis* tenable.[93]

To be love, God must be Triune since "love cannot be consummated by a solitary subject."[94] As Erickson states, "love, to be love, must have both a subject and an object."[95] Love without an other is merely narcissism, thus to be love and not just "loving," God had to exist in multiplicity.[96] Yet, in Tri-unity, Father, Son, and Spirit are one "by virtue of their eternal love."[97] In their relations, "they also realize themselves in one another by virtue of their self-surrendering love"[98]—a mutually sustaining cycle. Gunton, reiterates that "the three persons who make up the being of God; who, together, are the one God, are bound up together in such a way that only one word can be used to describe their relation: love."[99] Trinitarian Love compels God to create and thereby open God's self to loving and being loved by other.[100]

---

91. Pannenberg, *Systematic Theology*, 1:444–48. He states, "If the unity of God thus finds nuanced and concrete form only in the work of divine love, then the other attributes of the divine being may be shown to be either manifestations of the love of God or to have true meaning only insofar as their concrete manifestation is taken up into the sway of divine love" (1:445).

92. Boff, *Trinity and Society*, 144–46. Specifically he states, "God is eternally, without beginning, Father, Son and Holy Spirit, the inner reciprocity of their love" (144).

93. Ibid., 145. Differently than Pannenberg, Boff works from relational language of ontology rather than procession. Boff writes, "This understanding excludes the monarchy of One . . . in favour of the eternal communion of a simultaneous Three who are always one in, by, with, through and for the others, interpenetrating one another in love . . ." (ibid.).

94. Moltmann, *Trinity and the Kingdom*, 57.

95. Erickson, *God in Three Persons*, 221.

96. Ibid. However, neither he nor Moltmann explains why multiplicity must be three as opposed to more or fewer. Based on John Macmurry, Gunton theorizes that two's love for each other is inadequate and can only be fully love when two focus their mutual love on a third. Gunton, *Promise of Trinitarian Theology*, 92. Considering personhood, love is the "self-communication of the good" made possible by the giving of self to other while remaining other. Moltmann, *Trinity and the Kingdom*, 57. Giving of self must not be "self-destruction" as it "presupposes the capacity for self-differentiation" (ibid.). Insistence on personal existence only occurring in relation, requires that the one exist in relation to other(s). Ibid., 172–73.

97. Ibid., 175.

98. Ibid., 174.

99. Gunton, *Father, Son and the Holy Spirit*, 17.

100. Gunton, *Triune Creator*, 9–10.

Trinitarian Implications for Church Structures

In light of the hopeful understandings reviewed above, the tragedy of modern society is that "many have rejected God because the God of the Church seemed the source of unfreedom and oppression rather than of love."[101] The church has often reflected a god of the world rather than "the God of the Bible, who is a God of love."[102] Considering how to live according to God's Trinitarian relationality, it is essential to remember God's essence is the love relationship of Father, Son, and Holy Spirit. Humans, created in God's image as social creatures, must reflect God's love.[103]

From Trinitarian themes, an ecclesiology forms which expresses serious concern regarding the specialization of ministry. Any specialized ministry in the church occurs within the ministry of all members—the universal priesthood of all believers.[104] Emphasis on the professionalization of the pastoral function (expertise) has tended to lead to stagnancy, passivity, and alienation in the laity.[105] Full-participation of the church community is elemental.[106] However, the importance of the pastoral role in congregational life is not questioned—only the hierarchical understandings of such a role. Speaking for the Reformation's fulfillment, Moltmann challenges pastors, church leaders, and theologians to "press for" the "congregational church from below."[107]

Volf likewise correlates his egalitarian understanding of the Trinity to an egalitarian understanding of church. Acknowledging the limitations of our "creatureliness," humans cannot live the kind of interiority

101. Gunton, *Father, Son and the Holy Spirit*, 18.

102. Ibid.

103. This is the theme of Gunton's chapter 8 "The Triune Lord. Towards a Theology of the One and the Many" in *The One*, 210ff.

104. Moltmann, "The Diaconal Church," 33.

105. Ibid., 34.

106. Ibid., 40–42. See also Moltmann, *Open Church*, especially 113–26. Douglas Meeks states: "According to Moltmann, therefore, each and every form of practice in the church is a function of God's trinitarian history, and the equality of the Persons is the basis for the equality of the various ministries, or charismata, in the church. This means no one form of ministry can be considered more important than the others. At no time, for example, should the preaching and teaching or pastoral care or service to the world be considered the exclusive model or form of the church's ministry . . . I believe that Moltmann's main contribution to practical theology is that he places it in a trinitarian context" (Meeks, "Moltmann's Contribution," 61).

107. Moltmann, *Open Church*, 113–26.

experienced in the Trinity, but they can experience an "interiority of personal characteristics."[108] Volf and Lee suggest that the community of believers project the Trinity in three ways: catholicity,[109] equality,[110] and love.[111] The pastoral person is a part of this threefold projection, but must not dominate the church's Charismatic life. The giving of self is a part of the personal encounter: "This is the process of mutual internalization of personal characteristics occurring in the church through the Holy Spirit indwelling Christians."[112]

Viewing the relations of the Trinity as complementary *perichoretic* subjects, Volf concludes that ecclesial structures must be viewed as complementary and egalitarian. Therefore, he forcefully states:

> If one starts from the trinitarian model I have suggested, then the structure of the ecclesial unity cannot be conceived by way of the one, be it the Pope, the patriarch, or the bishop. Every ecclesial unity held together by a mon-archy, by a "one-[man!]-rule," is monist and thus also un-trinitarian.[113]

In such a church, the Charismata are recognized as universally distributed and are practiced by all in a "polycentric community" where members are participative, fulfilling their calling to serve God and the community in God's mission.[114]

---

108. Volf, *After Our Likeness*, 211.

109. Like the divine mutual inner-dwelling of the Trinity, "a member of the church is a catholic person because the other members of the church are part and parcel of his or her identity . . . a local church is a catholic community because it is related to other local churches . . ." (Volf and Lee, "Spirit and the Church," 34).

110. "The divine persons are distinct yet equal . . . Analogously, all members are fundamentally equal in that they have all been baptized by the Spirit and received gifts of the Spirit . . ." (Volf and Lee, "Spirit and the Church," 34).

111. "The equality and personal interiority of the divine persons are rooted in the perfect divine love . . . The love exhibited in the community of the Spirit should be modeled on the love of the divine persons for one another and for the world's sake . . ." (ibid., 34–35).

112. Volf, *After Our Likeness*, 211–12.

113. Ibid., 217.

114. Ibid., 221–45.

A Question of Conflict and Dissent

Mark Chapman queries that if some conflict is normal to human existence,[115] and if the Trinity is our model, how do we reconcile the discrepancy between the Trinity's perfect communion and conflictual human social existence?[116] Volf is helpful, reminding that human createdness limits our ability to emulate God.[117] The natural outworking of conflict in healthy collaboration recalls creatureliness. It reminds us of interconnectedness, of our having been made in God's image.[118] Unhealthy conflict recalls humanity's fallenness;[119] it emphasizes our need for saving by a God who is perfectly community and rescues us into that community. God's perfect communion may be unattainable in this life, but it guides us to attempt mutuality, equality, openness, and love. In such attempts it is possible to find that we are participating in God's divine dance.

Universal Priesthood of All Believers: Democracy or Holy Spirit?

One concluding consideration regarding an egalitarian understanding of the Trinity: is egalitarianism a product of good theology or societal and cultural upheaval? The assertion of some is that egalitarianism reflects societal or humanist understandings of human interaction more than biblical or theological understandings.[120] Volf counters that while those defending traditional hierarchy view egalitarianism as

> . . . projections onto God of the shallow democratic sentiments which emerged when modern, functionally-differentiated societies replaced traditional, hierarchically-segmented societies . . .

---

115. Conflict: "Two or more objects trying to occupy the same space at the same time" where space is defined in terms of land, time, concepts, etc. See, Leas and Kittlaus, *Church Fights*; Lewis, *Resolving Church Conflicts*; Augsburger, *Conflict Mediation across Cultures*, 18–20, particularly 20; Lederach, *Preparing for Peace*, 9.

116. Chapman, "Social Doctrine of the Trinity," 248ff.

117. Volf, "'Trinity is Our Social Program,'" 404–5.

118. Cunningham even suggests that there may be a Trinitarian connection to this kind of conflict: "God is capable of being internally conflicted, but chooses otherwise" (Cunningham, *These Three are One*, 241–42, quote from 242).

119. Volf, "'Trinity is Our Social Program,'" 404–5.

120. See Ratzinger, *Church, Ecumenism, and Politics*, 21–28; Ratzinger, *Salt of the Earth*, 186–94, 270–73; Zizioulas, *Being as Communion*, 214–25.

he sees hierarchical structures as,

> ... projections of the fascination with earthly hierarchies onto the heavenly community . . . less inspired by a vision of the Triune God than driven by a nostalgia for a "world on the wane" or by fears of chaos that may invade human communities if hierarchies are leveled, their surface biblical justification notwithstanding.[121]

The indwelling of the Holy Spirit in all members of the church pre-empts any one person having a greater say than another as the same Spirit may speak to and through all. Rather than understanding the church as "liberal democracy" *per se*, the church is to be Spirit led. It is the whole church body's responsibility to discern that leading; this may at times seem democratically driven.[122] Grenz, in his fine explanation of "democratic congregationalism"[123] states that,

> In a day when kings and councils decided the will of God, they [Baptists' English forbearers in the sixteenth century] asserted the radical idea that the church is constituted by the voluntary cov-enant of converted believers, who as an entire company under the guidance of their leaders discern Christ's will.[124]

Several dangers of such practice are that: 1) it can degrade into "ma-joritarian voting procedures with factions vying for control"; 2) "apathy of the membership, evidenced by declining participation in congregational meetings, can likewise render congregational rule ineffective"; and 3) for a large congregation it "is impossible for a great number of people to partici-pate actively in this system of government."[125]

Trinitarian ecclesiology makes no normative statement regarding congregational governance structures. Societal and cultural norms may dictate how congregations manage their structures, provided it is with a Trinitarian ecclesiology of non-domination and full participation. An organized body that sees itself institutionally constituted will live for its own survival rather than for God's purpose. Modern bureaucratic models,

---

121. Volf, "Social Program," 407–8.

122. See Guder, *Missional Church*, especially 142–220; Russell, *Church in the Round*; Van Gelder, *Essence of the Church*; Volf, *After Our Likeness*; Yoder, *Body Politics*.

123. Grenz, *Theology*, 553–57.

124. Ibid., 554.

125. Ibid., 557.

superimposed upon church structures, do not usually benefit Spirit-driven initiatives. Thus, ecclesial governance must focus on discerning God's will.[126]

Missional Themes

In both the biblical chapter and this theological chapter are implied missional concepts, which are briefly here made more explicit. In the Old Testament, YHWH is always referred to as having one flock. Notably, in the New Testament, Jesus specifically mentions bringing other sheep (Gentiles) into his flock. With God's activity on behalf of the marginalized, impoverished, weak, and downtrodden, the message of Christ reveals that shalom and justice are at the core of God's intention for humanity. While human participation is part of God's activity, it is always from a position of witness to God's grace rather than from a position of God's dependency upon human effort. It is notable that God chooses to work in human/divine partnership. By mutual discernment of God's work through the Spirit, Christians demonstrate God's unifying presence, a presence carried into the world by active participants in God's missional work.

Christ's followers are sent into the world because of Christ's missional coming to the world and his missional sending of the Spirit to us in the world. The perichoretic presence of God binds the church in mutuality, egalitarianism, and love. Pastors guiding congregations to respond in this manner must exemplify mutuality, egalitarianism, openness to other, and love in the communal discernment of the Spirit's missional promptings.[127]

Biblical and Theological Considerations: Toward Implications

In this second section, we have investigated biblical and theological themes that speak to the church in liminal times. Specifically, I identify how the shepherd metaphor and Trinitarian theology beneficially inform the pastoral role as an embedded and mutual role within congregational life. That shepherds have poor reputations in the Old Testament and New Testament indicates that when pastors are "hirelings," the potential for abuse

126. See Friend, "Leading from the Bottom Up," 6–11; Kujawa-Holbrook, "Calling All the Baptized," 17–21; Standish, "Mystics," 23–27.

127. Van Gelder, *Ministry of the Missional Church* is an excellent guide for furthering the discussion on how the church is sent by the Spirit into the world.

expounds. When God's people living under the Spirit's rule recognize Christ as Shepherd, then the priesthood of all believers has renewed meaning for discerning God's missional promptings.

The best understanding of the pastoral (shepherd elder) role recognizes this person as a fellow sheep wearing the Shepherd's bell. Always guiding the flock toward the Shepherd, this role occurs as part of a multiplicity of pastoral leaders. Embedded undershepherds guide fellow followers to witness God's missional activity in the world both by their words and by their example. This will require a reformulation of the pastor's place as well as of the pastoral role and purpose within the congregation.

PART THREE

Beyond Expertise—
Back into the Flock We Go

Chapter 7

Bell-Sheep Pastors:
Leaders Who Guide by Following

In part one, technical, expert leadership as practiced in modernity was named as a misguided praxis within the church because of how it disembeds pastors from the congregational system and, in particularly discontinuous situations, misdirects the church's approach to addressing adaptive change. Additionally, modern leadership methodology, with its emphasis on expert systems, creates disenfranchisement and undermines mission. Part two revisited some of the dangerous memories surrounding the shepherd metaphor in the Old and New Testament narratives and explored how social Trinitarian theology might inform ecclesial leadership.[1] It specifically identified the preeminence of Christ as the One Shepherd over the flock with congregational leaders serving as bell-sheep within the flock. Further, through social Trinitarian theology part two emphasized how the interconnected community of faith with an emphasis on leadership as a Spirit-led, polycentric, integrated reflection of God's revealed self offers the church a new way of envisioning congregational leadership.

Starting with this chapter, the praxis of part one will be placed in dialogue with the memories of part two.[2] Through this dialogue a model begins to emerge wherein the pastor becomes an integrated guide toward congregational discernment of meaning, where meaning is identified as

---

1. Regarding "dangerous memories," see chap. 3 n. 43.

2. Groome's movement 4 (appropriating). Groome, *Sharing Faith*, 249ff. See also Ray Anderson's "interpretive paradigms" and "experimental probes" (Anderson, *Shape of Practical Theology*, 26–31).

God's missional activity in the world. It is by way of congregational discernment of God's activity that a church can begin to embrace adaptive change.

Appropriation of Biblical and Theological Themes: Pastoral Implications

So, what are the implications for pastoral leaders?[3] What is the pastor's role in light of the biblical imagery of shepherd and its nearly exclusive Yahwistic/Christocentric usage and Trinitarian theological reorientation discussed in the previous chapters? What follows are suggestions on how congregations and pastoral leaders might reorient themselves.

Interiority: The Revised Ordination

Interiority and self-donation offer the first clues concerning the implications of Trinitarian ecclesiology for pastoral persons. Generally, the practice of ordination has been viewed in terms of setting a person aside for "special service" (expertise) in the local church.[4] By the nature of setting aside some through ordination, there is an assumption that such a person's service has more to offer the congregation than someone who is not "ordained." Viewing congregations through social Trinitarian theology places a high priority on interiority, changing the nature of the connection between the pastor and ordination. Congregational membership should automatically connect members to a setting aside for ministry as kingdom participation.[5] McClendon writes, "If *leadership* in the church is a gift among gifts granted in the fullness of Christ, then ordination (not provided in the New Testament) and hierarchy (opposed there) are not essentials of leadership."[6] This negates special privileges of pastoral ministry—perhaps including pay-

3. Note: there is a shift in terminology here to reflect the model shift this book is advocating from a singular, specialized pastor to a community of leadership by pastoral persons (lay or clergy). This reflects the work of Paul and Peter who seem to conflate "elders," "overseers," and "shepherds/pastors" as similar and related roles as well as social Trinitarian reflections.

4. For examples from the author's Baptist heritage see: Humphreys, "Ordination in the Church," 288–98; Grenz, *Baptist Congregation*, 67–72; Grenz, *Theology*, 563–70.

5. In more recent conversations, we have come to know this idea as Christian vocation, or calling. All members of Christ's flock are called to serve in his mission (*Missio Dei*). This service may or may not be in a congregational setting, and often should not be.

6. McClendon, *Doctrine*, 371.

ment for service given to the community.[7] It becomes critically important to recognize that traditionally perceived specialized ministries also exist in the ministries of "lay members" by nature of the Spirit's indwelling of the congregation.[8] The nature of all being sheep in the Christ's flock makes all responsible for following the One Shepherd. Congregational ecclesiology, in which each member has responsibility for the church, "is the death of clericalism."[9] All are called, and thereby all are set aside for ministry (ordained).[10] Hence, a plurality of leadership must begin to emerge which recognizes this extended calling.

Mutuality and Self-Donation: The Pastor in Community

If the Trinity is understood in terms of mutual giving of self so that no person of the Trinity is left deficient or receives more than that person gives (self-donation), then how can we recognize some persons in the church as more important than others?[11] Mutuality dictates that we all give ourselves one to another, without priority or rank. Often pastors fulfill ministries of pastoral care, counseling, teaching, and administration in return for a paycheck, but at the expense of their own spiritual, emotional and physical health. Burnout, divorce, rebellious children, and poor health are often the costs of traditional ministry. The church must recognize that the ministries of the pastoral person are part of the church's ministry to the pastor. In terms of the shepherding metaphor, the pastor is also one of the sheep. Moltmann calls for the "full integration of the clergy into the congrega-

7. This is a topic for further investigation. While some scriptural evidence exists to support the idea of paying "clergy," other passages argue against such practices, including the practice of Paul the tentmaker.

8. Moltmann, "The Diaconal Church," 33–36. McClendon includes the ministry of proclamation (prophecy) as he invokes Yoder's "rule of Paul" that "all present should be free to take the floor" (McClendon, *Witness*, 379).

9. Ibid. Others making similar points: Kitchens, *Postmodern Parish*, especially chapter 6, 85–99; Roxburgh, "Missional Leadership"; and Roxburgh and Romanuk, *Missional Leader*.

10. Volf contends that certain kinds of giftedness are directly tied to the offices which oversee the whole congregation. He states, "there would seem to be no need for ordained ministry. Yet this is not so . . . The specific necessity attaching the gifts of office is their reference to the entirety of the church: officeholders are responsible not for a part of the congregation or a narrow aspect of its life but the vital concerns of the congregation as a congregation" (Volf and Lee, "Spirit and the Church," 32).

11. Volf, "Trinity is our Social Program," 412–17.

tion" pointing out that "the pastor is first and foremost a member of the fellowship and only subsequently, and on this basis, is he or she called to a certain office."[12]

This could include calling pastors from within the congregation rather than simply filling an open job position. But more than simple authorization of service by a democracy, the congregation is entrusted with recognizing God's work in giving the gift of the pastoral persons to the church (Eph 4:1–12). This requires discernment by the congregation and preparation of the candidate through the congregation's self-giving; the congregation becomes the instrument by which pastoral persons are prepared to fulfill their calling. In this fashion and by the integration of the pastoral persons into the congregation, those entrusted with the care of the congregation become a part of the congregation under the care of others.

Pastoral Guides Following the One Shepherd: A Journey Theology of Leadership

The Church must remember that, as Moltmann and McClendon have demonstrated, history, including the history of church, is God's Trinitarian history.[13] To understand the openness of God in human history the church must remember that it is not the object of God's end; it is a sign of the Kingdom.[14] The Trinitarian inner-life welcomes God's people into God's own history. The church's journey is a journey to God's end found in the love of the Father, Son and Holy Spirit—a journey made possible because of God's diversity and differentiation. This journey recognizes that there is differentiation and diversity within the giftedness of the congregation even as the Father is not the Son who is not the Spirit, etc., but the three are one God of one purpose. The recognition of pastoral gifts—while not more appreciated than all other gifts—is one part of recognizing the Spirit's work in the congregation.[15]

12. Moltmann, *Hope*, 40.

13. Moltmann, *Church in the Power of the Spirit*, 50–65; McClendon, *Doctrine*, 318–22.

14. See specifically Moltmann, *Church in the Power of the Spirit* for a discussion of "sign theology."

15. McClendon, *Doctrine*, 367–70.

God's narrative is frequently revealed in the journey motif.[16] The church would do well to rediscover that God's work in humanity often occurs by means of the "journey" of discovery. Pastoral leaders would be wise to see their role as that of pointer to the journey's guide.[17] The often misquoted Proverb 29:18 ("Where there is no vision, the people perish . . .") is better translated, "Where there is no *revelation* . . . ."[18] The key issue according to Henry and Richard Blackaby is not to "sell" God's vision to the people, but to "bring followers into a face-to-face encounter with God so they hear from God directly, not indirectly through their leader."[19] Too often pastoral persons short-circuit the journey to get to the destination more quickly. However, that is not usually God's design. The pastoral persons are responsible for following the One Shepherd and for helping others also hear and follow the One Shepherd.

Mark Lau Branson illustrates that one way of helping a congregation experience together God's revelation is through Appreciative Inquiry, describing how asking the right questions can empower a congregation to discover God's revelation.[20] Another developing leadership practice is that of Open Space Technology where the wisdom of all, or the discernment

16. Consider Abram's journey, Jacob's journey, the exodus journey, exilic journey, Philip traveling from Jerusalem to Gaza, Saul's Damascus journey, and Paul's missionary journeys. Each of these journeys have an air of mystery that only God knows the path, but those on each path must follow the Spirit's leading to journey's end.

17. See 1 Pet 5:2ff. Traditionally, ποιμαίνω ("to shepherd") has been interpreted as "to lead" in the modern sense of domination, ruling, and administrating. What does it mean for the flock that their "undershepherd" is also one of the sheep? If we take seriously the mutuality and interiority of congregational life then this is precisely the case. ποιμαίνω as "to guide" might be better. Also the noun, ποιμήν, is often translated "pastor" or "shepherd" as in Eph 4:11. The 1 Peter passage is interesting as it is often sited as proof of a hierarchical pastoral role. However, often overlooked in interpreting this passage is that the "shepherd" is "among" the flock (NASB). Unfortunately, the NIV and others translate this passage as "over" the flock when a sense of "in the midst of" might be more appropriate. Bauer, *Greek-English Lexicon*, 258–59.

18. Blackaby and Blackaby, *Spiritual Leadership*, 69. Old Testament scholar Marvin Tate confirms this interpretation, stating that, "The meaning of v. 18 is tied up with the understanding of prophecy (vision) and law . . . Definite revelation(s) from God is (are) considered to be a necessary element in keeping a people from casting off restraint (lit., let loose as of the hair of the head in Lev. 10:6 or run wild as in Ex. 32:25)" (Tate, "Proverbs," 92; emphasis in original).

19. Ibid., 75.

20. Branson, *Memories, Hopes, and Conversations*. This power of the question is also Darrell Guder's concept for helping people engage God's missional journey. Guder, *Missional Church*, 246.

of all is engaged.[21] Both of these leadership practices will be more fully introduced in a later chapter. For now, consider how developing practices around mystical leadership (where mystical means seeking God and discerning missional impulses) might help pastoral leaders and congregations to live into our biblical and theological heritage.

This kind of "mystical leadership" encourages pastoral persons to seek encounters and experiences with God and to enable, equip, empower, and encourage the congregation to do so as well.[22] When encountering God, the congregation together discerns the will of God as a people fully engaged in seeking the Triune God's leading.[23] Even as the Father, Son, and Spirit each have a unique work in the divine processes of creation or salvation, so each congregational member has a unique work in discovering God's journey. The pastoral role is that of helping the congregation to ask the questions so that in community the church might seek God and rejoin God's journey. The pastor in community "wears a bell" to help others follow the One Shepherd.

Empowerment and Polycentrism

Finally, pastoral persons must see their role as that of equipping or empowering. Even as the Father sends the Son through the Spirit (Luke 1:35), and as the Father and the Son send the Spirit (John 14:26), and as the Son and the Spirit glorify the Father (John 16:14; 17:4–5) so must the church with its gifts work together for the "building up of the body of Christ" according to God's purposes (Eph 4:12). Mark Lau Branson's threefold congregational formation process is helpful: interpretive leadership, relational leadership, and implemental leadership.[24] While we will be exploring this model more fully later in this chapter, note that this process develops congregational leadership for the purpose of determining meanings (interpretive), developing and maintaining healthy personal interconnection (relational), and creating Spirit sensitive structures to carry out God's mission (implemental).[25] This mutually integrated process (*perichoresis*) depends on full congregational engagement with all elements. As Branson states:

21. Whitsitt, *Open Source Church*.
22. Standish, "Mystics," 23–27; especially 25–26.
23. Ibid., 26.
24. Branson, "Forming God's People," 97–107.
25. Ibid.

Some members of a congregation will specialize as teachers, activists, or nurturers; but people who are responsible for larger oversight must embody all three leadership capacities. When we lead by keeping meanings, relationships, and structures well integrated, we create a greater possibility for generative self-correcting praxis . . . By leading in this holistic and cohesive manner, we form and generate sustenance for the congregation in its vocation as a sign and agent of God's initiatives.[26]

Polycentrism: Expanding the Circle

Recognizing the symmetrical relationships of the Trinity allows the church to see itself in terms of a "polycentric community." Volf makes a threefold argument for the church being a "polycentric community": 1) the church is a "communion of interdependent subjects;" 2) "mediation of salvation" occurs through all members of the church; and 3) the church is constituted "through the communal confession in which Christians speak the word of God to one another."[27] This polycentric community is based in "the Christian call to faith and in the charismata."[28] Focusing on universal distribution of spiritual gifts, among other things, Volf creates a picture of the church interconnected, Spirit led, and varied.[29] Although Volf still acknowledges an ordained clergy[30] and that it is conceivable that a polycentric community could have traditional clergy, there is no reason to assume that it must be so.

In every congregation, there are those who serve as pastoral people without being officially recognized as such. They are persons who give leadership and care for their flock, however small. When the church does recognize their gifts and calling, the usual reaction is to push them into vocational ministry. While many find fulfillment in such a vocation, countless others find disillusionment and despair. Many of the latter leave the vocational ministry convinced that they are failures, or worse, that they were never "called to ministry" after all. It is time to recognize the calling of many to be pastoral persons, without insisting on a vocational manifestation of

26. Ibid., 106.

27. Volf, *After Our Likeness*, 224.

28. Ibid., 225.

29. Ibid., 228–33.

30. Ibid., 245–57.

said calling. In every congregation, it is necessary to hear the bells of those who follow the One Shepherd and to join in following their lead, whether they lead vocationally or not.

In a polycentric community, the interconnectedness of all allows many to participate in the full ministry of the church. Rather than a centralized pastoral person or team, many persons care for and are cared for in smaller units. Additionally, this concept does not assume a lifelong commitment. The Spirit who gifts persons for service has priority in calling and uncalling those in pastoral service of the church. To use our bell-sheep metaphor, the Shepherd gives and takes the bell based on his own assessment of what the flock needs. This requires that the church maintain a vigilant and discerning spirit. In this way, the church would be served by including ever-increasing numbers of people called to guide the church into God's presence. Multiplying those empowered to serve as pastoral persons multiplies those fulfilling their ministry to God as pastoral people in the church.[31] Polycentric communities are communities that recognize the many pastoral persons in the congregation, whatever their vocation.

The church's theology of the Triune God and its reconsideration of the biblical metaphor of shepherd drives it toward new considerations related to structure and roles. As this occurs, it is increasingly important that the church redefine those structures and roles accordingly, reinterpreting the metaphors with which to describe the church's leadership. As it does, the church will find itself being drawn into a greater dynamic relation with the God it seeks to emulate.

For pastoral persons, this will create enormous change in how they fulfill their calling. It will likely require sacrificing old paradigms and comfortable seats of authority. However, in return pastoral persons may find that their once lonely vocation is now a wonderfully interconnected and dynamically relational calling *within* a people that more intimately reflects the Tri-unity of God. The question then becomes, can pastoral leaders guide a church facing significant adaptive/discontinuous change as an integrated part of the flock? A particularly useful way of looking at leadership that promotes a plurality of leadership and a polycentric process of leadership is advocated by Mark Lau Branson. This leadership formation triad—when

---

31. This raises questions of training and preparation. There are those in the academic community who are suggesting that a reconnection of theological training to the local church might be a good idea as would be the need in a polycentric community. Anderson, *Ministry on the Fireline*, 197–209; Farley, *Theologia*; Muller, *Study of Theology*; and Banks, *Reenvisioning Theological Education*.

considered along with the tools for inquiry such as Appreciative Inquiry and Open Space Technology—becomes a particularly important model for helping congregations consider adaptive/discontinuous change.

A Model Takes Shape: Congregational Formations

Danièle Hervieu-Léger demonstrates that despite an apparent decline in organized religion, there has been a new resurgence of religious awareness in recent times because of a renewed need for meaning.[32] This need for meaning from religion is further expressed by Wuthnow who states,

> Meaning, so defined in terms of nested categories that encompass the individual ever more comprehensively, has been a particularly attractive concept in sociological studies of religion. For Berger and Luckmann, religion becomes a type of symbolic universe that transcends and orders reality wholistically, giving it a sense of sacredness. For Bellah (1970), religion also constitutes an encompassing type of symbolism that transcends the pragmatism of every day reality, differs from conceptual or denotative terminology, and embraces the individual in a transcendent framework that supplies meaning and motivation. Geertz (1973), too, stresses the transcendent meaning-supplying character of religious symbolism.[33]

Hervieu-Léger and Wuthnow advocate that Christian faith commitments by nature are meant to give meaning to life, not take it. That is what makes the failures of the ecclesial expert system so detrimental. The system must work for people versus making people work for the system. The critical issue is how to rehumanize the process. As was stated earlier, Banks identifies the classic problem with theological education—its abstract nature and its presently understood role of preparing students for professionalized clerical functions.[34] He then offers two solutions to this problem: 1) returning

---

32. Hervieu-Léger, *Religion as a Chain of Memory*, 23–33. Hervieu-Léger offers this rationale: "Religion is understood as the mechanism of meaning which enables humanity to transcend the deceptions, uncertainties and frustrations of every day life. This transcendentality occurs by reference to the vision of an ordered world which surpasses reality. There is a clear link, especially in Yinger (and less explicitly in several others), with the theology of Reinhold Niebuhr, defining religion as a 'citadel of hope built at the edge of despair,' and especially with the work of Paul Tillich" (ibid., 34).

33. Wuthnow, *Meaning and Moral Order*, 39–40.

34. Banks, *Reenvisioning Theological Education*, 20.

to a less abstract, more intuitive and practical theology, and 2) a revision of what ministry involves.[35] This requires a praxis-based theology where Christopraxis is the form of reembedding.

Praxis Based Theology: Christopraxis as Re-embedding

As illustrated earlier, Ray Anderson identifies Christopraxis as Christ's activity in the world through the Spirit. God is always at work and it is the responsibility of Christ's followers to participate in that work.[36] This praxis-based theology is understood by Mark Lau Branson as a "set of activities" where "its ends are embedded in the current activities."[37] Reflecting on Anderson and on Toulmin's perspective of the critical issues of modernity, praxis-based theology operates in a specific place and at a specific time. It seeks God's leadership at a moment in time regarding specific issues. These are not Descartes abstractions. Context plays a very significant role. The expectation is that God is working presently in our world and we are to join God's work. It expects that the church look out its doors and down its street to see God at work and then to walk out those doors and join into that work immediately, presently, and humanly.

Branson's Congregational Formation Model

Branson's congregational formation model is based in such concepts as a sound ecclesiological understanding of the local church, the Priesthood of all believers, the role of the Spirit in guiding and leading the church, the praxis based theory of theology, and the role of discernment in determining God's leading. At the root of these structures is the belief that God has empowered the church with Spirit-filled people equipped to do the work of the kingdom. These structures enable pastoral persons to guide congregations toward becoming people who together find meaning, relationships, and methods for living their faith. This requires that pastoral persons transform from "leaders" to "guides" (bell-sheep). The congregation becomes fellow actors who also seek God's work in the world. There are three significant

---

35. Ibid.

36. Anderson, *Shape of Practical Theology*, chapters 1–5, but especially chapters 2, 3, and 4.

37. Branson, "Forming God's People," 106.

elements to this model: Interpretive Leadership, Relational Leadership, and Implemental Leadership.[38]

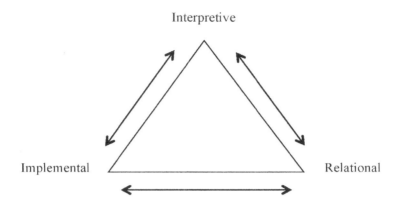

Interpretive

Implemental

Relational

Figure 2: Branson's Leadership Triad.

INTERPRETIVE LEADERSHIP

Interpretive leadership concerns itself with the discovery or rediscovery of meaning.[39] Through interpretive leadership, the church determines what it means to be a distinct people on mission with God.[40] Narrative is critical to developing a clear sense of God's presence. Appreciative Inquiry is a discovery process that allows leaders to engage the congregation in recovering God's activity in their storied past and present as a means for discerning God's leading for the future.[41]

38. Branson also develops this triad in Branson, "Ecclesiology and Leadership," 94–126. Also see, Branson, "Forming God's People," 97–107.

39. Branson asserts that, "Spirit-led interpretive leadership concerns the work of shaping 'communities of interpreters' by forming churches that learn how to deal with texts in such a way that they participate more fully in God's initiatives" (Branson, "Ecclesiology and Leadership," 120). Branson here cites Groome, *Sharing Faith*, 25 who is drawing from Gadamer.

40. Branson states that, "Interpretive leadership creates and provides the resources for a community of interpreters who pay attention to God, texts, contexts, and congregation" (Branson, "Forming God's People," 100).

41. For more on Appreciative Inquiry and congregations see Branson, *Memories, Hopes, and Conversations*.

Interpretive leadership is the critical component of a congregational structure wherein the community, as interpreters, share visionary leadership. Interpretive leadership creates a community that reviews societal and theological implications while reviewing the faith texts. It promotes the formation of commonly held bodies of knowledge as discovered in truthful, trustworthy, and honest intercommunity dialogue.[42] Leaders ask shaping questions while helping the congregation learn how to ask and answer its own questions.[43] Interpretive leadership clarifies meaning and purpose for other structures in this model, accessing its lifeworld and formulating new life together.[44]

RELATIONAL LEADERSHIP

Second, leadership is "relational."[45] If interpretive leadership gives meaning and defines the congregation, then relational leadership nurtures, shapes, and resources the social context wherein people gather as the church community. This is the arena where people interact with one another and for one another. Ecclesiology determines the nature of interaction: "If meanings are to be continually discerned by the interpretive community, and if those meanings are to be made tangible and visible, the whole process will be made possible by the congregation's numerous relational connections—its groups and networks."[46] Relational structure is not happenstance,

42. Branson, "Ecclesiology and Leadership," 120. Branson here is following Habermas's conceptualization of "communicative competencies." See Habermas, *Theory*, 2:120–21. Habermas uses the terms truth, sincerity, and normativeness of a statement. Ibid., 121.

43. Likewise, Browning and Anderson's outer-envelope, and Groome's five movements.

44. Branson, "Ecclesiology and Leadership," 120–21. See Habermas, *Theory*, 2:113–97.

45. Branson, "Ecclesiology and Leadership," 121; Branson, "Forming God's People," 102–4. Branson states, "Relational leadership creates and nourishes all the human connections in various groups, partnerships, friendships and families" (100).

46. Branson, "Forming God's People," 102. According to Branson, "Relational leadership concerns how social construction works generatively to form new muscles and synapses so we are healed and loved and grouped and partnered as the Body of Christ" ("Ecclesiology and Leadership," 121). The familial element of being the people of God is lived by how a congregation weeps with those who weep and rejoices with those who rejoice. It involves accountability, pastoral care, interest, friendship, hospitality, neighborliness, and even kinship.

but is purposeful in how persons relate one to another. Leaders help the church to become the people of God—one to another and to the world.[47] In so doing, shalom (justice, mercy, and grace) is expressed and experienced as demonstration of God's rule in a distinct (contrast) community.[48]

IMPLEMENTAL LEADERSHIP

Finally, "Implemental leadership attends to structures, activities, resources, and responsibilities in order to give meanings and relationships the necessary avenues for embodiment, equipping, resourcing, expression, organization, and endurance."[49] This is the praxis of acting where Christ acts. Congregational meaning, as discovered in interpretive leadership and as lived out in relational leadership, receives infrastructure in implemental leadership.[50] Here people determine how to allocate assets[51] and how to communicate and process mission. Most congregations focus their attention here, leaving meaning and relationship to chance. Implemental leadership, "is to shape and reshape activities and structures to be more coherent and consistent with generative meanings and relationships."[52] The values and meanings discovered through interpretive leadership and the high regard for one another developed through relational leadership both guide implemental leadership.

47. Branson, "Ecclesiology and Leadership," 121–22. Here Branson writes, "Relational leaders often need to bring the resources of conflict resolution and healing. They nourish the social imaginary concerning who is with whom, who has voice, and how personal and corporate character is formed. Networks of families and single persons become the corporate youth ministers of a congregation. Seniors and children learn to converse and serve together; newcomers and pillars share meals and stories; ethnic and economic boundaries are crossed" (122).

48. For a further discussion of the "contrast-society" as understood by Branson, see ibid., 94–112; see also, Lohfink, *Jesus and Community*, 157–63; Harvey, *Another City*, 21–31, 135–65.

49. Branson, "Ecclesiology and Leadership," 122–23, quote from 122.

50. This administrative functionality is where the churches, "form structures, develop strategies, delegate tasks, obtain and disperse resources, provide oversight, evaluate processes and results and coach numerous other leaders" (Branson, "Forming God's People," 104–5).

51. Assets include financial, property, reputation, human energy, creativity, experience, etc.

52. Branson, "Ecclesiology and Leadership," 122.

Leadership Cohesion

This leadership process is cyclical, ongoing, integrated, and praxis-based (see figure 2). Interpretive leadership develops meanings and defines relationships. Relational leadership determines how we work together to do the work of the kingdom and discover meaning while utilizing commonly held assets. Asset use leads to practical application, which takes place in relationships, and seeks meaning as confirmation of its purpose and intent. Two significant problems facing many churches are the lack of meaning (or forgotten meaning) behind their practice and application of assets, and the loss of key relationships that make practice part of community action. As meaning gives understanding to relational elements, those relationships help to determine how assets and resources are managed, requiring continual clarification of meaning.[53]

In the Face of Modernity

To be sure, there is no easy answer for overcoming the negative effects of modernity and its expert systems approach to life. But in addressing the congregation as a whole body and involving the participation of all, as Branson suggests, there is created a sense in which persons with expertise are mutually engaged and everyone has resources worth sharing. The disembedding of the ecclesial expert system into the academy encouraged preferential regard for persons with advanced training. What Branson proposes is a return of the knowledge and thereby the power to those who most need it and thus remove any two tier system of personal value in the church. Since God may speak through the Spirit to all of his people, and is often best heard in modes of corporate discernment, then each person must be seriously considered and no one person too seriously.

The modern agenda as established by Descartes and the rationalists led to dehumanizing conclusions. Christ's followers must return to a sense of wonder at how God works in mystery. Most mysterious of all is that God would take broken and fragmented people and use their frailties to form God's own people. It requires the wonder and mystery of Montainge who believed, but was never absolutely sure. Congregations must become experts together who know how little is known and are willing to live in the grace and mercy such knowledge requires. Most of all, believers need to

53. Ibid., 123–24.

become a people who live not by knowledge, theory, or abstraction alone, but a people who live by the practices of faith. Then it becomes possible to find the way in a very messy, but human process of being formed as God's people. The way of Christ is radically different from the adopted expert systems. The church's mission is to be a Gospel-centered people who live radically differently from the culture around them as witnesses to God's reign.[54]

A Way Forward

In light of failed praxis and the appropriation of Story/Vision, it becomes evident that pastoral leaders must take a different tactic than has been traditionally attempted in helping churches engage adaptive change. Rather than being solitary expert leaders doling out technical answers to the uninformed, a plurality of pastoral leaders must be embedded guides who guide the congregation's discovery of God's work in their midst and in the world around them. The chapters ahead look at how the communities of leadership developed above can engage the congregation in such discovery.

Particularly, in churches engaging adaptive change, communities of leadership become the means by which churches engage together in becoming God's people. This does not negate the reality of conflict. However, conflict can become a collaborative process by which communities discern God's promptings. Conflict in adaptive church contexts motivates the search for meaning.

---

54. Brownson et al., *StormFront*, especially 92–103, 105–29.

Chapter 8

Exploring Meaningful Conflict

As the realities of the liminal context come into contact with the cultural expectations around expertise, conflict will arise. Conflict might be thought of as "two or more objects trying to occupy the same space at the same time."[1] "Objects" include individuals, groups, or organizations and "space" could include land, property, (spheres of physicality) or ideas, goals, and intentions (spheres of meaning).[2] Unmet expectations and divergent norms fuel substantive conflict. To expand a bit further, congregations as systems are inclined toward homeostasis–sameness.[3] Conflict, as natural to change

1. Noting "conflict" is literally "to 'strike together,'" Leas and Kittlaus expound that "two pieces of matter attempting to enter the same space at the same time will conflict or strike together" (Leas and Kittlaus, *Church Fights*, 28).

2. Lewis, *Resolving Church Conflicts*, 5. Human sinfulness, self-esteem, pressures regarding personal social change, and vulnerability to power plays are sources for conflict and might be expressed as power struggles over differences: differing information, beliefs, interests, desires, values, and abilities to secure needed resources. Halverstadt, *Managing Church Conflict*, 2–4. David Augsburger summarizes, stating that: "Conflict exists in this tension between *same* and *other*: Conflict arises from the competition of *same* and *other*; conflict erupts as those who are *same* seek to control the *other* (and reduce its otherness), subordinate the other (and exploit its otherness), destroy the other (and annihilate its otherness), and exclude the other (escape from the threat of otherness)" (Augsburger, *Conflict Mediation across Cultures*, 16).

3. See Parsons and Leas, *Understanding Your Congregation*, 6–9. Also, Laszlo, *Systems View*, 35, 42; Wheatley, *Leadership and the New Science*, 75–90, 108–9; Senge, *Fifth Discipline*, 84–88.

and human social systems,[4] can be a constructive force[5] by creating enough imbalance to allow the needed shift in the systems to occur.[6] Engaging these change questions as guides of a congregational discernment process, pastoral leadership communities can avoid becoming "identified patients" of change[7] and thereby keep the pressure on the congregation for discerning God's designs and the communal need for change.[8]

4. David Augsburger states: "A common assumption among students of conflict is that the phenomenon of conflict, in its rich and varied forms, is an inevitable and universal feature of human groups" (Augsburger, *Conflict Mediation across Cultures*, 20). See also, Lederach, *Preparing for Peace*, 9; Lewis, *Resolving Church Conflicts*, 12; Steinke, *Healthy Congregations*, 14–22.

5. See Bossart's definition: "Conflict, in its proper sense, is not oriented ultimately toward upheaval and destruction but toward constructive and reconciling resolution of disruptive and divisive forces. Conflict thereby relates inseparably to both chaos and reconciliation. The disruption accompanying change often produces chaos. It is the initial stages in the experience of change. But chaos need not conclude the process. The ultimate goal includes both reconciliation and integration, but one does not get there through the process of cheap grace. One must come through the cross and reconciliation in the resolution of conflict. Conflict is a process, a means to an end. It connects the disruption and chaos of the old with the establishment of harmony and resolution of the new and not yet" (Bossart, *Creative Conflict*, 95).

Others confirm, conflict can be collaborative and fair, or overpowering and dirty depending on how power is shared and exercised. Constructive conflict is also described as "cooperative" or "exploratory;" destructive conflict is also described as "competitive" or "argumentative." See Lewis, *Resolving Church Conflicts*, 23–24; Leas, *Moving Your Church through Conflict*, 17–25; Augsburger, *Conflict Mediation across Cultures*, 42–72. Augsburger defines constructive conflict as conflict in which all parties are satisfied with the outcome while destructive conflict is conflict were some or all of the parties involved are dissatisfied. Augsburger, *Conflict Mediation across Cultures*, 42–72. Conflict can lead to exclusion when persons or groups believe that it is impossible to obtain two desired goals by the whole simultaneously. Leas and Kittlaus, *Church Fights*, 4–5. In church, conflict should encompass inclusive *shalom*, or wholeness, health, and security for all. Halverstadt, *Managing Church Conflict*, 3–10.

6. In adaptive change leadership, "orchestrating conflict," particularly conflict from raised awareness regarding the lack of a technical solution, is essential. Heifetz and Linsky, *Leadership on the Line*, 101–22. Heifetz and Linsky guarantee that, "conflict will arise with potential for deep ongoing change. They state, "When you tackle a tough issue in any group, rest assured there will be conflict . . . But deep conflicts, at their root, consist of differences in fervently held beliefs, and differences in perspectives are the engine of human progress" (101).

7. Parsons and Leas, *Understanding*, 23–24, 30–36. See also Friedman, *Generation*, 210–12; Steinke, *Healthy*, 42–52, 59–63. Heifetz and Linsky indicate that one way leaders are distracted from change is by making them the focus of the conflict through marginalization by diversion, seduction, or personal attack. Heifetz and Linsky, *Leadership on the Line*, 31–48.

8. Because social systems maintain equilibrium, change creates distress that the

To help the community engage change through the conflict process, pastoral leaders recognize that while substantive conflicts are expressed over implemental issues and experienced in relational contexts, it is actually occurring regarding latent interpretive questions. Focusing on interpretive issues allows the system to relax,[9] disengaging it from distracting relational and implemental questions, in order to clarify God's agenda.[10] This implemental focal point becomes the designated sphere of discovery, guiding future action in the other two spheres of leadership engagement. It will be helpful to investigate Appreciative Inquiry and Open Space Technology as exemplary processes for addressing these interpretive questions.

The Nature of Substantive Conflict

Generally, people experience conflict as intrapersonal, interpersonal, and substantive.[11] Intrapersonal conflict concerns two issues or interests within an individual that are at odds with one another, causing inner turmoil.[12] Interpersonal conflict is conflict when persons are "striking against the other primarily over their incompatibility as persons"—i.e., personality conflicts.[13] The third area, substantive conflict, is the focus of this study and is conflict over "facts, means, ends, or values."[14] Individuals or groups struggle with these areas as major transitions occur, such as a move toward intercultural

system will seek to ignore, destroy, or minimize. To this Heifetz and Linsky state: "There are really two tasks here. The first is to raise the heat enough that people sit up, pay attention, and deal with the real threats and challenges facing them. Without some distress, there is not incentive for them to change anything. The second is to lower the temperature when necessary to reduce the counterproductive level of tension. Any community can take only so much pressure before it becomes either immobilized or spins out of control. The heat must stay within a tolerable range—not so high that people demand it be turned off completely, and not so low that they are lulled into inaction" (Heifetz and Linsky, *Leadership on the Line*, 107–8). See also, Parsons and Leas, *Understanding*, 69–72; Steinke, *Healthy*, 86.

9. Steinke, *Healthy*, 57–67, 86; Freidman, *Congregation*, 208–10. This relates to Heifetz and Linsky's chapter 9, "Anchor Yourself" where they discuss handling attacks. They suggest leaders protect themselves from attacks by absorb the attack, without owning it, to refocus on the issues rather than on themselves. See Heifetz and Linsky, *Leadership on the Line*, 187–206.

10. Blackaby and Blackaby, *Spiritual Leadership*, 119–46.

11. Leas and Kittlaus, *Church Fights*, 29–35.

12. Ibid., 29–30.

13. Ibid., 30–31.

14. Ibid., 31.

church life or the apparent social marginalization of the church in the West. As adaptive situations are realized, people or groups perceive the opportunities/difficulties differently. Ultimately, goals reflect the church's values and it is possible that not everyone shares the same values.[15]

That said, there is a danger for congregational leaders who assume the correctness of their own understandings and the wrongness of those who might disagree. Dissent in the age of expertise is often viewed as disloyalty. However, from a position of humility and flockliness, dissent may be viewed as being: 1) an alternate option whose value must be considered and discerned (some may be more appropriate, and others less so), and/or 2) an ill-informed opinion that presents an opportunity for reshaping. Assuming every voice of dissent is only ill-informed opinion denies the leader of his or her opportunity to find another way in which God might be leading God's people to a desired goal. It also robs the people of the character shaping activity in discernment, which God might be attempting to do in helping them to identify the values and beliefs underlying each particular action plan. Dissent does not necessarily offer a better option, any more so than it automatically offers a worse option.

The process of discernment is the opportunity to learn again and discover a fresh the presence of the Sprit-mediated Christ and the direction in which the Spirit of Christ leads. It encourages us to once again surrender to Pneumacracy—the ruling of the Spirit—and the presence of Christ our Shepherd in midst of his church. A bell-sheep approach invites others to come with her or him to find Christ in our midst. Any method of discernment that takes seriously dissent, even when it seems ill-informed, must encourage God's people to emerge the values and meanings latent within each position, so as to clarify intention and purpose behind the action. Action and activity not guiding us further into God's preferred future is to be rejected while that which does is to be embraced. The manner with which leaders engage dissent has significant implications for conflict, which will be discussed more fully later in chapter 8. But for now it is enough to recognize dissent as a shaping force.

When discouraged or denied its proper place in shaping the conversation, it becomes a force for passive aggressiveness or subversion. When encouraged and welcomed, it becomes a force for reshaping people's understanding of God vision for the community. This could mean that the community's understanding of God is reshaped and thus they are further

15. Ibid., 31–34.

formed into the image of Christ. Or it could mean that God's vision becomes more clear to his people and the outcome of that vision (plans, actions, and activities) becomes more closely related to that vision.

Regarding spheres of meaning, this conceptualization suggests that, "conflicting goals are two purposes or objectives that cannot occupy the same group at the same time."[16] In transitional churches, the struggle is between incompatible understandings of reality trying to occupy the same community. Generally, people and groups believe that they share a common definition of reality, however conflict arises when two or more definitions of reality clash.[17] As Lederach states, "Conflict situations are those unique episodes when we explicitly recognize the existence of multiple realities and negotiate the creation of a common meaning."[18] Sociologically, perceived scarcity of resources may exacerbate these clashes of "realities."[19] The goal is to develop these conflicts in such a manner that they become exploratory and transformative.[20] This is why the presence of dissent is helpful. Dissent is a means by which voices in community may raise their desires and concerns. In the raising of these desires and concerns, the community may identify important values that shape its meaning-making and then either to spiritually shape the community's actions to match those values or to have those values to be reshaped in spiritual formation of the community. This helps leaders to identify and make known displaced and latent conflict over values, norms, and meaning

Displaced/Latent Conflict

In contexts of discontinuous change, conflict expressed over implemental issues and experienced in relational spheres[21] is best recognized as displaced

16. Ibid., 28.

17. Augsburger, *Conflict Mediation across Cultures*, 17.

18. Lederach, "Of Nets, Nails and Problems," 39.

19. Bossart, *Creative Conflict*, 34.

20. This is possible by engaging conflicted persons in critical conscientization as agent-subjects-in-relationship. Groome, *Sharing Faith*, 19–20, 100–104, 429–30. Freire states: "Knowing, whatever its level, is not the act by which a Subject transformed into an object docilely and passively accepts the contents others give or impose on him or her. Knowledge, on the contrary, necessitates the curious presence of Subjects confronted with the world. It requires their transforming action on reality. It demands constant searching" (Freire, *Education for Critical Consciousness*, 93).

21. See Lewis, *Resolving Church Conflicts*, 12; Bossart, *Creative Conflict*, 34; Halverstadt, *Managing Church Conflict*, 27; Leas and Kittlaus, *Church Fights*, 43; and Gangel and

or latent interpretive conflict regarding values, norms, and meaning.[22] Displaced conflict is defined as "a manifest and underlying conflict which is not dealt with in the argumentation."[23] Latent conflict is "conflict that should be occurring and is not. It is repressed or displaced. It needs consciousness raising to be dealt with."[24] Lederach describes key issues related to displaced and latent conflict.

In congregations where conflict appears interpersonal, but is based in substantive issues, handling it in a cursory "kiss and makeup" fashion leaves the conflictual issues buried producing further hurt, anger, frustration, and fear. Peaceful relationships occur by revealing latent conflict and the balancing of power, not through authoritarian leadership tactics that are usually practiced in these contexts. Substantive conflict disrupts the static or "homeostatic" nature of relationship, and, according to systems theory, creates discomfort and unease, but also opportunity for change.[25] It would be presumptuous to think that any process could wholly fit every situation. However, the process discussed below can help access latent and substantive conflict. Branson's triadic leadership communities assist congregations by unearthing transitional conflict issues.

Consequences of Failing to Address Conflict

Leas and Kittlaus state, "Where groups tend to suppress conflict, there will be an accumulation of feeling, leading toward a potentially dangerous conflict."[26] Regular expression of conflict and dissent with their related emotions allows communities to learn how appropriately to handle conflict and its emotional consequences.[27] Additionally, "the larger the number of

---

Canine, *Communication and Conflict*, 131–32.

22. "Changing the status quo generates tension and produces heat by surfacing hidden conflicts and challenging organizational culture" (Heifetz and Linsky, *Leadership on the Line*, 107).

23. Bossart, *Creative Conflict*, 13.

24. Ibid.

25. See Wheatley, *Leadership*, 75–78; Friedman, *Generation*, 23–26. Friedman uses the term "homeostasis" which is the family systems theory equivalent to "equilibrium" in the wider field; both terms imply balance. Regarding disequilibrium and leadership, see Heifetz and Linsky, *Leadership on the Line*, 153–60.

26. Leas and Kittlaus, *Church Fights*, 47.

27. Ibid., 47–48. Kouzes and Posner speak of the mutuality and reciprocity of relationships, developing that relationships help prevent escalation of conflict, and provide

conflicts, the greater the stability of the organization."[28] With numerous conflicts, persons oppose particular individuals on certain issues, but ally with some of the same individuals on other issues. Therefore, it is difficult to vilify people with whom you are sometimes in agreement.[29] Lewis warns that conflict is unavoidable—the only question is whether or not that conflict will be constructive or destructive.[30]

> The evidence is overwhelming that a persistent management style of avoidance or repression of conflict ultimately has destructive effect on a person, a relationship, or an organization . . . Organizational research reveals that the most effective organizations are ones that develop processes for managing conflict. Rather than suppress conflict, managers of high performance organizations in all environments tend to deal openly with conflict and work with a problem until a resolution is reached that best meets total organizational goals . . . [E]ffective organizations tend to affirm conflict.[31]

Surfacing and resolving conflict is a catalyst to creativity and growth, whereas suppressing or neglecting conflict is harmful, stifling, and potentially explosive.[32]

Communal Leadership and Conflict Resolution

As communities of leadership, pastoral leaders—paid or unpaid—should responsibly guide the church into and through constructive conflict. A pastor should avoid taking sole or primary responsibility for managing or mediating conflict.[33] By taking the responsibility for conflict upon himself

———

stability and predictability for the dealing with difficulties. Kouzes and Posner, *Leadership Challenge*, 156–57.

28. Leas and Kittlaus, *Church Fights*, 46.

29. Ibid., 46–47.

30. Lewis, *Resolving Church Conflicts*, 23–24.

31. Ibid., 24.

32. See especially Bossart, *Creative Conflict*. Also note Augsburger, *Conflict Mediation across Cultures*, 17, 21; Halverstadt, *Managing Church Conflict*, 3; Leas, *Moving Your Church through Conflict*, 7–12; Leas and Kittlaus, *Church Fights*, 35–41; Lederach, *Preparing for Peace*, 9–10; Lewis, *Resolving Church Conflicts*, 24.

33. However, Halverstadt demonstrates that in circumstances where a "malevolent cycle" of conflict is occurring, it requires a pastoral/manager's intervention. This person moves conflict from "win/lose" to a more "benevolent cycle" of looking for how *shalom* can be maintained in the congregation. Halverstadt believes this possible even when

or herself, a pastor becomes the focus of conflict and allows others to deflect responsibility for their work in meaning finding.[34] Rather, integrated pastoral leaders can help the congregation become a community that recognizes conflict and processes it meaningfully and appropriately.[35] Leas identifies four areas where the leader's role helps to keep conflict healthy: 1) Empower individuals to use their best efforts in the conflict; 2) Arouse confidence in the group and its leadership; 3) Provide or help the group to discover common goals; and 4) Provide or help the group discover the means of achieving the goals.[36] As we have discovered already, the more pastoral leaders can veer away from attempting to answer questions or fix problems and focus more on controlling processes of discovery, the better off they will be and the more likely they are to help a congregation to discover God's missional work.

This "transformational leadership" helps others to "feel strong enough to deal with the issues that are confronting the organization."[37] This view of leadership fits well with Branson's triad for congregational leadership, Heifetz and Linsky's approach to adaptive change, and the appreciative approach to meaning discovery, discussed below.

---

parties are unable to agree on resolutions to problem solving or when one party is unwilling "to follow a benevolent process." Ultimately, for Halverstadt the goal is "constraining win/lose resolutions and obtaining win/win resolutions" (Halverstadt, *Managing Church Conflict*, 7–10).

Augsburger offers a differing view of conflict processing that he terms a "neither-nor" solution where it is neither one nor the other party's solution. Nor is the solution a "win/win" where one gets some desired outcomes and the other also gets some outcomes. Rather, both parties work toward solutions not owned by either party, but is a "joint creation—a mutually constructed, equally supported, communally concluded process" (Augsburger, *Conflict Mediation across Cultures*, 51–53).

34. Heifetz and Linsky, *Leadership on the Line*, 38ff.

35. This may require surfacing or escalating a conflict situation. Heifetz and Linsky refer to this as "turning up the heat." Heifetz and Linsky, *Leadership on the Line*, 107–17. Preparation for conflict is important and pastoral leaders need to equip congregations with processes and means for engaging in healthy conflict. See especially Leas, *Leadership and Conflict*.

36. Ibid., 29.

37. Ibid., 31.

Conflict and the Three Spheres of Congregational Leadership

Conflict often surfaces in relational spheres over implemental questions (how money is spent, raised, or saved; who should utilize facilities for what kind of events and when; how are properties secured and people kept safe). Heated issues create additional friction in relationships, which can become a distraction from the work of discerning God's agenda in a diverse community. Or, as described below, they can become tools for guiding congregations toward discernment.

Conflict Surfaces in the Relational Sphere

It is an important truism that conflict in churches, as elsewhere, is by its nature experienced relationally (see figure 3): "One irony linked to an accurate view of conflict is that the participants must be connected . . . Some link must still connect the conflicting parties for conflict to be present."[38] This has important implications for congregational systems. It would be a hasty and unwise conclusion to assume that conflict experienced in the relational sphere is interpersonal.

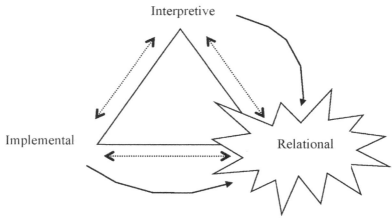

Figure 3: Latent Conflict Perceived in Relational Sphere.

Yet, this is precisely what happens in many circumstances. Individuals develop Friedman's anxious presence and focus on content issues rather

38. Gangel and Canine, *Communication and Conflict*, 131.

than on how the current imbalance in the system might advance further health in that system. As systems theory also indicates, the process of focusing on a particular element of the system, thus creating an "identified patient," allows the system to deflect more critical and substantive matters. Thus, in determining that the conflict is relational, the hard work of clarifying interpretive issues is left undone. However, Leas makes this observation: "It is only through interaction with others that one develops, and it is only through interaction with others that one can experience the fulfillment that one seeks."[39] While relational conflict may be a mask for latent interpretive conflict, it cannot be ignored. Perhaps the most significant moment in transitioning from this arena of conflict to determining actual conflictual issues is the commitment made to preserve the relationship. These relationships become the "holding environment for containing the stresses of their adaptive efforts."[40] Heifetz and Linsky state that, "a holding environment is a space formed by a network of relationships within which people can tackle tough, sometimes divisive questions without flying apart."[41] As Branson says:

> We are reconciled agents of reconciliation. If meanings are to be continually discerned by the interpretive community, and if those meanings are to be made tangible and visible, the whole process will be made possible by the congregation's numerous relational connections—its groups and networks. Within the congregation, families and friendship need leadership so that gospel meanings can be embedded and healthy relationships can be nurtured. In groups that discern, plan, and work, relational dynamics make the difference between dysfunction and banality on one hand, and lives that exhibit sanctification and justice on the other.[42]

---

39. Leas, *Leadership and Conflict*, 24.

40. Heifetz, *Leadership on the Line*, 103.

41. Ibid., 102. Heifetz also defines the holding environment as *"any relationship in which one party has the power to hold the attention of another party and facilitate adaptive work"* (ibid., 104–5; emphasis in the text). This asset is critical as it creates the balance necessary to "maintain a level of tension that mobilizes people" (ibid., 106). At its foundation, the holding environment is based on trust. Trust is based on a sense of predictability: predictability of values and of skills. People have to believe that a leader has their best interests in mind. Ibid., 107–08. This recalls the question of trust, expert systems, and expertise associated with modernity discussed in chapter 4. However, Heifetz and Linsky point out that a holding environment has limits and there are times when it becomes necessary to pull back from the change process.

42. Branson, "Forming God's People," 25.

Relationships are essential to the church's being. However, it is important to remember that although conflict is experienced relationally, it is often not primarily interpersonal conflict.

Since conflict is intrapersonal, interpersonal, or substantive, and since intrapersonal is focused in a single individual, and interpersonal has already been dismissed above, conflict experienced relationally is usually substantive.[43] Substantive conflict may be over facts, means, ends, or values. Therefore, the question is whether this conflict relates to implemental issues (means and ends) or interpretive issues (facts, values, and meanings)?

Surfaced by Issues in Implemental Sphere

To clarify this conclusion, it is necessary to focus on the issues related to implemental leadership. As Branson describes it, implemental leadership is where decisions are made regarding the allocation of assets.[44] These assets may be time, energy, space, money, promotion, or emphasis. In churches that are in the midst of cultural transition, these elements become critical to members as they vie for resources to promote the growth of their particular projects and groups. In-group favoritism, where boundaries may be ethnic, age related, or ideological, means that the lack of resources to do everything will create conflict as security issues come into play. As Bossart states:

> One type of conflict comes from the various segments of a system where the objects of need are scarce or unavailable for all. Power arises as that commodity needed to help our acquisition of those scarce objects and a sense of self-worth. If our needs are not satisfied, or we do not sense equilibrium in our system, we tend to fall into conflict, or competition, for the power needed for our sense of well-being.[45]

The critical issue here demonstrates that while change in the transitional church is in process, it is not felt until it impacts the security issues of a group of people, at which point conflict occurs. Heifetz and Linsky clarify that people do not resist change, but do resist loss.[46] While relational sphere is the area of "identified patient" or "symptomatic realization" it is in the

---

43. Leas and Kittlaus, *Church Fights*, 24.

44. Branson and Martínez, *Churches, Cultures, and Leadership*, 56–57.

45. While quoted earlier in this paper, what appears here is a fuller quotation of that section of Bossart. Bossart, *Creative Conflict*, 11.

46. Heifetz and Linsky, *Leadership on the Line*, 11–13.

arena of implementation that an imbalance in systemic "homeostasis" is realized. Therefore, if the conflict is experienced in the relational arena and surfaced in the implemental arena, it must then be driven by conflict in the interpretive arena.

Generated by Discrepancy in Interpretive Sphere

Branson, speaking about interpretive leadership, states, "Spirituality, then, is defined as attentiveness to and participation in the initiatives of the Holy Spirit."[47] When discussing implemental leadership, Branson states, "Whenever community members are hearing the Holy Spirit's call in their lives, leaders must give attention to specific practices."[48] Thus when speaking of the search for meaning in a congregational setting, it is clear that it is the Spirit's meaning that is being sought. The difficulty that arises comes in determining what initiatives are of the Spirit and which are humanly driven. Lewis develops the notion that in any congregation (or other organization, for that matter) an individual's personal goals, an individual's goals for that congregation, and the congregation's goals all bear on emerging conflict. He writes,

> Conflict in an organization, whether a local church, a large business, or a family, results in large part from the clashing of these three completing sets of goals . . . In a local church, conflict sometimes erupts when the pastor and a small group of lay persons determine the priorities the church will pursue, only to find a large portion of the congregation either turned off or angry about the new direction . . . The purpose of the church is not merely to be the setting in which all human needs are met. To be faithful to its mission requires focus. It means saying no to some human wants and yes to others. Faithfulness demands purposefulness on the part of individual members and the church and the willingness to deal with the conflict that is generated as they search for a common vision.[49]

The change in focus, even if agreed upon by all, will still create conflict as the resources shift to manage and support that change. Many members do not understand how such a shift will impact their personal goals for

47. Branson, "Forming God's People," 25.

48. Ibid., 27.

49. Lewis, *Resolving Church Conflicts*, 19.

the organization and thus, their personal understanding of meaning and security become threatened. Therefore, conflictual encounters likely are initiated by this change in meaning and purpose.

Backdoor Is the Way Forward

How then shall a congregation move beyond this conflictual moment? As has been stated earlier, conflict allows congregations and individuals the opportunity to grow together in relationship as well as allowing for revival of creative processes. In this particular context, conflict can become the conduit through which a community of believers can renew themselves to their stated purpose.

As figure 4 illustrates, the nature of conflict is that certain parts of the system are under particular stress. The relational arena and the implemental arena are under threat and are the least likely arenas to be able to work toward a substantive solution. Besides, as has been stated, these are not truly the areas needing to be addressed, but are, according to systems theory, content issues. The area of least active conflict is interpretive. Therefore, by working at implemental and relational issues and interests by way of meaning issues, the elevated threat to the system is lessened since meaning "appears" to have less importance. It is also an area in which there has been previous agreement, if in theory only.

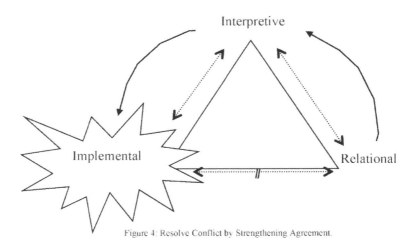

Figure 4: Resolve Conflict by Strengthening Agreement.

This process helps to affirm the conflicting parties as significant parts of the whole body. There is a recommitting of all involved to seeking again the initiatives of the Spirit. Henry Blackaby describes a similar process in his booklet, *What the Spirit is Saying to the Churches*:

> What happened next, we believed, was God indicating to us [God's] will. We were a living Body. If the consensus was 45 percent negative and 55 percent positive, we did not immediately proceed. We had seen two things: (1) that God was definitely moving in a positive direction; but that (2) the timing was not right, because 45 percent had no clear word in that direction. So we waited until God brought the rest to one heart and mind. We realized that some good directions were often lost in the timing. God was in charge and was present bringing us to the "same mind" (Rom. 12:16; 15:5–6; 1 Cor. 1:10), and we needed to wait on [God] until [God] had adjusted all of us to [God's self].[50]

In this pattern, the sanctity of the human involvement in God's initiatives is preserved.[51]

Summary of Conflict and Congregational Leadership

To sum up, consider how the Branson congregational leadership model, systems theory, and conflict awareness operate together in adaptive contexts.

First, it is apparent that conflict is rarely experienced in only one arena of the model. As has been demonstrated, in adaptive situations, conflict is experienced relationally, surfaced implementally, and generated interpretively. No part of the system escapes from the effects of conflict. This sense of systemic awareness should cause church leaders pause in ignoring the conflicts occurring within congregations.

Second, by avoiding direct conflict about secondary issues, pastoral leadership can help the congregation to lessen anxiety and create ways of helping the system to become a healthier system. In the process, such a pattern allows for a greater level of sensitivity to those for whom direct conflict is an affront. This reaffirms the interpretive work and the relational work of the community church. This also means avoiding the desire to attribute conflict over substantive issues to mere personality clashes.

---

50. Blackaby, *What the Spirit is Saying*, 33–34.
51. Groome, *Sharing Faith*, 160–61.

Finally, conflict offers important health benefits to the local congregation. It reminds us of the need to seek God's initiatives. It restores a need for one another in community. And it draws congregations into awareness that there is an intersection between God's initiatives and participation in community. The leadership triad helps congregational leaders understand how conflict occurs in congregational systems and demonstrates one way to help conflict be positive and transforming. Conflict becomes a means by which congregations are drawn to the work of discerning God's missional impulses thus opening the opportunity for imagination and experimentation to be unleashed.

Chapter 9

Empowering Imagination and Experimentation

As human beings, we have a unique ability to change our social reality by becoming conscious of the way our stories and histories have influenced our way of living and then to choose to live differently.[1] This is not mere theorizing about how things ought to be, but intentional activity with consequences of loss and gain toward a new way of life.[2] Further, because our nature is social, we have the ability to make new ways of living in community with one another.[3] It is with these understandings that we now engage in what Anderson describes as an "exploratory probe."[4]

Pastor in a Community of Pastoral Leaders

In expert systems, pastors are involved in a process of prescribing answers to problems and describing their understanding of God's vision. What is suggested here is that the church is better served by a more broadly diffused access to knowledge and a process of imagination that is rooted in spiritual practices of corporate study and discernment. The biblical and theological investigation in chapters 4, 5, and 6 and the application of these "memories" in chapter 7 point to the integration of the pastor as one bell-sheep with others in a Spirit-filled community of priests.

---

1. Groome, *Sharing Faith*, 110–12, 116–17, 123–31.
2. Ibid., 95–98. See Taylor, *Modern Social Imaginaries*, 23–26.
3. Groome, *Sharing Faith*, 100–108, 130.
4. Anderson, *Shape of Practical Theology*, 26–29.

In every congregation there are numerous leaders who go unrecognized and untapped. Pastors have a unique opportunity to involve the congregation in recognizing and engaging those whom God has already chosen. This is an imperfect process of realizing God's bell sheep, but as people are recognized as being Spirit sensitive and alert to God's promptings, congregations can undertake the practice of commissioning these as guides to God's missional activities. By betraying "pastoral privilege," pastors make themselves less the focus of the congregation's objectification and likewise allow the congregation to become agent-subjects-in-relationship.[5] It is important to recognize that encouraging communal leadership is not an expansion of specialized leadership to include more people. Rather, leaders create environments and help others access resources that allow God's people to become aware of the Spirit's work in their histories in anticipation of God's work in their future and then to experiment with engaging that work in their current ministry.[6] Such congregations recognize that some leaders engage the external community, operating at the cusp of the church's outward reach—the point of missional engagement.

One of the possibilities of expanding the leadership community is that new centers of leadership emerge, creating polycentric leadership within the congregation. This creates opportunity for greater conflict because these centers may have conflicting understandings of God's activity. As will be demonstrated below, this allows for new opportunities for discernment. It need not be that every leadership center operates on an exact and unified plan, although it is unlikely that God would create confusion and thus the general thrust of each center should be in the same general direction—in witness of God's reign.[7] The pastor's unique role in this process is the preparation of the community to discern and follow God's promptings including equipping others to likewise prepare the community.

Preparing others as bell-sheep pastoral leaders inevitably includes the passing on of technical skills and knowledge received through formalized theological education. There are difficulties as to how this might be accomplished, but too often pastors assume the "laity" are unable to obtain or are uninterested in obtaining these specialized pastoral skills. Perhaps re-embedding these expectations back into the congregation will be a starting

---

5. Groome, *Sharing Faith*, 19–20.

6. Roxburgh and Romanuk, *Missional Leader*, 143ff.

7. Groome, *Sharing Faith*, 14–18, 124–28, 162–63, 228–29. Guder, *Continuing Conversion*, 35–39; Hunsberger, "Missional Vocation," 77–109.

place for further advancing the belief that all of God's people are called to be priests one to another. Rather than expecting lay leaders to only utilize particular technical skills they possess from their own fields of employment, all fields related to training "clergy" are available for training lay pastoral leaders in a congregational setting—pastoral care, hermeneutics, preaching, worship leadership skills, etc. However, a critical component to this preparation is training lay leaders to identify adaptive and technical situations. This allows a wider awareness and promotes broader congregational access to understanding the limits of pastoral expertise.

Pastoral Leaders Engaging Community in Discernment

As guides, these pastoral leaders engage the congregation and the community in the process of discerning God's presence in the Spirit's missional promptings. Discernment in this sense seeks God's activity and responds to the Spirit's callings as the Spirit sends the church into the world. It recognizes that God's activity in the church is preparatory for the sending of the church as witness to God's reign. This requires stepping away from the tendency toward expert problem solving and stepping into the challenge with a positive focus on how it provides opportunity for discovering where God is at work and how we can and must be witnesses of that work. In so doing, these pastoral leaders live is such a way as to exemplify Christ's pre-eminence as Shepherd of the flock as they live out their role as bell-sheep.

Often times this work is discerned by conversations with neighbors. For instance, a church social worker, in conversation with neighborhood associations, apartment managers, city agencies, and local schools, discovers that there is a desire to hold a community event to offer a job fair, health services, and community gathering. This external discovery in conjunction with internal desires by the church to engage its neighbors in a relevant and meaningful way, leads the church to host, in partnership with these other groups, a community job and health fair with relevant participation by all.[8]

There is intentional need to create the kind of space or opportunities for such discernment to occur as part of the regular and ongoing life of a congregation. Many of the processes for leadership analysis that have

8. This is a description of the process pursued by Dr. Cynthia Kinnison at FSBC Phoenix during her tenure as the Church Social Worker at the church from 1997–2003. For more information on how churches can engage congregations in community ministries see Kinnison, "Helping a Church Embrace."

served the church in modernity perpetuate systems of analysis that might be deemed pastor-centric. However, there are emerging models for pastoral leaders to consider that allow for the Spirit of God to emerge God's desires for his people through his people.

Two such models are Appreciative Inquiry and Open Space Technology. The pages that follow will briefly describe the processes and considerations for both Appreciative Inquiry and Open Space. It is important to recognize how both foster Christianly humanizing approaches to discovery that reflect the biblical and theological memories of the previous chapters. One of the strengths of both Appreciative Inquiry and Open Space Technology is their ability to connect people to their stories and to one another, thus making people more fully rooted in our created nature; they are fully humanizing in the Trinitarian sense of our interconnectedness.

Appreciative Inquiry: Finding Meaning in a Positive Past

Appreciative Inquiry (hereafter, "AI") empowers congregations to access narratives of God's faithfulness in their own stories as well as in the biblical and historical narratives thus informing their discovery of God's work in their present context. By focusing on the positive and life-giving stories, pastoral leaders use questions to promote critical consciousness by church members as agent-subjects-in-relationship, thus encouraging the congregation to become participants in changing their social context toward God's agenda. As pastoral leaders engage others to ask questions, determine themes, and develop provocative proposals they also uncover important spiritual resources in the life of the congregation.[9] It is also likely that they will uncover or create conflict in this process, further developing opportunities for discovery of meaning.

"Appreciative Inquiry is the study and exploration of what gives life to human systems when they function at their best."[10] A more in-depth definition is offered by Jane Magruder Watkins and Bernhard Mohr:

> Appreciative Inquiry is a collaborative and highly participative, system-wide approach to seeking, identifying, and enhancing the "life-giving forces" that are present when a system is performing

9. Branson, *Memories, Hopes, and Conversations*, 61–63.

10. Whitney and Trosten-Bloom, *Power of Appreciative Inquiry*, 1. See also the Appreciative Inquiry Commons, Weatherhead School of Management, http://appreciativeinquiry.case.edu/.

optimally in human, economic, and organizational terms. It is a journey during which profound knowledge of a human system at its moments of wonder is uncovered and used to co-construct the best and highest future of that system.[11]

Both definitions emphasize that whatever AI is, it has its basis in human systems. This natural link to the systems theory perspective promotes that human social systems have within them something of value for the functioning of that organization or group.[12] The social dynamic of interaction and the various ways in which those systems are structured, communicate, operate, and create meaning are by their nature human.[13]

Appreciative Inquiry and Human Systems Orientation

Whitney and Trosten-Bloom in their *Power of Appreciative Inquiry*, identify six substantive reasons that AI works to promote human connections. First, AI "builds relationships enabling people to be known in relationship, rather than role."[14] Connections are built on who people are rather than on what they do. Second, AI "creates an opportunity for people to be heard."[15] People long to participate in meaningful ways but too often are overlooked or ignored. AI creates a space and time for the often marginalized to participate fully. Third, "it generates opportunities for people to dream, and to share their dreams."[16] The natural creative nature of human beings is nurtured and expression of this nature is encouraged.

Fourth, AI "creates an environment in which people are able to choose how they contribute."[17] Similarly to Freire, Groome, and others who have

11. Watkins and Mohr, *Appreciative Inquiry*, 14. With appreciation to Mark Lau Branson for bringing this quote to the attention of the author in Branson, *Memories, Hopes, and Conversations*, 19.

12. Regarding AI and the new sciences, see also Branson, *Memories, Hopes, and Conversations*, 32–36.

13. As Whitney and Trosten-Bloom state, "Appreciative Inquiry works because it treats people like people, and not like machines . . . Appreciative Inquiry enables leaders to create natural human organizations—knowledge-rich, strength-based, adaptable learning organizations" (Whitney and Trosten-Bloom, *Power of Appreciative Inquiry*, 19).

14. These six reasons for Appreciative Inquiry are located in Whitney and Trosten-Bloom, *Power of Appreciative Inquiry*, 20–21.

15. Ibid.

16. Ibid.

17. Ibid.

demonstrated the importance of non-coercion in leading, people can choose to participate or not participate promoting the kind of self-determination and emancipation described above. Fifth, AI "gives people both discretion and support to act."[18] Empowerment is a critical part of the AI process throughout. Finally, AI, "encourages and enables people to be positive."[19] Most people know the energy and emotional drain that occurs when being constantly bombarded by the negative. AI focuses people's attention on the positive and life-giving, energizing them to act with enthusiasm. In AI, that which is most humanizing, life giving, and hope-filled becomes the focus of attention, transforming the community or organization in the process.

AI is appreciative in that it both appreciates as recognitions (of "the best in people and the world around us" as well as of "those things which give life, health, vitality, and excellence" including "past and present strengths, successes, assets, and potentials") and it appreciates as adding value (or "value enhancement").[20] It is inquiry-centered in that it works by means of asking questions, studying, searching, exploring, delving into, and exploring the topic in question.[21]

Processes for Appreciative Inquiry

There are five processes, which, when applied as steps, form the heart of the AI experience. However, the steps may be applied in a variety of formats as exemplified later in this section. The five processes are as follows. There is first a need to "choose the positive as the focus of inquiry."[22] Similar to determining the generative theme in Groome's shared Christian praxis, choosing the positive initiates a filter which encourages the participants to consider specifically what it is they are about in this process and leave aside that which is unhelpful, but perhaps more habitual in our conversations. The second process is that we "inquire into the stories of life-giving forces."[23] This is a process of inquiry and questioning that helps participants search

18. Ibid.

19. Ibid.

20. Ibid., 2–3.

21. Ibid., 3. According to the authors, "The spirit of inquiry is the spirit of learning. It implies a quest for new possibilities, being in a state of unknowing, wonder, and a willingness to learn. It implies an openness to change."

22. Branson, *Memories, Hopes, and Conversations*, 28.

23. Ibid.

for and find both the common and the forgotten stories that have positively shaped their organization. The third process is to "locate the themes that appear in the stories and select topics for further inquiry." Here, the self-organizing nature of human systems promotes the idea that surrounding the area of focus certain recurring themes will emerge. As these themes are surfaced, they must be consciously communicated as part of the awareness process (Freire). Fourth, the group needs to "create shared images for a preferred future."[24] This process of picturing the future creates a conscious image of how life might look based on the hopes aroused by looking at the past. And fifth, the participants must "find innovative ways to create that future."[25] This is the moment when the horizons of the past and future merge in the present as praxis.

One of the benefits of AI is that practitioners offer several different methods of approaching these five processes. Branson uses the Four I Model: Initiate, Inquire, Imagine, and Innovate.[26] Whitney and Trosten-Bloom suggest the 4-D Cycle: Select affirmative topic, Discovery, Dream, Design, and Destiny.[27] Others have suggested a 5-D Model, which includes the idea of selecting a topic with the word "Define."[28] Whichever model is chosen, all five of the processes must be encountered.[29]

Considerations Regarding Appreciative Inquiry

AI has much in common with the concepts studied above. First, AI is a process of awakening awareness in people.[30] The terms "discovery" and "initiate/inquire" get at this idea. Sue Annis Hammond states, "Watching a long-held assumption be questioned and replaced tends to inspire people to question other long-held assumptions. In my opinion, this is the first

24. Ibid., 29.

25. Ibid.

26. Ibid., 65ff; chapters 4 and 5 of Branson are the procedural instructions with information, scripts, and schedules in the chapters that follow.

27. Whitney and Trosten-Bloom, *Power of Appreciative Inquiry*, 6–10; pages 6–10 is an overview while chapters 6–10 are more in-depth on each of these topics.

28. This model is advocated by the Clergy Leadership Institute, http://www.clergyleadership.com.

29. Branson, *Memories, Hopes, and Conversations*, 28.

30. This beautifully matches Clemens Sedmak's perspective that "theology is an invitation to wake up: to be mindful and attentive" (Sedmak, *Doing Local Theology*, 1–3; quote from pg. 1).

step necessary for any organizational change."[31] Whitney and Trosten-Bloom write, "[I]nquiry and change are simultaneous; that inquiry is intervention—and perhaps, the most effective means to transformation."[32] These and other statements seem closely connected to Heifetz and Linsky, and Groome (Freire) all of whom contend for the process of questioning as a means to awakening the minds and hearts of participants for becoming subjects of change and transformation in their respective environments. Further, the emphasis on question-raising by leaders, not with a specific answer in mind, but rather as a method of uncovering the tools within a community for change, is another link to the above-mentioned values. Likewise, there is a deep and abiding respect for people in AI as well as in adaptive change theory and shared Christian praxis. These are processes that can be engaged by a community of leaders within a congregational system.

Open Space Technology: Finding Meaning in the Wisdom of All

An emerging tool for spurring social imagination is that of Open Space Technology.[33] Having developed as an application in business and governmental sectors, this method for engaging people in imagination and collaboration has developed proponents for its use in congregational life. Like AI, Open Space Technology allows for congregations to discern God's activity in their midst by trusting that Spirit imbued resources and abilities of the congregation are sufficient to the work God has called them to engage. This occurs when the community engages one another to discern just how God through the Spirit of Christ might be at work.

Open Space Technology (hereafter, "OST") is rooted in fostering essential human connectedness in adaptive contexts for the sake of discerning meaning and discovering new ways. Diverse communities benefit by the process of valuing the work of participants as they engage in this work. As Harrison Owen states, "Open Space Technology is effective in situations where a diverse group of people must deal with complex and potentially conflicting material in innovative and productive ways. It is particularly

---

31. Hammond, *Thin Book of Appreciative Inquiry*, 18.

32. Whitney and Trosten-Bloom, *Power of Appreciative Inquiry*, 58.

33. The title of this section comes from the sub-title for Whitsitt, *Open Source Church*.

powerful when nobody knows the answer, and the ongoing participation of a number of people is required to deal with the questions."[34]

OST "creator" Harrison Owen identifies several important concepts that guide OST in being particularly helpful toward promoting healthy human systems. He starts with the hypothesis that "human systems, from families to the Family of Nations, share a common characteristic. They are all Complex Adaptive Systems. Like all other open, natural systems found anywhere in the cosmos, self-organization is simply what they do."[35] Owen describes how the circle, with its egalitarian construction and communal emphasis allows for self-organization that encourages and promotes full participation of people in relationship with one another.[36] To be truly generative, people collaborate in a process of imagination that is fueled by "passion and responsibility."[37] Additionally, Owen identifies empowerment as a significant outcome of the OST process.[38] One way in which this empowerment is manifest is through the voluntary self-selection process by which people choose to participate allowing those who have the passion and will take responsibility for the theme under consideration.[39]

OST's power comes from engaging humans as fully human in the positive Christian sense. As Trinitarian theology reminds, the essential nature of human being is connection to others. The fostering of human relationships lies at the core of OST as it "opens space" for people to hear, speak, imagine, and create with others and God the solutions to a group's concerns.

Furthermore, Owen describes the OST as a tool for engaging people in the "griefwork" that adaptive change brings. The natural response to loss,

34. Owen, *User's Guide*, 15.

35. Owen, *Power of Spirit*, 59.

36. Ibid., 46.

37. Ibid., 47.

38. Owen, *User Guide*, 85.

39. Owen, *Power of Spirit*, 47. More specifically, Owen insists that if people "don't care, they *shouldn't* come. Not everybody cares about the same things, and having uncaring people in an Open Space circle is, to put it bluntly, a drag. They contribute nothing, and they gain nothing."

which is what people resist according to Heifetz and Linsky, is grief.[40] This is the moment in transformation when the realization of loss sets in and people must work through the loss such change requires before moving on to new opportunity. "In Christian terms, one might speak of life, death, and resurrection. Contemporary theorists would prefer Steady State, Periodic Doubling, chaos, and renewal at a higher order of complexity. Different words, same process––I think."[41]

As a final indication of how OST functions from a human systems perspective, it is notable how the literature identifies significant human conditions as part of its expression: "fun and substance,"[42] "despair," "wonder and imagination," "vision," and "love."[43] These are human traits that often are lost in organizations and "strategic planning" for problem solving. In OST, whole people are engaged in transformational processes that are linked "with the millennia-old experience of humankind as we have sought to understand ourselves in all of our dimensions—physical, biological, and spiritual."[44]

Processes for Open Space Technology

According to Harrison Owen, there are "four principles" and "one law" that guide the OST experience. The four principles of OST are: 1) Whoever comes are the right people, 2) whatever happens is the only thing that could have, 3) whenever it starts is the right time, and 4) when it's over it's over.[45] These four principles reflect important collective elements or concepts reinforced throughout the OST material. A first concept of OST is the faith that the resources present with in a group are sufficient to creatively finding

40. Heifetz and Linsky, *Leadership on the Line*, 26–30.

41. Owen, *Power of Spirit*, 66.

42. Owen, *Expanding Our Now*, 25.

43. Owen, *Power of Spirit*, 72–77. A note about Owen's use of "vision": compared to what Owen describes as a current fad–the byproduct of a group "seeking to instill rationale and purpose into an organization,–Vision Statements," vision is "the picture of some future state that we hold in our head" that drives us by its "sheer power." "Vision is Spirit bursting out in new and powerful ways . . . Vision is prerational or subrational, the very ground and foundation from which rationality emerges. Given vision, you may figure out how to implement it, but you never think your way to vision. It is always a gift of chaos, the product of transformative High Learning" (ibid., 77).

44. Ibid., 66.

45. Whitney and Trosten-Bloom, *Power of Appreciative Inquiry*, 70.

resolution to the group's focused question.[46] This diversity of resources within a group when combined with passion about a topic and the responsibility for that issue makes the group's ability to engage that topic superior to that people working in isolation.[47] From a Christian faith perspective, we believe that God's Spirit provides through giftedness and talents what is needed for the tasks in which God calls God's people to participate.

Along with the four principles, there is one law: the law of two feet.[48] The law of two feet states that "if at any time you are neither learning or contributing, you should use your two feet and move to a more productive place."[49] This law allows us to focus our attention on those things that give us life or "keeps our attention on what we really care about, what has genuine heart and meaning for us." Owen determines that the role of "fit" is essential in helping people identify what role they might have in a system:

> When we become prisoner to the strictures of the formal system (custom, regulation, procedures, ways of thinking about things), all of which may have been very good ideas once upon a time, we are effectively taken out of the ongoing search for fitness. As individuals we lose the opportunity to build new skills and new competencies. And the organization of which we are a part will lose an effective agent (us) in the ongoing pursuit of high performance.[50]

A second important element of process is the circle and creation of space for people to interact. Some of this space is formal as in the case of the circle. Other space is informal: coffee area, sitting space, walking space. Owen describes the nature of the space as being essential to redefining environment and interactions.[51] The importance of the openness of the middle of the circle determines the tone of egalitarianism and equality of engagement. As Owen states, "When everybody, no matter their rank or position, sits on the same level, eye-to-eye, with nothing in the way, an extraordinarily powerful statement is made about equality of participation, and the conditions for a truly collaborative effort are created."[52] This issue

46. Ibid., 22.

47. Ibid., 22–23.

48. Owen, *Wave Rider*, 175–79.

49. Ibid., 175.

50. Ibid., 176.

51. Owen, *User Guide*, 66–67.

52. Ibid., 68.

of equality and egalitarianism is an important connection to Trinitarian theology and the nature of being members of God's flock.

A third element of process is the creation of a community bulletin board and the opening of the village marketplace. Both of these mechanisms are essential communication tools. The community bulletin board is the place where issues are raised and identified for open space conversation. This creates interest and allows for important negotiations as to where overlap might exist in issues and where folks will meet and engage in conversations. And as Owen identifies, this community bulletin board and marketplace allows for people to sort themselves by the meaning-making they wish to engage. People self-organize by identifying the areas of interest into which they wish to invest so as to maximize input and influence in the community.[53]

And a fourth element of process for introduction is the reporting of the news. In OST, morning announcements and evening news become places for the spirit of the people to be nourished by the gathering and interaction.[54] This is an open microphone opportunity to give away power to the community (betray pastoral privilege) for self-reporting what God might be doing in their meetings. And, with a nod to Heifetz and Linsky's admonition to "give the work back to the people" in adaptive change contexts, the OST facilitator "must constantly turn the freedom and responsibility back to the participants."[55] This self-reporting prevents the sterilization of God's message as it is allowed to come from those to whom it has come. As Owen, describes, OST has its potential for abuse, but more often the community has mechanisms already built in to prevent such abuses from being sustained, so long as the facilitator holds the space as equal and open space.

Considerations for Open Space Technology

One of the appealing elements of OST is the pervasive and essential spirituality that runs throughout the material. In his book *The Spirit of Leadership*, Harrison Owen easily engages spiritual language in discussion of leadership and its relational expressions.[56] This is refreshing and essential, however, it

53. Ibid., 102–4.

54. Ibid., 113.

55. Ibid., 116–18; quote from 117.

56. Owen, *Spirit of Leadership*, 51ff. In this chapter, "Spirit of Leadership," Owen states that "I take it as a given that Spirit is the most critical element of any organization.

will require translation from a non-Christian context to the church. Such translation is not difficult, but necessary.

As with AI, there are important connections to the material posted earlier in this work. The common language of human systems, as well as similar connections to Heifetz and Linsky make for obvious compatibility with the concepts driving leadership as understood in the earlier chapters of this book. A most notable connection to Heifetz and Linsky is how Owen recognizes leadership as an act of *love*.[57] Owen recognizes love as being both "unconditional acceptance" and "radical challenge."[58] At the core, this is what makes Christian leadership, Christian; love is the essence of Christ's actions and activity and all who lead others to follow him must likewise love as Christ loves.

Engaging Conflict as an Opportunity

Conflict reminds leaders that when people experience change then they also normally experience loss. This loss is expressed as grief with all of its emotional components. However, as pastoral leaders recognize this conflict—experienced in relationships and expressed regarding resources—they can utilize AI or OST as processes, which allow the system to relax and at the same time further discover meaning. By absorbing attacks, asking life-giving questions toward discovery of meaning, and creating space to engage in the making of meaning, pastoral leaders can avoid becoming the focal point of the failed expert system, thus keeping the congregation focused on the work of change. Also, by dispersing pastoral leadership throughout the congregation, the pastor can absorb heated attacks while

---

With Spirit of the appropriate quantity, quality, and direction, almost anything is possible. Without Spirit, the simplest task becomes a monumental obstacle. Furthermore, it is in the domain of Spirit that leadership operates. Though it may be true that leaders have a multitude of very practical tasks, they have one task that outweighs all others: to care for Spirit" (ibid., 52).

57. Heifetz and Linsky note, "The sources of meaning most essential in human experience draw from our yearning for connection with other people. The exercise of leadership can give life meaning beyond the usual day-to-day stakes . . . because, as a practical art, leadership allows us to connect with others in a significant way. The word we use for that kind of connection is love . . . Love gives meaning to what you do, whether in a corporation, a community, a classroom, or a family" (Heifetz and Linsky, *Leadership on the Line*, 209).

58. Owen, *Spirit of Leadership*, 122–30.

still encouraging other pastoral leaders to continue engaging in the AI or OST investigative and imaginative work.

Engaging in Story / Vision Discovery

To a large degree, the role of pastoral leaders is to determine what elements of God's Story/Vision speak to the contextual issues and then to engage the congregation in interpreting those texts. With training opportunities for lay leaders, pastoral leaders might help the congregation as a whole begin to discover God's Story/Vision in the church's context. This process could be enhanced through regular preaching services and special educational opportunities (i.e., home Bible studies, Winter Bible Study, Adult VBS, etc.). As pastoral leaders guide others in discovery of God's Story/Vision, they do so with a generative theme in mind, but not necessarily a specific understanding of how that theme is lived. This is for the congregation to discover as a congregation.

Engaging in Lament and Redemption

While AI and OST promote positive perspectives, they are not intended to ignore problems. Branson notes that lament is part of the awareness process.[59] As stories are told, and latent conflict arises, they also allow unhealth to be surfaced and addressed. This provides opportunities for healing as important areas for lament, confession, and repentance emerge that allow the congregation to move further into God's missional work. By ignoring areas of brokenness and sinful conformity to systems of the world's brokenness, a congregation will be unable to move forward as witnesses of God's reign because they reject God's work of reconciliation and restoration. Lament, confession, and repentance allow the congregation to experience a continuing conversion toward congregational life as a testimony of the faithful leading of a Good Shepherd who brings other sheep into the fold.[60]

---

59. Branson, *Memories, Hopes, and Conversations*, 52–54.
60. Guder, *Continuing Conversion*, throughout, but especially 87–96, 145ff.

Community as Witness of God's Missional Activity

As the congregational community begins to identify God at work in the world around them, they would also begin to understand their part as persons engaged in witnessing and to that work.[61] Pastoral leaders guide the community to consider what the Spirit is saying, where Christ is at work, and how their participation reflects the Father's love. As the community begins to understand its part without authoritarian impositions, and as new centers of leadership begin to emerge, the mission of God becomes a more integral part of the community's ethos. As a contrast society, they demonstrate how God's people are distinct from the world of power and division.[62] This begins when the community's leadership surrenders itself to the community, abandoning authoritarian, expert-visionary leadership, and giving themselves to guide the church to follow the One Shepherd, Jesus Christ.

A Provocative Experiment

So how might pastors respond to discontinuous and disruptive change in light of this study's considerations? Thomas Groome's five part process that has framed these chapters is a helpful framework for guiding pastoral actions. The first response should be to recognize that many of the situations confronting the church are such that the skills and expertise of the pastor alone is insufficient for the kinds of changes congregations are experiencing. The many changes require recognition by pastors that congregations are operating in a new context requiring adaptive leadership. Rather than trying to fix their respective churches, pastors need to resist the tendency for problem solving and to realize that members of their churches need to be led in a process of becoming aware of what God is doing in their midst and how God's work often requires significant change from them. The goal of church leaders should be to lead the church to following Christ into a new social imagination of God's missional activity.[63]

---

61. Van Gelder, *Confident Witness*.

62. Lohfink, *Jesus and Community*; Harvey, *Another City*.

63. Blackaby and Blackaby's language of helping people discover and move "on to God's agenda" is helpful here. Blackaby and Blackaby, *Spiritual Leadership*, throughout but especially 119–46.

For instance, a pastor might begin *focusing*-conversations, formally and informally, upon the question of God's missional activity in their midst and what the church's part might look like within that mission. These conversations could take place in the various venues already engaged: council and committee meetings, deacon meetings, choir rehearsals, Bible study classes, business meetings, fellowships, etc. As the church begins to think about God's activity, the pastor should guide congregational leaders in *naming the current praxis*. This is a congregational practice where leaders ask questions to clarify how the church sees its life and practice in relation to the changing world around them. Likely, a variety of narratives will be raised ranging from fear and anger as well as joy and engagement.

As these narratives surface, pastoral leadership—those already identified as congregational leaders (pastors, elders, ministers, Bible study leaders, deacons, committee members, and other key leaders)—can begin raising a *critique* of how cultural influences, rather than biblical narratives, have shaped the church's response. Again, engagement with the congregation by way of interviews and communal discussions will help the church leadership to notice trends. Some of these may come from past denominational and church history; other trends may be seen as more indirectly coming from culturally shaping factors such as politics, media, education, family histories, and others. By questioning broadly across the congregation, these leaders allow the congregation to become agent-subjects-in-relationship, engaging their world with the potential for naming and renaming it.

As these social forces are recognized, pastoral leaders, with the pastor preparing and maintaining the environment, begin to *access* anew how the gospel narrative speaks into current questions and missional witness. Pastoral leaders consider how the reign of God—realized in community and proclaimed by that community in the world—might look in the current context. Bible studies, sermon series, communal discernment exercises, and other venues are organized to allow the congregation to consider how they might be transformed by the Spirit's renewing of the mind, rather than being conformed by submission to the world (Rom 12:2). This should be a process that leads to both hope and conviction: hope in God's continuing mission and the church's part in that mission; conviction, lament, and repentance for the church's part in past departures from God's mission and the wounding those departures may have caused for others.

As the church recognizes God's missional activity and identifies areas where engagement is required, pastoral leaders can engage the congregation in the AI process of uncovering past and current moments where they have personally and corporately participated in God's missional promptings. The church and its leadership also must engage its neighbors in the AI process to discover how God is at work in the community outside the church's doors. They investigate what God has provided to people as evidence of God's work of preparing the various peoples around the church for engagement with the church as the church moves toward God's activity. The church's leaders can develop from these stories a wider vision than if it only focuses internally.

Further, this allows the congregation to begin to envision how to *appropriate* God's story/vision to their experiences. As stories are communicated in gatherings, newsletters, small groups, and worship, the church can share experiences when people acted against the social norm to offer Christ-like love, compassion, and care. They can begin to identify strengths already in their narratives, and realize God's faithfulness in preparing them for this moment, as the church begins to consider how they can participate more actively in God's missional activity.

This movement allows the church to consider those provocative opportunities before opening before them as to how they *respond* to live out the Christian faith. How do our worship, Bible study, pastoral care, and community ministry change? The church is allowed to imagine and probe how they can receive God's reign when it means their own participation and that of their neighbors. As resources are allocated and reallocated, conflicts will arise. However, each conflict is an opportunity to reevaluate interpretive understandings, through AI processes, OST, or other approaches to interpretive leadership.

Throughout this entire process, pastoral leaders will empower, engage, and encourage other pastoral leaders to step into the church's conversation and to play important roles in helping the congregation to discern God's activity. Following Spirit-led initiatives, the community of pastoral leaders expands to include those who are responsible for guiding others. In the end, it is hoped that the church has made a transition toward discovering the journey on which only God could be credited with having led them.

A Final Word

This book is a bridge between the current state of the church as a culturally captivated entity and a future church where shared leadership guides us into life as a significant aspect of our witness to God's ability to discover and engage God's mission in the world. Being this kind of church involves loss and pain, but an appreciative perspective tells us that "For momentary, light affliction is producing for us an eternal weight of glory far beyond all comparison, while we look not at the things which are seen, but at the things which are not seen; for the things which are seen are temporal, but the things which are not seen are eternal" (2 Cor 4:17–18). May God's people be found embracing the transformation such a journey provokes as they are transformed to his image!

Bibliography

Achtemeier, Paul J. *1 Peter*. Hermeneia. Minneapolis: Fortress, 1996.

Anderson, Ray S. *Ministry on the Fireline: A Practical Theology for an Empowered Church.* Pasadena, CA: Fuller Seminary Press, 1998.

———. *The Shape of Practical Theology: Empowering Ministry with Theological Praxis.* Downers Grove, IL: InterVarsity, 2001.

———. *The Soul of Ministry: Forming Leaders for God's People.* Louisville: Westminster John Knox, 1997.

Anonymous. "A Cash Call." *The Economist* (February 17–23, 2007) 71–73.

———. "The End of the Cash Era." *The Economist* (February 17–23, 2007) 13.

Augsburger, David W. *Conflict Mediation across Cultures: Pathways and Patterns.* Louisville: Westminster John Knox, 1992.

Aune, David E. "The Influence of Roman Imperial Court Ceremonial on the Apocalypse of John." *Papers of the Chicago Society of Biblical Research* 18 (1983) 5–26.

———. *Revelation 17–22*. Edited by Bruce M. Metzger. Word Biblical Commentary 52c. Nashville: Thomas Nelson, 1998.

Banks, Robert. *Reenvisioning Theological Education: Exploring a Missional Alternative to Current Models.* Grand Rapids: Eerdmans, 1999.

Barclay, William. *The Gospel of Luke*. Daily Study Bible. Philadelphia: Westminster, 1975.

Barr, James. *The Semantics of Biblical Language.* Oxford: Oxford University Press, 1961.

Bauer, Walter. *A Greek-English Lexicon of the New Testament and Other Early Christian Literature.* Edited by F. Wilbur Gingrich and Frederick Danker. 2nd rev. ed. Chicago: University of Chicago Press, 1979.

Beasley-Murray, George R. *John*. Word Biblical Commentary 36. Waco, TX: Word, 1987.

Bevans, Stephen B. *Models of Contextual Theology*. Maryknoll, NY: Orbis, 2005.

Blackaby, Henry T. *What the Spirit Is Saying to the Churches.* Atlanta: Home Mission Board of the Southern Baptist Convention, Lay Evangelism Department, 1988.

Blackaby, Henry T., and Richard Blackaby. *Spiritual Leadership: Moving People onto God's Agenda.* Nashville: Broadman & Holman, 2001.

Blackaby, Henry T., and Claude V. King. *Experiencing God: Knowing and Doing the Will of God.* Nashville: LifeWay, 1990.

Bock, Darrell L. *Luke 1:1—9:50*. Baker Exegetical Commentary of the New Testament 3. Grand Rapids: Baker, 1994.

Boff, Leonardo. *Trinity and Society*. Eugene, OR: Wipf & Stock, 1988.

Borchert, Gerald L. *John 12–21*. New American Commentary 25B. Nashville: Broadman & Holman, 2002.

Borowski, Oded. *Every Living Thing: Daily Use of Animals in Ancient Israel*. Walnut Creek, CA: AltaMira, 1998.

Bossart, Donald E. *Creative Conflict in Religious Education and Church Administration*. Birmingham, AL: Religious Education, 1980.

Branson, Mark Lau. "Ecclesiology and Leadership for the Missional Church." In *The Missional Church in Context: Helping Congregations Develop Contextual Ministry*, edited by Craig Van Gelder, 94–125. Grand Rapids: Eerdmans, 2007.

———. "Forming God's People." In *Leadership in Congregations*, edited by Richard Bass, 97–107. Herndon, VA: Alban, 2007.

———. *Intercultural Church Life and Adult Formation: Community, Narrative, and Transformation*. Ann Arbor: UMI, 1999.

———. *Memories, Hopes, and Conversations: Appreciative Inquiry and Congregational Change*. Bethesda, MD: Alban, 2004.

———. "Reflecting on the Gospel: On Changing Stories." March 1, 2007. http://www.allelon.org/articles/article.cfm?id=310.

Branson, Mark Lau, and Juan F. Martínez, *Churches, Cultures, and Leadership: A Practical Theology of Congregations and Ethnicities*. Downers Grove, IL: InterVarsity, 2011.

Brown, Francis, with S. R. Driver and Charles A. Briggs. *A Hebrew and English Lexicon of the Old Testament: With an Appendix Containing the Biblical Aramaic*. Oxford: Clarendon, 1975.

Brown, Raymond E. *The Gospel according to John (xiii–xxi)*. Anchor Bible 29A. New York: Doubleday, 1984.

Browning, Don S. *A Fundamental Practical Theology: Descriptive and Strategic Proposals*. Minneapolis: Fortress, 1991.

Brownson, James V., et al. *StormFront: The Good News of God*. Grand Rapids: Eerdmans, 2003.

Bruce, Frederick. F. *The Book of the Acts*. New International Commentary on the New Testament 44. Rev. ed. Grand Rapids: Eerdmans, 1988.

———. *The Epistle to the Hebrews*. New International Commentary on the New Testament 58. Grand Rapids: Eerdmans, 1979.

Buxton, Graham. *Dancing in the Dark: Participating in the Ministry of Christ*. Waynesboro, GA: Paternoster, 2001.

Carey, John. "Medical Guesswork." *Business Week* (May 29, 2006) 72–79.

Carroll, Jackson W. *God's Potters: Pastoral Leadership and the Shaping of Congregations*. Grand Rapids: Eerdmans, 2006.

Carter, Waren. *Matthew and Empire: Initial Explorations*. Harrisburg, PA: Trinity, 2001.

Chae, Young S. *Jesus as the Eschatalogical Davidic Shepherd*. Wissenschaftliche Untersuchungen zum Neuen Testament-2.Reihe 216. Tübingen: Mohr Siebeck, 2006.

Chapman, Mark D. "The Social Doctrine of the Trinity: Some Problems." *Anglican Theological Review* 83/2 (Spring 2001) 239–54.

Clergy Leadership Institute. "Appreciative Inquiry." http://www.clergyleadership.com/appreciative/ai.html.

Collins, Paul M. *Trinitarian Theology: West and East*. Oxford: Oxford University Press, 2001.

Cormode, Scott. "Multi-Layered Leadership: The Christian Leader as Builder, Shepherd, and Gardner." In *Journal of Religious Leadership* 1/2 (Fall 2002) 69–104.

Cunningham, David S. *These Three are One: The Practice of Trinitarian Theology*. Cambridge, MA: Blackwell, 1998.

Davids, Peter H. *The First Epistle of Peter*. New International Commentary on the New Testament 60. Grand Rapids: Eerdmans, 1990.

Dietterich, Paul M. "What Time Is It?" *Transformation* 1/3 (Fall 1994) 1–7.

Dirksen, Murl. "Shepherding the Herds of the Simakiyya Villagers." http://www.vkrp.org/studies/cultural/simakiyya-study/info/shepherding-villagers.asp.

Drane, John. *The McDonaldization of the Church: Consumer Culture and the Church's Future*. Macon, GA: Smyth & Helwys, 2001.

Duguid, Iain M. *Ezekiel*. NIV Application Commentary. Grand Rapids: Zondervan, 1999.

———. *Ezekiel and the Leaders of Israel*. Supplements to Vetus Testamentum 56. New York: Brill, 1994.

Dunn, James D. G. *The Acts of the Apostles*. Narrative Commentaries. Valley Forge, PA: Trinity, 1996.

Elliot, John H. *1 Peter: A New Translation with Introduction and Commentary*. Anchor Bible 37b. New York: Doubleday, 2000.

Erickson, Millard J. *God in Three Persons: A Contemporary Interpretation of the Trinity*. Grand Rapids: Baker, 1995.

Evans, Craig A. "King Jesus and His Ambassadors: Empire and Luke/Acts." In *Empire and the New Testament*, edited by Stanley E. Porter and Cynthia Long Westfall, 120–39. Eugene, OR: Pickwick, 2011.

Farley, Edward. *Theologia: The Fragmentation and Unity of Theological Education*. Philadelphia: Fortress, 1983.

Fiddes, Paul S. *Participating in God: A Pastoral Doctrine of the Trinity*. Louisville: Westminster John Knox, 2000.

Forrester, Duncan B. *Truthful Action: Explorations in Practical Theology*. Edinburgh: T. & T. Clark, 2000.

France, R. T. *The Gospel of Mark: A Commentary on the Greek Text*. New International Greek Testament Commentary 2. Grand Rapids: Eerdmans, 2002.

Freedman, Harry, and Maurice Simon, eds. and trans. "Exodus Rabbah, Shemot." In *Midrash Rabbah* 2. London: Sorcino, 1992.

Freire, Paulo. *Education for Critical Consciousness*. New York: Continuum, 2005.

———. *Pedagogy of the Oppressed*. New York: Continuum, 2005.

———. *Politics of Education: Culture, Power, and Liberation*. Westport, CT: Bergin & Garvey, 1985.

Friedman, Edwin H. *Generation to Generation: Family Process in Church and Synagogue*. New York: Guilford, 1985.

Friend, Howard E. "Leading from the Bottom Up." *Congregations* 31/2 (Spring 2005) 6–11.

Fukuyama, Francis. "Social Capital and Civil Society." Working Paper, International Monetary Fund Institute, April 2000.

———. *Trust: The Social Virtues and the Creation of Prosperity*. New York: Free Press, 1995.

Galtay, John, and Douglas L. Johnson, eds. *The World of Pastoralism: Herding in Comparative Perspective*. New York: Guilford, 1990.

Gangel, Kenneth O., and Samuel L. Canine. *Communication and Conflict Management in Churches and Christian Organizations*. Nashville: Broadman, 1992.

Garland, David E. "A Life Worthy of the Calling: Unity and Holiness Ephesians 4:1–24." *Review and Expositor* 76/4 (Fall 1979) 517–27.

———. *Reading Matthew: A Literary and Theological Commentary on the First Gospel*. New York: Crossroads, 1993.

Gaveneta, Beverly Roberts. *Acts*. Abingdon New Testament Commentaries 5. Nashville: Abingdon, 2003.

Giddens, Anthony. *The Consequences of Modernity*. Stanford: Stanford University Press, 1990.

———. *Modernity and Self-Identity: Self and Society in the Late Modern Age*. Stanford: Stanford University Press, 1991.

Giles Jere L., and Jerome Gefu. "Nomads, Ranchers, and the State: The Sociocultural Aspects of Pastoralism." In *The World of Pastoralism: Herding Systems in Comparative Perspectives*, edited by John G. Galaty and Douglas L. Johnson, 99–118. New York: Guilford, 1990.

Grenz, Stanley J. *The Baptist Congregation: A Guide to Baptist Belief and Practice*. Valley Forge, PA: Judson, 1985.

———. *Rediscovering the Trinity: The Trinity in Contemporary Theology*. Minneapolis: Fortress, 2004.

———. *Theology for the Community of God*. Grand Rapids: Eerdmans, 2000.

Groome, Thomas H. *Sharing Faith: A Comprehensive Approach to Religious Education and Pastoral Ministry: The Way of Shared Praxis*. Eugene, OR: Wipf & Stock, 1991.

Guder, Darrell L. *The Continuing Conversion of the Church*. Grand Rapids: Eerdmans, 2000.

———, ed. *Missional Church: A Vision for the Sending of the Church in North America*. Grand Rapids: Eerdmans, 1998.

Gunton, Colin. *Father, Son and Holy Spirit: Toward a Fully Trinitarian Theology*. London: T. & T. Clark, 2003.

———. *The One, the Three and the Many: God, Creation and the Culture of Modernity*. Cambridge: Cambridge University Press, 1993.

———. *The Promise of Trinitarian Theology*. Edinburgh: T. & T. Clark, 1991.

———. *The Triune Creator: A Historical and Systematic Study*. Grand Rapids: Eerdmans, 1998.

Habermas, Jürgen. *The Theory of Communicative Action: Reason and the Rationalization of Society*. Vol. 1. Translated by Thomas McCarthy. Boston: Beacon, 1984.

———. *The Theory of Communicative Action: Lifeworld and System*. Vol. 2. Translated by Thomas McCarthy. Boston: Beacon, 1987.

Haenchen, Ernst. *John 2: A Commentary on the Gospel of John, Chapters 7–21*. Hermeneia. Edited and translated by Robert W. Funk. Philadelphia: Fortress, 1984.

Hall, John, and Hannah Elliot. "Pastors: Leaders of the Flock but Alone in the Crowd." Associated Baptist Press (October 3, 2006). http://www.abpnews.com/1401.article.

Halverstadt, Hugh. *Managing Church Conflict*. Louisville: Westminster John Knox, 1991.

Hammond, Sue Annis. *The Thin Book of Appreciative Inquiry*. Bend, OR: Thin Book, 1996.

Harvey, Barry A. *Another City: An Ecclesiological Primer for a Post-Christian World*. Harrisburg, PA: Trinity, 1999.

Heifetz, Ronald A. *Leadership Without Easy Answers*. Cambridge, MA: Belknap, 1994.

Heifetz, Ronald A., and Marty Linsky. *Leadership on the Line: Staying Alive through the Dangers of Leading*. Boston: Harvard Business School Press, 2002.

Heitink, Gerben. *Practical Theology: History, Theory and Action Domains*. Grand Rapids: Eerdmans, 1999.

Hendricksen, William. *New Testament Commentary: Exposition of the Gospel According to Luke*. Grand Rapids: Baker, 1978.

Herms, Ronald. *An Apocalypse for the Church and for the World: The Narrative Function of Universal Language in the Book of Revelation.* New York: Walter de Guyter, 2006.

Hervieu-Léger, Danièle. *Religion as a Chain of Memory.* New Brunswick, NJ: Rutgers University Press, 2000.

Hobbs, Walter C. "Faith Twisted by Culture: Syncretism in North American Christianity." In *Confident Witness–Changing World: Rediscovering the Gospel in North America,* edited by Craig Van Gelder, 94–109. Grand Rapids: Eerdmans, 1999.

Hoehner, Harold W. *Ephesians: An Exegetical Commentary.* Grand Rapids: Baker Academic, 2002.

Horrell, J. Scott. "Toward A Biblical Model of the Social Trinity: Avoiding Equivocation of Nature and Order." *Journal of the Evangelical Theological Society* 47/3 (September 2004) 399–421.

Humphreys, Fisher. "Ordination in the Church." In *The People of God: Essays on the Believer's Church,* edited by Paul Basden and David S. Dockery, 288–98. Nashville: Broadman, 1991.

Hunsberger, George R. "Missional Vocation: Called and Sent to Represent the Reign of God." In *Missional Church: A Vision for the Sending of the Church in America,* edited by Darrell L. Guder, 77–109. Grand Rapids: Eerdmans, 1998.

———. "Shaping Up the Size of the Church." *Reformed Review* 47/2 (Winter 1993) 135–38.

Huntzinger, John David. "The End of Exile: A Short Commentary on the Shepherd/Sheep Metaphor in Exilic and Post-Exilic Prophetic and Synoptic Gospel Literature." PhD diss., Fuller Theological Seminary, 1999.

Inouye, Arlene R. "Revisioning the American Evangelical Church and Pastoral Leadership for the 21st Century." DMin project, Fuller Theological Seminary, 2001.

Jenson, Robert W. *Systematic Theology: The Triune God.* Vol. 1. Oxford: Oxford University Press, 1997.

Jeremias, Joachim. "ποιμήν." In *Theological Dictionary of the New Testament,* translated by Geoffrey W. Bromiley, 6:485–502. Grand Rapids: Eerdmans, 1968.

Jobes, Karen H. *1 Peter.* Baker Exegetical Commentary on the New Testament. Grand Rapids: Baker Academic, 2005.

Johnston, Philip S. "Civil Leadership in Deuteronomy." In *Interpreting Deuteronomy: Issues and Approaches,* edited by David G. Firth and Philip S. Johnston, 139–56. Downers Grove, IL: InterVarsity, 2012.

Kant, Immanuel. "The Conflict of the Faculties." In *Religion and Rational Theology,* edited and translated by Allen W. Wood and George di Giovanni, 239–309. Cambridge: Cambridge University Press, 1996.

Kinnison, Cynthia A. "Helping a Church Embrace Community Ministries." DMin project, Golden Gate Baptist Theological Seminary, 2001.

Kinnison, Quentin P. "The Social Trinity and the Southwest: Toward a Local Theology in the Borderlands." *Perspectives in Religious Studies: Journal of the National Association of Baptist Professors of Religion* 35/3 (Fall 2008) 261–81.

Kitchens, Jim. *The Postmodern Parish: New Ministry for a New Era.* Bethesda, MD: Alban, 2003.

Klein, William B. "Ephesians." In *Ephesians–Philemon.* Expositor's Bible Commentary 12. Grand Rapids: Zondervan, 2006.

Knight, George W., III. "Two Offices (Elders/Bishops and Deacons) and Two Orders of Elders (Preaching/Teaching Elders and Ruling Elders): A New Testament Study." *Presbyterion* 11/1 (Spring 1985) 1–12.

Koester, Craig R. *Revelation: A New Translation with Introduction and Commentary.* Edited by John J. Collins. Anchor Yale Bible 38A. New Haven, CT: Yale University, 2014.

Köstenberger, Andreas J. "Jesus the Good Shepherd Who Will Also Bring Other Sheep (John 10:16): The Old Testament Background of a Familiar Metaphor." *Bulletin for Biblical Research* 12/1 (2002) 67–96.

———. *John.* Baker Exegetical Commentary on the New Testament 4. Grand Rapids: Baker Academics, 2004.

Kouzes, James M., and Barry Z. Posner. *The Leadership Challenge.* San Francisco: Jossey-Bass, 2002.

Kubo, Sakae. *A Reader's Greek-English Lexicon of the New Testament and Beginner's Guide for the Translation of New Testament Greek.* Grand Rapids: Zondervan, 1975.

Kujawa-Holbrook, Sheryl A. "Calling All the Baptized." *Congregations* 31/2 (Spring 2005) 17–21.

Lane, Julie M., and Quentin P. Kinnison. *Welcoming Children with Special Needs: Empowering Christian Special Education through Purpose, Policies, and Procedures.* Bloomington, IN: WestBow, 2014.

Lane, William L. *The Gospel according to Mark: The English Text with Introduction, Exposition, and Notes.* New International Commentary on the New Testament 41. Grand Rapids: Eerdmans, 1974.

Laniak, Timothy S. *Shepherds after My Own Heart: Pastoral Traditions and Leadership in the Bible.* Downers Grove, IL: InterVarsity, 2006.

Larkin, William J. *Acts.* IVP New Testament Commentary 5. Downers Grove, IL: InterVarsity, 1995.

Laszlo, Ervin. *The Systems View of the World: A Holistic Vision for Our Time.* Cresskill, NJ: Hampton, 2002.

Leas, Speed. *Leadership and Conflict.* Nashville: Abingdon, 1986.

———. *Moving Your Church through Conflict.* Bethesda, MD: Alban, 2002.

Leas, Speed, and Paul Kittlaus. *Church Fights: Managing Conflict in the Local Church.* Philadelphia: Westminster, 1973.

Lederach, John Paul. "Of Nets, Nails and Problems: A Folk Vision of Conflict in Central America." PhD diss., University of Colorado, 1988.

———. *Preparing for Peace: Conflict Transformation across Cultures.* Syracuse: Syracuse University Press, 1995.

Letham, Robert. *The Holy Trinity: In Scripture, History, Theology, and Worship.* Philipsburg, NJ: P&R, 2004.

Levin, Jay H. *A Guide to the Euro.* Boston: Houghton Mifflin, 2002.

Lewis, G. Douglass. *Resolving Church Conflicts: A Case Study Approach for Local Congregations.* San Francisco: Harper & Row, 1981.

Lincoln, Andrew T. *Ephesians.* Word Biblical Commentary 42. Nashville: Thomas Nelson, 1990.

Lohfink, Gerhard. *Jesus and Community.* Philadelphia: Fortress, 1982.

Lummis, Adair T., "What Do Lay People Really Want in Pastors? Answers from Lay Search Committee Chairs and Regional Judicatory Leaders." *Pew and Pulpit Research Reports* 3 (Spring 2003). Durham, NC: Duke Divinity School, 2003.

Marshall, I. Howard. *1 Peter*. IVP New Testament Commentary 17. Downers Grove, IL: InterVarsity, 1991.

Martin, Troy W. *Metaphor and Composition in 1 Peter*. Society of Biblical Literature Dissertation Series 131. Atlanta: Scholars, 1992.

McClendon, James William, Jr. *Systematic Theology: Ethics*. Vol. 1. Rev. ed. Nashville: Abingdon, 2002.

———. *Systematic Theology: Doctrine*. Vol. 2. Nashville: Abingdon, 1994.

———. *Systematic Theology: Witness*. Vol. 3. Nashville: Abingdon, 2000.

McDougall, Joy Ann. "The Return of Trinitarian Praxis? Moltmann on the Trinity and the Christian Life." *The Journal of Religion* 83/2 (April 2003) 177–203.

Meeks, M. Douglas. "Moltmann's Contribution to Practical Theology." In *Hope for the Church: Moltmann in Dialogue with Practical Theology*. Edited and translated by Theodore Runyon, 57–74. Nashville: Abingdon, 1979.

Merrill, Eugene H. *Deuteronomy*. The New American Commentary 4. Nashville: Broadman & Holman, 1994.

Metz, Johann Baptist. *Faith in History and Society: Toward a Practical Fundamental Theology*. Translated by David Smith. New York: Seabury, 1980.

Michaels, J. Ramsey. *1 Peter*. Word Biblical Commentary 49. Waco, TX: Word, 1988.

Miller, Patrick D. *Deuteronomy*. Interpretation. Louisville: John Knox, 1990.

Min, Anselm K. "The Dialectic of Divine Love: Pannenberg's Hegelian Trinitarianism." *International Journal of Systematic Theology* 6/3 (July 2004) 262–64.

Molnar, Paul D. *Divine Freedom and the Doctrine of the Immanent Trinity: In Dialogue with Karl Barth and Contemporary Theology*. Edinburgh: T. & T. Clark, 2002.

Moltmann, Jürgen. *The Church in the Power of the Spirit*. Translated by Margaret Kohl. Minneapolis: Fortress, 1993.

———. "The Diaconal Church in the Context of the Kingdom of God." In *Hope for the Church: Moltmann in Dialogue with Practical Theology*, edited and translated by Theodore Runyon, 21–36. Nashville: Abingdon, 1979.

———. *History and the Triune God: Contributions to Trinitarian Theology*. Translated by John Bowden. New York: Crossroad, 1992.

———. *The Open Church: Invitation to a Messianic Lifestyle*. Translated by Margaret Kohl. London: SCM, 1978.

———. *Theology of Hope: On the Ground and the Implications of a Christian Eschatology*. Translated by John W. Leitch. Minneapolis: Fortress, 1993.

———. *The Trinity and the Kingdom: The Doctrine of God*. Translated by Margaret Kohl. Minneapolis: Fortress, 1993.

Mounce, Robert H. *The Book of Revelation*. New International Commentary on the New Testament 66. Grand Rapids: Eerdmans, 1980.

Muller, Richard. *The Study of Theology: From Biblical Interpretation to Contemporary Formulation*. Grand Rapids: Zondervan, 1991.

Nelson, Richard D. *Deuteronomy: A Commentary*. Old Testament Library. Louisville: Westminster John Knox, 2002.

Neuhaus, Richard. "Moltmann vs. Monotheism." *Dialog* 20/3 (Summer 1981) 239–43.

Norsworthy, David R. "Rationalism and Reaction among Southern Baptists." In *Southern Baptists Observed: A Perspective on a Changing Denomination*, edited by Nancy Tatom Ammerman, 71–97. Knoxville: University of Tennessee Press, 1993.

Ogbonnaya, A. Okechukwu. *On Communitarian Divinity: An African Interpretation of the Trinity*. St. Paul, MN: Paragon, 1994.

Ogden, Greg. *Unfinished Business: Returning the Ministry to the People of God*. Grand Rapids: Zondervan, 2003.

Osborne, Grant R. *Revelation*. Edited by Moisés Silva. Baker Exegetical Commentary of the New Testament. Grand Rapids: Baker Academic, 2002.

Owen, Harrison. *Expanding Our Now: The Story of Open Space Technology*. San Francisco: Berret-Koehler, 1997.

———. *Open Space Technology: A User's Guide*. 3rd ed. San Francisco: Berrett-Koehler, 2008.

———. *Power of Spirit: How Organizations Transform*. San Francisco: Berrett-Koehler, 2000.

———. *The Spirit of Leadership: Liberating the Leader in Each of Us*. San Francisco: Berrett-Koehler, 1999.

———. *Wave Rider: Leadership for High Performance in a Self-Organizing World*. San Francisco: Berrett-Koehler, 2008.

Painter, John. "Tradition, History and Interpretation in John 10." In *The Shepherd Discourses of John 10 and Its Context*, edited by Johannes Beutler, and Robert T. Fortna, 53–74. New York: Cambridge University Press, 1991.

Pannenberg, Wolfhart. *Systematic Theology*. Vol. 1. Grand Rapids: Eerdmans, 2001.

Parsons, George, and Speed B. Leas. *Understanding Your Congregation as a System*. Washington, DC: Alban, 1993.

Paul, Shalom M. *Amos*. Hermenia. Minneapolis: Fortress, 1991.

Perkins, Pheme. *Ephesians*. Abingdon New Testament Commentaries 10. Nashville: Abingdon, 1997.

Polhill, John B. *Acts*. New American Commentary 26. Nashville: Broadman, 1992.

Preskill, Stephen, and Stephen Brookfield. *Learning as a Way of Leading*. San Francisco: Jossey-Bass, 2009.

The Princess Bride. Directed by Rob Reiner. ACT III Communications. DVD. 20th Century Fox, 1987.

Ratatouille. Directed by Brad Bird. Pixar Animation. DVD. Walt Disney Pictures, 2007.

Ratzinger, Joseph. *Church, Ecumenicism, and Politics: New Essays in Ecclesiology*. New York: Crossroad, 1988.

———. *Salt of the Earth: The Church at the End of the Millennium: An Interview with Peter Seewald*. Translated by Adrian Walker. San Francisco: Ignatius, 1997.

Ricoeur, Paul. *Interpretation Theory: Discourse and the Surplus of Meaning*. Fort Worth: Texas Christian University Press, 1976.

———. *Time and Narrative*. Vol. 3. Translated by Kathleen Blamey and David Pellauer. Chicago: University of Chicago Press, 1985.

Ritzer, George. *The Globalization of Nothing*. Thousand Oaks, CA: Pine Forge, 2004.

———. *McDonaldization of Society*. 4th ed. Thousand Oaks, CA: Pine Forge, 2004.

Robson, James. "The Literary Composition of Deuteronomy." In *Interpreting Deuteronomy: Issues and Approaches*, edited by David G. Firth and Philip S. Johnston, 19–59. Downers Grove, IL: InterVarsity, 2012.

Rofé, Alexander. *Deuteronomy: Issues and Interpretation*. Edited by David J. Reimer. Old Testament Studies. New York: T. & T. Clark, 2002.

Roxburgh, Alan J. *Joining God, Remaking Church, Changing the World*. New York: Church Publishing, 2015.

————. "Missional Leadership: Equipping God's People for Mission." In *Missional Church: A Vision for Sending of the Church in North America*, edited by Darrel Guder, 183–220. Grand Rapids: Eerdmans, 1998.

————. *The Missionary Congregation, Leadership, and Liminality*. Harrisburg, PA: Trinity, 1997.

————. *The Sky Is Falling: Leaders Lost in Transition*. Eagle, ID: ACI, 2005.

————. *Structured for Mission: Renewing the Culture of the Church*. Downers Grove, IL: IVP Academic, 2015.

Roxburgh, Alan J., and Mike Regel. *Crossing the Bridge: Church Leadership in a Time of Change*. Ventura, CA: Precept, 2000.

Roxburgh, Alan J., and Fred Romanuk. *The Missional Leader: Equipping Your Church to Reach a Changing World*. San Francisco: Jossey-Bass, 2006.

Russell, Letty M. *Church in the Round: Feminist Interpretation of the Church*. Louisville: Westminster John Knox, 1993.

Schreiter, Robert J. *Constructing Local Theologies*. Maryknoll, NY: Orbis, 2004.

Schüssler Fiorenza, Elizabeth. *In Memory of Her*. New York: Crossroad, 1983.

Sedmak, Clemens. *Doing Local Theology: A Guide for Artisans of a New Humanity*. Maryknoll, NY: Orbis, 2002.

Senge, Peter. *The Fifth Discipline: The Art and Practice of the Learning Organization*. New York: Currency/Doubleday, 1990.

Simmons, Patti. "Supporting Pastoral Excellence." *Congregations* 29/1 (Winter 2003) 29.

Simpson, E. K. "Ephesians." In *Commentary on the Epistles to the Ephesians and the Colossians*. New International Commentary on the New Testament 49. Grand Rapids: Eerdmans, 1979.

Sire, James W. *The Universe Next Door*. 3rd ed. Downers Grove, IL: InterVarsity, 1997.

Smith, D. Moody, Jr.. *John*. Abingdon New Testament Commentaries 4. Nashville: Abingdon, 1999.

Smolander, Kari, et al. "Future Studies of Learning Software Organizations." In *Professional Knowledge Management*, edited by Klaus-Dieter Althoff et al., 134–44. Berlin: Springer, 2005.

Standish, Graham. "Mystics." *Congregations* 31/2 (Spring 2005) 23–27.

Stassen, Glen H., and David P. Gushee. *Kingdom Ethics: Following Jesus in Contemporary Context*. Downers Grove, IL: InterVarsity, 2003.

Steinke, Peter L. *Healthy Congregations: A Systems Approach*. Washington, DC: Alban, 1996.

Tate, Marvin, Jr. "Proverbs." In *Broadman Bible Commentary: Proverbs–Isaiah*, edited by Clifton J. Allen, 5:1–99. Nashville: Broadman, 1971.

Taylor, Charles. *Modern Social Imaginaries*. Durham, NC: Duke University Press, 2005.

————. *A Secular Age*. Cambridge, MA: Belknap, 2007.

Taylor, Harold. *Applied Theology 2: Tend My Sheep*. SPCK International Study Guide 19. Cambridge: SPCK, 1998.

Tolbert, Malcolm O. "Luke." In *Broadman Bible Commentary: Luke–John*, edited by Clifton J. Allen, 9:1–187. Nashville: Broadman, 1970.

Torrance, Thomas F. *The Christian Doctrine of God, One Being Three Persons*. Edinburgh: T. & T. Clark, 1996.

Toulmin, Stephen. *Cosmopolis: The Hidden Agenda of Modernity*. Chicago: University of Chicago Press, 1992.

Turner, John D. "The History of Religions Background of John 10." In *The Shepherd Discourses of John 10 and Its Context*, edited by Johannes Beutler, and Robert T. Fortna, 33–52. New York: Cambridge University Press, 1991.

U.S. Office of Naval Research. "Ocean Water: Salinity." Science and Technology Focus, http://www.onr.navy.mil/focus/ocean/water/salinity1.htm.

Van Gelder, Craig, ed. *Confident Witness–Changing World: Rediscovering the Gospel in North America*. Grand Rapids: Eerdmans, 1999.

———. *The Essence of the Church: A Community Created by the Spirit*. Grand Rapids: Baker, 2000.

———. *The Ministry of the Missional Church: A Community Led by the Spirit*. Grand Rapids: Baker, 2007.

Vatican Council. *Dogmatic Constitution on the Church: Lumen Gentium, Solemnly Promulgated by His Holiness, Pope Paul VI on November 21, 1964*. Boston: St. Paul, 1965.

Volf, Miroslav. *After Our Likeness: The Church in the Image of the Trinity*. Grand Rapids: Eerdmans, 1998.

———. "'The Trinity is our Social Program': The Doctrine of the Trinity and the Shape of Social Engagement." *Modern Theology* 14/3 (July 1998) 403–23.

Volf, Miroslav, and Maurice Lee. "The Spirit and the Church." *Conrad Grebel Review* 18/3 (Fall 2000) 20–45.

Wagner, E. Glenn. *Escape from Church, Inc.* Grand Rapids: Zondervan, 1999.

Watkins, Jane Magruder, and Bernard J. Mohr. *Appreciative Inquiry: Change at the Speed of Imagination*. San Francisco: Jossey-Bass/Pfieffer, 2001.

Weatherhead School of Management, Case Western University. "Appreciative Inquiry Commons." http://appreciativeinquiry.case.edu.

Wenger, Etienne, Richard McDermott, and William M. Snyder. *Cultivating Communities of Practice: A Guide to Managing Knowledge*. Boston: Harvard Business School Press, 2004.

Wheatley, Margaret J. *Leadership and the New Science: Discovering Order in a Chaotic World*. San Francisco: Berrett-Koehler, 1999.

Whitney, Diana, Amanda Trosten-Bloom, and David Cooperrider. *The Power of Appreciative Inquiry: A Practical Guide to Positive Change*. San Francisco: Berrett-Koehler, 2003.

Whitsitt, Landon. *Open Source Church: Making Room for the Wisdom of All*. Herndon, VA: Alban, 2011.

Work, Telford. *Deuteronomy*. Brazos Theological Commentary on the Bible. Grand Rapids: Brazos, 2009.

Wuthnow, Robert. *Meaning and Moral Order: Explorations in Cultural Analysis*. Berkley: University of California Press, 1987.

Yoder, John Howard. *Body Politics: Five Practices of the Christian Community Before the Watching World*. Scottdale, PA: Herald, 2001.

Zizioulas, John. *Being as Communion: Studies in Personhood and the Church*. Crestwood, NY: St. Vladimir's Seminary Press, 2002.

Appendix A

Thomas Groome's Concepts
of Shared Christian Praxis

To accomplish education for conation, Groome utilizes a "focusing activity" and "five movements." The following briefly explains the shared Christian praxis process.[1]

Focusing Activity

A *focusing activity* establishes "a common 'generative theme' (Freire's phrase) that shapes the core curriculum of the whole event."[2] This generative theme is a historical question, value, belief concept, or event that "is likely to draw participants into active engagement because it has import and meaning for their lives."[3] The central or core issue is existential and experiential. Crisis within the faith community forces the church into a reflective process whereby they evaluate practice and its social, historical and applied meaning. Such crises compel the community to ask, "What then should we do?" and, "How then should we live?" Action, reflection,

---

1. Groome overviews this process (Groome, *Sharing Faith*, 146–48), developing each movement in following chapters.

2. Ibid., 156.

3. Ibid. It should be easily identifiable to all participants and have symbolic qualities that focus the attention of the participants without becoming the focus of the participants. Further, its "generative" nature should "engage participants with something of interest to their very 'being' in the world." For Browning the evaluation process begins with the inner-core questions facing every congregation in crisis. Browning, *Fundamental Practical Theology*, 55–58.

and experience drive the conversation between theory and action.[4] Theologically, the focusing activity is based on 1) God's continuing activity of self-revelation in the daily lives of people, and 2) human ability to enter such revelatory events as agent-subjects, who recognize, reflect upon, and participate in God's self-revealing work.[5] After this initial activity, participants engage five movements for understanding and changed action.

Movement 1: Naming/Expressing "Present Action"

Naming/expressing "present action" enables "participants to name or express an aspect of their own and/or their society's present praxis."[6] A grounded awareness essentially "reconstruct[s] the former praxis" or becomes critically attentive to current praxis in order "to become capable of a new and different praxis."[7] Participants express this awareness as a consciousness of

4. Anderson, *Shape of Practical Theology*, 26–29. Focusing begins by selecting a theme raised by the facilitator/leader or by participants. Groome, *Sharing Faith*, 164. This generative theme should "attend to both present praxis and to Christian Story/Vision" (ibid., 165).

Groome identifies four guidelines for an effective focusing activity: 1) it "sponsors a common praxis or turns people to attend to an aspect of present praxis that reflects the generative theme;" 2) "it should elicit [participants] active participation as agent-subjects in the teaching/learning dynamic;" 3) it "is to establish, and should at least move participants toward, a shared sense of their common curriculum, and as it pertains to present praxis;" and 4) "as the focusing activity proposes a theme, or sense of the shared curriculum, it should be a 'manageable' one for these participants on this occasion" (ibid., 170–71).

Focusing establishes the "core of the curriculum to be attended to throughout the whole event," and should engage the learners' interests while evoking a sense of communal awareness and shared praxis. Ibid., 156–57. There is some interesting overlap here with Wenger et al., *Cultivating Communities of Practice*, 70–77. Wenger et al., identify in "stage 1—: potential" the elements of discovery and imagining as ways of bringing forward the shared values and practices of a newly forming community. This is not unlike Groome's process of identifying a common theme of interest for focusing the communal attention in the learning event.

5. Groome, *Sharing Faith*, 159–60; likewise, Blackaby, *What the Spirit is Saying*. Similar to Anderson, *Shape of Practical Theology*; Blackaby and Blackaby, *Spiritual Leadership*, especially 69–72; Blackaby and King, *Experiencing God*; Anderson, *Shape of Practical Theology*; Guder, *Continuing Conversion*; Guder, *Missional Church*; Brownson et al., *StormFront*.

6. Groome, *Sharing Faith*, 175. Naming creates awareness, which "is not a theoretical activity as an ahistorical sense of theory" (176).

7. Ibid., citing Freire, *Politics of Education*, 54. Anderson speaks of awareness in terms of "inherited narratives and practices that tradition has delivered to us . . . " emphasizing,

their own praxis, society's praxis, or both.[8] Through expression of action, the critical consciousness awakens. Communal interaction creates a synergistic environment that carries this transformational work throughout the community.

Movement 2: Critical Reflection on Present Action

Critical reflection on present action provides greater engagement between subjects where the aim for engagement is mutual respect and greater understanding among participants.[9] Communal nurturing and critical education are mutually compatible.[10] Reflecting on present action, "critical and social reasoning" promotes the uncovering of "reasons for present praxis" as well as identifying how praxis is influenced by "context in place and time." This allows participants to "scrutinize the interests, assumptions, prejudices, and ideologies that it embodies."[11] Browning reminds the

---

as do Groome and Freire, the manner in which current practices and stories engage the investigative process during the evaluation of current praxis. Anderson, *Shape of Practical Theology*, 27; Browning, *Fundamental Practical Theology*, 11. Browning insists that the interpreter cannot separate himself or herself from context in which he or she evaluates; an awareness of ones own interpretive pre-suppositions is critical. Browning also recognizes that both the interpreter and the context are changed in the dialogue. *Fundamental Practical Theology*, 47–8, 77–93, 243–45.

8. Groome clarifies that "the personal is always somehow social," noting that engagement on one level is connected to engagement on the other. Groome, *Sharing Faith*, 177–78. Groome demonstrates several rationale for this first movement as a dialogical process. First, Groome demonstrates that "use of language and symbols both arises from and shapes our consciousness, identity, and agency" (179). Specifically, he cites Freire, stating that "'the learners must assume from the beginning the role of agent subjects'; this requires that the pedagogy honor 'the radical, human need for expression'" (ibid; citation from Freire, *Politics of Education*, 49, 21). Second, the dialogical nature of opening one's perspective to others "is essential for responsible freedom and social transformation" (Groome, *Sharing Faith*, 179–80). He again cites Freire, writing, "that 'speaking one's word' in dialogue is intrinsically related to 'transforming reality'" (180; Groome notes this as a theme throughout but references Freire, *Politics of Education*, 51ff).

9. Groome references Habermas, stating: "Habermas's ideals of communicative competence: that interaction be marked by mutual respect for one another; be free from domination or manipulation; have no compulsion to agreement or consensus other than the persuasiveness of a particular perspective as it is tested by the discernment of the teaching/learning community" (Groome, *Sharing Faith*, 192). See Habermas, *Communicative Action*, vol. 1; and Habermas, *Communicative Action: Lifeworld*, vol. 2.

10. Groome, *Sharing Faith*, 194–95.

11. Ibid., 188. This is accomplished first by critical personal reasoning: participants

church that communities are products of their environments with futures tied to their histories.[12]

This movement promotes "analytical and social remembering [which] prompts participants to a critical analysis of the sociohistorical and biographical sources of present praxis and the historical influences that shape" their recognition and naming of it.[13] This is first about uncovering the personal story shaping both praxis and interpretations of societal praxis.[14]

---

reflect on how society personally shapes them and on how they personally shape society. Second, participants reflect at a systems level regarding how the whole functions together. Ibid., 200–201. This connects well to what Heifetz and Linsky, Wheatley, Senge, and others have demonstrated regarding the systems theory approach to understanding life where the whole is greater than the sum of the parts. See Senge *Fifth Discipline*, 4–9; Wheatly, *Leadership and the New Science*, 139ff. See also Laszlo, *Systems View*. For family systems theory work, specifically focused on the church see Friedman, *Generation*, throughout, but as introductory material, 14–39.

12. Graham Buxton's insight on the future is significant. Quoting Ray Anderson's concepts of *futurum* and *adventus*, Buxton suggests that God is revealing himself in the past, present and future. Therefore, our decisions are not just based on past or present revelation leading to a future we can predict (*futurum*). Rather is based on "God's future" (*adventus*) that is "outside human control or manipulation—the present apprehends the future in terms of that which is yet to be or come, and asks what yet can be done to bring that future into reality" (Buxton, *Dancing*, 27–28).

Consequently, Browning employs particular tools to unpack the environment, enable informed decision-making about God's activity, and identify potential application for human participation in that activity: "[P]ractical reason needs the . . . larger interpretive and hermeneutic process in order to have a sense of the wider reality in which it functions" (Browning, *Fundamental Practical Theology*, 40). Browning identifies four "outer-envelope" elements: "descriptive theology," "historical theology," "systematic theology," and "strategic (or fully) practical theology." Anderson uses the designations "communities of memory," "historical consciousness," "interpretive paradigms," and "experimental probes" (Anderson, *Shape of Practical Theology*, 26–31).

13. Groome, *Sharing Faith*, 188–89. "The outer-envelope of practical reason is made up of tradition-saturated images and visions of the way the world is at the ultimate edges of experience," writes Browning (*Fundamental Practical Theology*, 40). This "descriptive theology" means the social sciences. Browning states that, "this first movement is horizon analysis" which analyzes "the cultural and religious meanings that surround our religious and secular practices." Here sociology, psychology, anthropology, ethnology, and others explain the nature of human interaction within various circumstances, informing the congregation about the nature of their experience. To the questions "What then should we do?" and "How then should we live?" descriptive theology reflects on human responses in similar circumstances, providing insight into the human engagement of life. He explains that descriptive theology is similar to sociology if sociology is understood hermeneutically. Ibid., 47.

14. This is "'re-membering' in the sense that it brings to mind one's various 'memberships' (class, race, nationality, gender, sexual orientation, age, etc.) and how they and

Analytical and social remembering is "social archeology" that "focuses on the history of that context and ethos over time."[15] Emphasizing the "practical and emancipatory" elements of Christian pedagogy, Groome insists that knowing present praxis's "historical genesis" makes praxis changeable.[16] The facilitator's questions initiate unearthing of the community's "dangerous memory."[17]

Critical reflection introduces creative and social imagining allowing participants to "see the intended consequences of present praxis for both self and society and empowers them to imagine and make ethical choices for praxis that is personally and socially transforming."[18] Imagination allows participants "to see consequences, possibilities, and responsibilities of present praxis, personal and social, and how it can or should be reformed for the well-'being' of all."[19]

Movement 3: Making Accessible Christian Story and Vision

In *making accessible Christian story and vision*, participants engage the Christian Story/Vision and investigate the texts and interpretations that inform the generative theme.[20] Drawing on Gadamer and Ricoeur, Groome

their ideologies have shaped one's present agency" (Groome, *Sharing Faith*, 202).

15. Ibid., 203. This is a process of uncovering, recovering, or discovering the communities of memory, which inform a peoples' praxis. Anderson, *Shape of Practical Theology*, 26–30.

16. Groome, *Sharing Faith*, 203–4. Groome states that this is so because "without such remembering present praxis can take on an aura of inevitability, appear unchangeable, thus robbing participants of their sense of historical agency" (203).

17. Ibid., 204.

18. Ibid., 189. Groome's use of "social imagining" here brings to mind Charles Taylor: "By social imaginary, I mean something much broader and deeper than the intellectual schemes people may entertain when they think about social reality in a disengaged mode. I am thinking, rather, of the ways people imagine their social existence, how they fit together with others, how things go on between them and their fellows, the expectations that are normally met, and the deeper normative notions and images that underlie these expectations" (Taylor, *Modern Social Imaginaries*, 23).

19. Groome, *Sharing Faith*, 205.

20. Ibid., 215. This is Browning's historical theology: "This is where the traditional disciplines of biblical studies, church history, and the history of Christian thought are located. In this scheme, these disciplines and all their technical literary-historical, textual, and social scientific explanatory interests are understood as parts of a larger practical

determines the nature of the hermeneutical moment included within this third movement. He distinguishes between the meaning of the text for the author and what the text has come to mean elsewhere.[21] Groome offers three guidelines for movement three: 1) remember one's own pre-understandings,[22] 2) utilize the hermeneutics of retrieval, suspicion, and creative commitment regarding the text,[23] and 3) employ the "marks of authenticity" for explanation and application of the Christian Story/Vision.[24]

hermeneutical enterprise" (Browning, *Fundamental Practical Theology*, 49). This follows with Anderson's "historical consciousness" (Anderson, *Shape of Practical Theology*, 26–31).

21. Groome, *Sharing Faith*, 224. Ricoeur helps by opening the way for the meaning behind the text to create meaning in front of the text. Paul Ricoeur, *Interpretation Theory*, 87. Groome cites Gadamer's language of conversation to liken the process of determining the "meantness" and the "meaning" of the texts. Groome compares this to Ricoeur's understanding of applicability of the text as an ethical obligation. Groome, *Sharing Faith*, 224–25.

22. Each person brings to the text the baggage of culture, experience, presupposition, value, etc. To offset these external influences, Groome suggests that the first criterion for interpretation is the reign of God. Ibid., 227. This overarching (meta) symbol for the Christian Story/Visions determines a "sense of what prototype of Christian faith *always* means *for us*" (ibid., 228, emphasis in the original). Second, Groome suggests that the educator recall the "interests" and "perspectives" they bring to the hermeneutical process. As with Freire, making conscious held assumptions allows participants to critically reflect, transform, or at least acknowledge honestly the existence of these assumptions. Ibid., 229–30. Third, the facilitator's awareness of the participants' known assumptions, as he or she brings the community into dialogue, enables the facilitator to ask questions connecting to the time and place of the group. Ibid., 230.

23. Regarding the hermeneutics of retrieval, suspicion, and creative commitment to the "text," Groome initially commends employment of a "'hermeneutic of retrieval' to reclaim and access the truths and values symbolically mediated in the Christian texts. Ibid., 231. See also Anderson, *Shape of Practical Theology*, 88–90. Groome asserts that God communicates today to the faith community in relevant and meaningful ways even as in the past. Groome, *Sharing Faith*, 231–32. See also Blackaby, *What the Spirit is Saying*. Second, Groome proposes a "'hermeneutic of suspicion' to uncover mystifications and distortions in the dominant interpretations of Christian Story/Vision in order to reclaim its 'dangerous memories'" (Groome, *Sharing Faith*, 232). Third, Groome contends for a "hermeneutic of creative commitment." This hermeneutic of creative commitment allows the text to creatively engage the current context "beyond the dominant understandings of Story/Vision." Each text has a surplus of meaning extending beyond each moment's reflective need. Ibid., 234. See Browning, *Fundamental Practical Theology*, 247–49. Commitments must be practical and ethical, reminding participants of God's reign. Groome, *Sharing Faith*, 235.

24. Ibid., 227, 230, 235. Regarding "marks of authenticity," the Christian Story/Vision must be understood and lived. This is first measured by the continuity an explanation has with "constitutive truths and values of the *whole* Story/Vision." Thus, any interpretation

This book demonstrates the hermeneutic of suspicion as essential for social imagination. Communities generally avoid the hard work of change,[25] and that avoidance occurs in adopting commonly accepted interpretations without critique, while marginalizing texts that speak a more dangerous message.[26] The hermeneutic of suspicion questions why the dominant interpretation is accepted and why the more dangerous, yet life-giving, text is not accepted.[27]

Browning suggests that the guiding question at this stage of investigation is, what do the texts *"really* imply for our praxis when confronted as honestly as possible?"[28] It propels a congregation back to the texts to identify a clearer understanding of God's voice as it relates to their particular moment. It requires exploration of how texts might inform new understanding through meanings previously overlooked.[29]

Movement 4: Dialectical Hermeneutics to Appropriate Story/Vision to Participants' Stories and Visions

Regarding the *dialectical hermeneutics to appropriate story/vision to participants stories and visions,* Groome states that the "purpose of movement 4 is to enable participants to critically appropriate the faith community's

---

"should be in harmony with what's at the 'heart' of the Christian faith" (ibid., 236). Emphasized in *Sharing,* however, it has been altered here to emphasize the important statement Groome makes about the holistic nature of accurate interpretations over and against "proof-texting." The second measurement relates to an interpretation's consequential (i.e., ethical) nature. The needs of the poor, the freedom of the dominated, and the participation of the marginalized take priority over the wants of the rich, the liberty of the powerful, and the preservation of social structures of exclusion. Ibid., 236–37. Finally, the communal nature of an interpretation measures an interpretation's authenticity. The church is responsible for the meaning of its texts. As such, interpretations outside the official teaching, the research of scholarship, and the discernment of the people are rejected. Ibid., 237–38.

25. Heifetz and Linsky, *Leadership on the Line,* 31–48.

26. Groome, *Sharing Faith,* 233.

27. Ibid., 203–4, 234.

28. Browning, *Fundamental Practical Theology,* 49, emphasis in original.

29. Perhaps more than understanding this as "what have we understood the Bible to say about this issue?" or "what does church history teach us about this problem?" historical theology demands reexamination of known texts and identification of others previously unknown to us. Ibid.

Story/Vision to their own lives and contexts."[30] If theology is enacted and performed locally, then the faith Story/Vision must be internalized, or "appropriated."[31] Two questions clarify the formative and authoritative texts of the Christian tradition in relation to the broad themes of praxis: "What new horizon of meaning is fused when questions from the present practices are brought to the central Christian witness?" and "What reasons can be advanced to support the validity claims of this new fusion of meaning?"[32] One answer acknowledges the revelatory nature of God's presence in the moment of praxis: God is already working in this situation; followers must discover that work and join God in it.[33] Anderson is helpful here.

Rather than understanding Christ as a static, historical person, ascended and gone, Anderson's Christopraxis views Christ as present in the Spirit.[34] Christ's activity in the world accomplishes his purposes; the church joins him in his work, becoming the church he desires upon his return.[35] The missional activity of the church is, "the ongoing ministry of

30. Groome, *Sharing Faith*, 250. Sedmak states that "theology is done locally" (Sedmak, *Doing Local Theology*, 3). See also Schreiter, *Constructing Local Theologies*, 1–21.

31. This is Browning's third movement, where theory and action meet: "Systematic theology, when seen from the perspective of Gadamer's hermeneutics, is the fusion of horizons between the vision implicit in contemporary practices and the vision implied in the practices of the normative Christian texts" (Browning, *Fundamental Practical Theology*, 51). Here "systematic theology" relates more closely to the hermeneutic questions of Groome's movement 4 than traditionally understood as texts and historical reasoning (Groome's movement 3). Anderson understands this as "interpretive paradigms." See Anderson, *Shape of Practical Theology*, 26–28.

32. Browning, *Fundamental Practical Theology*, 51–52.

33. Groome, *Sharing Faith*, 254–56. Groome states: "[M]ovement 4 of shared Christian praxis reflects the conviction that as people encounter God's self-disclosure through Christian Story/Vision, they have a 'natural' (but graded) ability and affinity to recognize and personally appropriate its truth and values for their lives" (ibid., 256). See also Anderson, *Shape of Practical Theology*, 37–46; Blackaby and King, *Experiencing God*; Blackaby, *What the Spirit is Saying*; Harvey, *Another City*, 150–65.

34. As Anderson remind, the Spirit of Christ is the Holy Spirit. Anderson, *Shape of Practical Theology*, 102–9. Following Anderson, Graham Buxton says, "Christian ministry is fundamentally about participation in the ongoing ministry of Christ himself, who invites us into all the he is doing today by the power of the Spirit" (Buxton, *Dancing*, 1). While Christocentric, Christopraxis is a fully Trinitarian concept as presented by Anderson. Christ's work is carried on by the Spirit in us and remains Christ's work to the Father on behalf of the world. See Ibid., 39–46.

35. Anderson, *Shape of Practical Theology*, 106–12. Again, Buxton states: "It is not the task of the church to decide how and when to make God known: it is the privilege and responsibility of those who confess Christ to discern the will of the Father, and in

Christ through the power and presence of the Spirit of Christ [which] constitutes the praxis of God's mission to the world through the church and its ministry."[36] This hermeneutic suggests that the work of the Spirit interprets the word of the Spirit.[37] Hence, the critical question is not "what would Jesus do?" but "what is Jesus doing?"[38]

Movement 5: Direction/Response for Lived Christian Faith

In direction/response for lived Christian faith, participants make "a decision for knowing, desiring, and doing with others what is humanizing and life-giving for all; it also provides a community of conversation whose communal probing and testing dynamic prompts participants to make

---

obedience to respond to the Sprit who ever seeks to glorify Christ in the world . . . The implications of this are profound, for to view the ministry in this light is to emphasize the crucial relationship between the ministry of Christ and the ministry of the church. This is what I mean by describing the ministry of the church as Christological. Any local church which attempts to influence and persuade without reference to Christ ceases to be a part of the true church of God" (Buxton, *Dancing*, 17). Anderson identifies the church as first, "missional," and second, "ecclesial": missional because only in participation of Christ's mission does the church have reason to exist and ecclesial as identifying the community within which Christ is fulfilling his mission. Anderson, *Shape of Practical Theology*, 30–34.

36. Anderson, *Shape of Practical Theology*, 31. Christ's work past, present, and future must be clearly understood in light of Pentecost. The resurrected and living Christ actively works in his church through the person of the Spirit. Ibid., 35–46.

37. Ibid., 47–60; esp. 51–54. He denies any new revelation or any self-serving or ungodly interpretation of scripture. Ibid., 55. The Spirit who is the mediated presence of Christ in us breathed the words of Scripture. There is no division in him and there can be no duplicity between his works and his words. Likewise, failure to participate in Christ's activity in the world today because it does not match preconceived notions will not hold up to scrutiny. Anderson uses the issue of sexual parity in pastoral ministry to explain how the Spirit's work interprets the Spirit's Word. Since God is consistent in how he works, it is important to understand biblical antecedents. In the Old Testament and the New Testament, women are called out for service, including authority over men. For Anderson, Gal 3:28 is normative, while 1 Tim 2 (and elsewhere) are expedient answers to difficult contextual questions. Thus, Pentecostal Christians, living in the fulfillment of Joel as confirmed by Peter in Acts 2:17–18, should view the work of Christ in calling women and men to pastoral service as a Work of Christ interpreting the Word of Christ. Ibid., 77–101; esp. 90–101.

38. This is Blackaby's focal consideration. Blackaby, *What the Spirit is Saying*. Similar to Anderson, *Shape of Practical Theology*, 77–101, 102–12.

self-conscious and intentional decisions."[39] Theologically, participants enter God's grace and participate in "renewed Christian praxis, faithful to God's reign."[40] This process concludes not only with the intention of working through the issue, but with the added dimension of helping participants consider how to enter their world as active participants, subjects able to transform the world around them.[41]

Beyond what to do, the more intriguing question faced by the community at movement five is, "Who are we to become as a result of this process?"[42] A community experiences conversion in this critical moment.[43] God's purpose has always been to create a people and to make them into God's own image.[44] This fifth movement is the crux of that process regarding the generative theme in consideration.[45]

39. Groome, *Sharing Faith*, 267.

40. Ibid.

41. Ibid. There are four arenas where these changes operate. First is the cognitive, affective, and behavior/decision-making process. Orthodoxy," "orthopraxis," and "right relationship" describe the results. It is not enough to simply believe the right things, but one also must do them and in relation rightly with others (268–69). Second, these changed minds, hearts, and relationships should have effectiveness on the personal, interpersonal, and social levels (269–70). Third, decision-making occurs on both the personal and communal level. Groome notes that there is no clear distinction as overlap is inevitable, however there should be consciousness of when each is specifically considered (270). Fourth, decisions must be recognized as having both internal consequences for the community as well as external consequences for the world in which a community lives. The world-at-large will be changed by the nature of a changed ecclesial community and this consciousness should be considered in movement 5 (270–71).

42. Ibid., 271. Branson's warning against the fragmentation of "being" from "doing" is worth mentioning here ("Ecclesiology and Leadership," 102 n. 10). Groome is not creating a false dichotomy where doing and being are considered separately, but rather an integrated understanding that as a community is converted, being and doing are both changed.

43. Ibid.

44. See Lohfink, *Jesus and Community*.

45. Browning identifies this as a "strategic or fully practical theology." Here the reflective church synthesizes its praxis. Confronted by the discrepancy between its practice and God's activity in the world, and having consulted descriptive, historical, and systematic theologies, the resultant understanding as to how the congregation should live is strategic or fully practical theology. Anderson calls these "experimental probes" because they assume no particular answer; rather, these probes are opportunities to discover Christ at work, *ergo* praxis. Anderson, *Shape of Practical Theology*, 26–30. Informed by descriptive, historical, and systematic theologies, congregations answer the inner-core questions through strategic, practical, and theological investigations. As Browning states, "Strategic practical theology is the culmination of an inquiry that has been practical throughout" (*Fundamental Practical Theology*, 57).

Appendix B

Basic Assumptions of Appreciative Inquiry and Open Space Technology

In both Appreciative Inquiry (AI) and Open Space Technology (OST) there are important underlying assumptions that make them useful for congregational contexts. The following are brief explanations of those assumptions for each of these methods.

AI Assumptions

There are ten basic assumptions in AI.[1] The first is the recognition that "in every organization, some things work well."[2] These resources and narratives may be taken for granted or even hidden by years of neglect and/or forgetfulness; however, they do still exist.[3] Second, "what we focus on becomes our reality."[4] As Branson states it, "the 'reality' of an organization is defined by whatever participants think about, talk about, work on, dream about, or

---

1. While Whitney and Trosten-Bloom offer four basic assumptions, I prefer Branson's list as it is both comprehensive and approachable. See Branson, *Memories, Hopes, and Conversations*, 24–27. Branson notes dependence upon the work of Hammond, Cooperrider, and Campbell for his list. Ibid., 127 n. 5. Whitney and Trosten-Bloom also offer eight principles about Appreciative Inquiry that more closely align with Branson's assumptions. I will reference these as well. See Whitney and Trosten-Bloom, *Power of Appreciative Inquiry*, 51–79.

2. Branson, *Memories, Hopes, and Conversations*, 25.

3. Whitney and Trosten-Bloom, *Power of Appreciative Inquiry*, 61–64.

4. Branson, *Memories, Hopes, and Conversations*, 25.

plan."[5] As athletes use a technique of vision projecting to enhance performance and success, likewise focusing on the positive creates a more positive reality.[6] Third, "asking questions influences the group." The power of the question is also emphasized in Freire, Groome, and Heifetz and Linsky. AI states that what we question turns the focus upon that subject.[7] Fourth, "people have more confidence in the journey to the future when they carry forward parts of the past." The fear of change and the loss it requires can be lessened if parts of the past are carried into the new future. "The future will be a little less strange, and participants can envision their own roles in that future."[8]

Fifth, "if we carry parts of the past into the future, they should be what is best about the past."[9] It seems a better way to word this might be "*since we carry parts of the past into the future . . . .*" Social scientists indicated that our past makes our present and future; that is why it is so important to know and manage the implications of the past socially, psychologically, and emotionally. Thus, it is wise to choose the best of a congregation's past to carry forward rather than dysfunctional practices and embedded behaviors that "end up undermining core purposes and values."[10] Sixth, "it is important to value differences." Unearthing differing narratives and values can be an important part of the communal learning process. These different narratives are comparable to the "dangerous memories" mentioned by Groome.[11] The AI process allows people with differing perspectives to hear each other in a constructive and life-giving way.[12]

Seventh, "the language we use creates our reality."[13] As social creatures, our language is the means by which we construct and communicate perception, belief, value, and emotion. In so doing, we influence our world

5. Ibid.

6. See also Whitney and Trosten-Bloom, *Power of Appreciative Inquiry*, 72–74.

7. Branson, *Memories, Hopes, and Conversations*, 25. See also Whitney and Trosten-Bloom, *Power of Appreciative Inquiry*, 72–74, 66–69.

8. Branson, *Memories, Hopes, and Conversations*, 25. For an interesting addendum to this thought as action in the present, see also Whitney and Trosten-Bloom, *Power of Appreciative Inquiry*, 72–74.

9. Branson, *Memories, Hopes, and Conversations*, 26.

10. Ibid.

11. Groome, *Sharing Faith*, 204.

12. Branson, *Memories, Hopes, and Conversations*, 26. See also Whitney and Trosten-Bloom, *Power of Appreciative Inquiry*, 69–71.

13. Branson, *Memories, Hopes, and Conversations*, 26–27.

and in effect change it, making it into our communicated vision. This links to Freire's perspective that giving voice and the power to reflect to the un-conscientized and the oppressed effectively gives them power to transform their environment.[14] Metaphors and images "can carry a visual or affective punch that requires little explanation."[15] However, the interpretive work surrounding the metaphors and images are part of the imaginative pro-cess that cannot be left undone.[16] The images we use to describe ourselves and which we allow others to use in describing us have formative powers. Care must be used in choosing which metaphors and images are selected to describe an organization or group because of the reality forming power they contain.[17] Eighth, "organizations are heliotropic." Organizations, like plants, naturally turn or lean toward that which gives energy—regardless of the energy source being healthy or unhealthy. In AI, memories and imagi-nation can be "engaged to nourish participants with the best and most life-giving" sources of energy.[18]

Ninth, is a practical matter: "outcomes should be useful." While dia-logue as a means of opening hearts, minds, and ears is beneficial, something should happen in the organization as a result of the interpretive process and the vision expressed therein. In the long-term, AI helps people envision a future that they can actually create.[19] Finally, "all steps are collaborative." Participation by all is not only encouraged, but in many ways the process expects, even demands it. This is not coercive, as we have already con-firmed. However, it does allow for the fullest participation of people willing to fully participate. Participants form an "interpretive community" where "at its best, this contributes to the formation of a learning community in which all participants . . . have access, voice, and responsibilities."[20]

14. Freire, *Pedagogy of the Oppressed*, 80–83; Freire, *Education for Critical Conscious-ness*, 110–13.

15. Branson, *Memories, Hopes, and Conversations*, 30.

16. Ibid.

17. See also Whitney and Trosten-Bloom, *Power of Appreciative Inquiry*, 53–58.

18. Branson, *Memories, Hopes, and Conversations*, 27. See also Whitney and Trosten-Bloom, *Power of Appreciative Inquiry*, 66–69.

19. Branson, *Memories, Hopes, and Conversations*, 27.

20. Ibid. See also Whitney and Trosten-Bloom, *Power of Appreciative Inquiry*, 75–78.

APPENDIX B

OST Assumptions

Identifying the assumptions that are at the core of Open Space Technology is a bit more difficult than with AI where the assumptions are clearly spelled out. According to Smolander, Schneider, Dingsøyr, et. al., there are four basic assumptions that guide Open Space Technology. To their four I would add two additional ones.

Smolander, et.al., identify the first assumption as being that the OST "event must focus on an issue of concern, and when the purpose becomes clear, the appropriate event and project structures will follow as a natural expression or embodiment of the purpose."[21] This is supported by Harrison Owen's statement the OST "runs on two fundamentals: passion and responsibility."[22] Passion connects to interest and responsibility is about getting things done.[23] Thus, when leaders identify the focus and communicate it to people who self-select themselves into the conversation, the outcomes that follow will be the right outcomes.

Second, "people can and will self-organize based on their interests."[24] Smolander et al., insist that in OST responsibility and participation unleash creative potential and energy.[25] By allowing people to organize around their own interests, leaders evoke the concept of self-organization, a principle identified by biologist Stuart Kauffman, physical chemist Ilya Prigogine, and others, which allows organisms and organic organizations to adapt to increasingly complex contexts with high efficiency.[26]

Third, "experts and analysts are needed among the participants."[27] In other words, the resources present in the group gathered are sufficient to the required task. Smolander, et. al. clarify that "there should be no expert help from outside the group."[28] The voluntary nature of OST insists that people are free to choose to participate and with whom they will participate. According to Owen, this is the best guarantee that the most essential quality in the group is present: they truly *care* about the topic and the out-

21. Smolander et al., "Future Studies," 141.
22. Owen, *User's Guide*, 23.
23. Ibid.
24. Smolander et al., "Future Studies," 141.
25. Ibid.
26. Owen, *Wave Rider*, 80-91, 94.
27. Smolander et al., "Future Studies," 141.
28. Ibid.

comes.[29] Adding outside experts removes the agency of the people who care for the issues and will carry them out within in a given context.

Fourth, "[Chaos] represents an opportunity for growth, organizational learning, and improved effectiveness."[30] Building off of chaos theory and the growing understanding that chaos gives way to greater organization and effectiveness, Owen points out that the absence of chaos in biological and physic terms (also known as a "state of equilibrium") is equivalent to death.[31] The chaotic nature of change is a natural part of the world in which we live and likely should be.[32] However, rather than seeing the chaos as problematic or as a challenge to overcome, it might and likely should be viewed as an opportunity for new awareness and learning.[33]

As a fifth assumption, I add that Owen and OST, take seriously the spiritual dimension of leadership work and the nature of discovery. In both his books *The Spirit of Leadership* and *The Power of Spirit*, Owen profoundly argues that leadership in these disruptive contexts is as much about summoning, discerning, and nurturing spirit.[34] It would be disingenuous to assume a Christian perspective from Owen's work. However, it is not a difficult leap from spirit to the kind of Pneumacracy (rule of the Holy Spirit) proposed in the body of this work. Further, Owen evokes spirit as a great equalizer in the search for meaning and practice in the midst of change. Again, it is not a difficult stretch to recognize the similar Trinitarian egalitarian and priesthood of all believers connections made earlier in this book and realize the way in which such connections are made possible in human systems due to the Holy Spirit's presence.

Finally, like in AI, OST views people from a positivist perspective with appropriate allowance for brokenness and the lament and grief such brokenness causes. Smolander, et. al. state, "This method has a very optimistic view of people. There is a basic belief that good things will happen

29. Owen, *User's Guide*, 25.

30. Smolander et al., "Future Studies," 141.

31. Owen, *Wave Rider*, 32.

32. Ibid., 49.

33. Owen, *Spirit of Leadership*, 21–23. Also, Owen, *Power of Spirit*, 15–20. A few helpful reminders are the biblical narratives of exodus, exile, and crucifixion. The upheaval of the moment ultimately led to new and powerful expressions of God's mission of reconciliation, which God's people learned in the midst of these experiences. Owen picks up on the later of these (Crucifixion/Resurrection) in *Power of Spirit*, 19-20.

34. See Owen, *Spirit of Leadership*, throughout but especially 51ff., and Owen, *Power of Spirit*, throughout, but especially 135ff.

if people get together to discuss topics of mutual interest."[35] Overall, this is an accurate assessment, however, it is much too simplified. Owen writes at length in *The Spirit of Leadership* about the importance of lament and grief when endings come or things fall apart.[36] Elsewhere, Owen states, "There comes a time when nothing but the truth will do. And it is not so much about telling the truth as letting the truth emerge."[37] He goes on to discuss how story telling allows the narratives of the organization to emerge and the truth to be confronted and when appropriate, mourned (lament).[38] Like AI, OST creates space for stories of brokenness to be told, for repentance to occur, and for discovery of new ways of living congregational life that better reflect the *missio Dei* of reconciling God's world.

35. Smolander et al., "Future Studies," 141.
36. Owen, *Spirit of Leadership*, 105ff.
37. Owen, *Power of Spirit*, 176. This quote is in chapter 12: "Healing a Broken Spirit."
38. This agrees nicely with the need for lament discussed briefly in chapter 9.

Appendix C

Shared Christian Praxis, AI, OST, and Adaptive Change Theory: A Dialogue

In this concluding appendix, I consider, sometimes reconsider, the connections between these conceptualizations of change leadership: adaptive change theory, education for connation/critical consciousness (shared Christian praxis), and Appreciative Inquiry and Open Space Technology. I focus primarily on similarities, however, where it seems appropriate I also consider important dissimilarities as well. The dialogue between these conversation partners will be approached using Heifetz's balcony language because it seems an apt metaphor for this reflective process.

On The Balcony: Reflection, Praxis and Critical Consciousness, and Inquiry

Heifetz and Linsky comment that the first moment of adaptive change is getting onto the balcony.[1] They remark that getting to the balcony is a means of gaining perspective by briefly and momentarily taking oneself out of the fray.[2] One particular expression of this balcony process is the interpretive process of "listening to the song beneath the words."[3] I find here similarities to AI literature regarding the role of Appreciative Inquiry in the "interpretive work—the discovery of meanings and the forming of local

---

1. Heifetz and Linsky, *Leadership on the Line*, 51ff.
2. Ibid., 51–54.
3. Ibid., 64–67.

meanings"[4] and to the OST literature regarding the role of emerging organizational mythology and story.[5] This process of "meaning-making" (Whit-
ney/Trosten-Bloom's term) is rarely a process of manufacturing meaning as
it is of discovering existing meaning within a community/organization. The
importance of this lies in self-reflection, communal awareness that leads to
the empowerment of a person and a people for making change in a situation of adaptive change.[6] Moreover, this is precisely the argument of Freire
and Groome for the role of education.

"Conscientization," "critical consciousness," or "connation" (Freire
and Groome) name the process of becoming aware of oneself and one's
world, and thereby accessing the power within to transform one's environment.[7] It is connected to praxis as the process of reflection within the ac-
tive/reflective cycle of praxis.[8] At one point, Groome describes this process
as uncovering the "dangerous memories" of a community. These memories
are uncovered as part of a process of becoming aware of the untold or
under-represented realities of a community. As Branson states, "It is not
likely that participants will always agree on what is 'the best.'"[9]

Groome goes further reminding educators that the process of reflecting on present praxis will unearth painful stories and passionate sorrows
and fears.[10] These stories are part of the process of waking up to the realities
of praxis as part of the investigation into how that praxis functions for some
and does not function for others. Owen uses a fragrantly provocative metaphor of the Dead Moose Society, describing how dysfunction, brokenness,
and pain are often like a dead moose that everyone ignores, until someone

4. Branson, *Memories, Hopes, and Conversations*, 24; Whitney and Trosten-Bloom,
Power of Appreciative Inquiry, 165–68.

5. Owen, *Power of Spirit*, 175–93; 209–12. Owen states: "The impact of storytelling time is palpable. All of a sudden everything that everybody was whispering behind
closed doors is right out there on the table. The pretense is over, and the sense of relief
is apparent" (178).

6. Owen, *User's Guide*, 116–18. See also Wenger et al., *Cultivating Communities of
Practice*, 210–11.

7. Groome, *Sharing Faith*, 123.

8. Ibid., 137. Freire reminds us that, "Let me emphasize that my defense of the
praxis implies no dichotomy by which this praxis could be divided into a prior stage of
reflection and a subsequent stage of action. Action and reflection occur simultaneously"
(Freire, *Pedagogy of the Oppressed*, 128).

9. Branson, *Memories, Hopes, and Conversations*, 26.

10. Groome, *Sharing Faith*, 208–10.

tells the story about the dead moose under the table.[11] In what may almost appear pastoral-care oriented, Owen reminds leaders that griefwork must be work performed by the grieving—those who owned and loved or where wounded by the dead moose—but the leader's job is that of "being fully present with others in their moment of grief [which] is a defining moment of our own humanity."[12] From an AI perspective, Branson likewise remarks that even in a process of positive inquiry there is room for lament as a positive move toward confession, grace, and gratitude.[13] However, this can only occur when people are willing to engage the questions surrounding praxis.

This is another similarity within the reflection/critical consciousness/inquiry/ getting to the balcony process: the power of the question. These processes emphasize that the power of leadership in the midst of adaptive situations comes not from knowing answers (expertise), but from asking the right question and letting the participants discover God's answers. Heifetz and Linsky, in the context of speaking about the role of giving the work back to the people, state, "They [observations] shift the group momentarily onto the balcony so that they can get a little distance from and perspective on what they are doing . . . You might use a question [to follow up an observation] because you do not know the answer and therefore cannot render an interpretation."[14] Groome and Freire are more forceful. Freire rejects fully the "banking process" of education contending that only in "problem-posing" education is found the "essence of consciousness" and the embodiment of communication.[15] Groome reminds the educator that in shared Christian praxis, there is an expectation that the educator shift his or her mindset from "answer person" to "question poser."[16]

From the Balcony: You Find That for Which You Look

A second interesting area of discussion in this investigation is the question of what is it we look for while on the balcony. Here there is some discrepancy between our conversation partners. Heifetz and Linsky are clearly operating from a problem-oriented perspective. Their focus is on surfacing

11. Owen, *Power of Spirit*, 179–80.

12. Ibid., 197.

13. Branson, *Memories, Hopes, and Conversations*, 52.

14. Heifetz and Linsky, *Leadership on the Line*, 135–36.

15. Freire, *Pedagogy of the Oppressed*, 79, 80–81.

16. Groome, *Sharing Faith*, 182.

adaptive situations and leading people through loss for the sake of change.[17] Thus, while utilizing a similar approach to AI as it relates to questioning and the role of the leader, Heifetz and Linsky are still operating in a deficit-based model.[18] The fundamental difference between problem solving and AI has to do with what it is you are expecting people to look at and address. As Branson describes it, problem-solving focuses on the inadequacies where as AI asks the question, "What do we want more of?"[19]

This discrepancy may be the one real weakness in Groome and Freire's approach. Even Freire's use of the term "problem poser" manifests the deficit model. It is highly conceivable that the shared Christian praxis of Groome and the critical consciousness of Freire can be modified toward the positive focused model of AI. Groome and Freire both openly affirm the assumption of AI that "people individually and collectively have unique gifts, skills, and contributions to bring life."[20] It also matches OST's assumptions that, "whoever comes is the right people" and that those attending have the resources needed to address the concerns of the organization.[21] Freire states that "dialogue further requires an intense faith in humankind, faith in their power to make and remake, to create and re-create, faith in their vocation to be more fully human . . . ."[22] Groome uses the verbiage of "appropriating" sources of wisdom to decisions "for lived Christian faith toward God's reign."[23] Both of these writers see the resources within the community and acknowledge that when these resources are accessed and applied, transformation is possible—perspectives very similar to AI and OST perspectives.

Likewise, Heifetz and Linsky implicitly recognize the assets within a community; otherwise, how could giving the work away be anything other than cruelty? Heifetz and Linsky state that adaptive challenges require "experiments, new discoveries, and adjustments from numerous places in the organization or community." They further recognize that "changed

17. Heifetz and Linsky, *Leadership on the Line*, 89, 92–95.

18. For a comparison of the two forms of change (deficit-based and positive change) see Whitney and Trosten-Bloom, *Power of Appreciative Inquiry*, 17; also Branson, *Memories, Hopes, and Conversations*, 21–24, especially 22.

19. Branson, *Memories, Hopes, and Conversations*, 21–23.

20. Whitney and Trosten-Bloom, *Power of Appreciative Inquiry*, 2.

21. Owen, *Expanding*, 11, 29–30.

22. Freire, *Pedagogy of the Oppressed*, 90.

23. Groome, *Sharing Faith*, 115.

attitudes, values, and behaviors" are possible.[24] These all imply the kinds of assets necessary in AI and OST for change to occur. Furthermore, when viewed through the AI's lens of "what do we want more of?" change is less about what we lose and more about what we gain, perhaps minimizing some of the resistance, fear, and danger with which Heifetz and Linsky are so rightfully concerned.[25] This is not to imply that danger does not still exist in the AI process, but as Whitney and Trosten-Bloom remind us, "if you want to transform a situation, a relationship, an organization, or community, focusing on strengths is much more effective than focusing on problems."[26]

Behind the Balcony: Shared Christian Praxis and Congregational Appreciative Inquiry

The final area of dialogue I consider is that between shared Christian praxis, OST, and AI. Here we find common approaches to engaging people of faith in addressing areas of change. An important word in this framework is that of "conversion." The OST conversation at this point is more difficult to connect as there is not as of yet any work making explicit connections between the Christian story/vision and OST, like Branson's *Memories, Hopes, and Conversations* does for AI. However, it is worthy of mention that what Owen describes as "transformation" is certainly very similar to the "conversion" language described hereafter.[27]

Groome remarks that, "in a very real sense, all the activities and dynamics of a conative pedagogy is [sic] an education for ongoing conversion."[28]

24. Heifetz and Linsky, *Leadership on the Line*, 13.

25. Recall Branson's assumption four: "People have more confidence in the journey to the future when they carry forward parts of the past." This assumes assumption five, which reminds congregations to take the best of the past into the future. Branson, *Memories, Hopes, and Conversations*, 24, 25–26.

26. Whitney and Trosten-Bloom, *Power of Appreciative Inquiry*, 18.

27. See Owen, *Power of Spirit*, 4-8. He states, "A major theme of this work is transformation of organizations. When the subject is transformation, the world itself tells us that we are dealing with a process in which something (unnamed) goes through, or across, forms—trans-forms, as it were. The focus is not on the forms, which is what most people talk about, but rather that which goes through the forms, which is what I think we *should* be talking about. And that 'something,' so far as I am concerned, is Spirit" (ibid., 8, emphasis in original).

28. Groome, *Sharing Faith*, 129.

There are four kinds of conversion in shared Christian praxis: intellectual, moral, religious, and social.[29] These conversions are centered on the idea of changed praxis, a kind of reprogramming, but one in which the participants are active. Similarly, Branson writes that, "a helpful way of understanding conversion is to see it as adopting a different narrative."[30] This process of adopting or being adopted into the Christian narrative challenges the other existing narratives we carry socially, culturally, locally, and personally.[31] The AI processes engage the conversion-oriented narrative in scripture.[32]

What Branson's AI and shared Christian praxis bring to this discussion are the ways in which the Christian story/vision call for a change of heart as the Father draws us into God's reign by the Son's demonstration of love, and through the power of the Spirit. Encountering texts and their engagement with contemporary contexts puts congregations in surprising opportunities to choose life: "As people intentionally choose and realize the fullness of life that God wills for all creation, such praxis brings them 'closer to God.'"[33] Closeness to God enables people to see with thanksgiving God's blessings and mercies. Accordingly, Branson reminds us that Paul encouraged the Philippians as follows: "Brothers and sisters, think about the things that are good and worthy of praise. Think about the things that are true and honorable and right and pure and beautiful and respected."[34] As we enter into the change opportunity, we must first realize that God goes before and is making the way. This is a positive development for our discovery. In so doing, we discover that which is most important: God is present with us and initiates ahead of us.

29. Ibid., 130.

30. Branson, *Memories, Hopes, and Conversations*, 54.

31. Ibid., 54–55.

32. Ibid., 55–63.

33. Groome, *Sharing Faith*, 272.

34. Phil. 4: 8, NCV. Quoted from NJB in Branson, *Memories, Hopes, and Conversations*, 64.

General Index

adaptive/adaptation, xix, xxiv, 5 (n. 5)
    8–11, 29, 33, 36, 64, 108, 113,
    119, 125 (n.13), 128, 129, 132,
    162, 165–70
    and discontinuous change, xiii,
    5–6, 49, 62, 91, 98–99, 110,
    135
    leadership, xix, 27, 30, 38, 91,
    105, 115, 122, 135
    systems, 129
Anderson, Ray S., xix, xx (n. 4), xxi,
    xxvi, 25, 33 (n. 42), 91 (n.2),
    100, 102 (n. 43), 121, 150–51
    (n. 7), 152 (n. 12), 153 (n.15),
    154 (n. 20), 156–57, 158 (n.
    45)
Appreciative Inquiry (*also* AI), 95, 99,
    101, 108, 124–28, 133, 134,
    136–37, 159–61, 165–70
authority, 37 (n. 2), 38–42, 49, 51–53,
    61, 65 (n. 92), 66, 157 (n. 37),
bell sheep, 44, 49, 61, 64, 66, 91,
    91–105, 109, 121–23
Blackaby, Henry T., xxvi, 95, 119, 135
    (n. 63), 157 (n. 38)
Boff, Leonardo, 69 (n. 9), 71–72,
    74–75, 78–79, 81, 82
Branson, Mark Lau, xiii–xv, xix, xxvi,
    8, 33 (n. 41), 38 (n. 6), 95, 96,
    98, 100–104, 111, 113, 115,
    116, 117, 119–20, 127, 134,
    158 (n. 42), 159, 167, 168, 169
    (n. 25), 170

Browning, Don S., xix, xxi, xxii,
    xxvi, 102 (n. 43), 149 (n. 3),
    151–52, 153 (n. 20), 155, 156
    (n. 31), 158 (n 45)
Collins, Paul M., 71 (n. 17),
Cunningham, David S., 69 (n. 6), 70
    (n. 10), 76, 85 (n. 118),
David, king of Israel, 41–42, 44, 46
    (n.36), 47, 48, 50, 55 (n. 23),
    56
deskill(ing), xiv, 27, 31
differentiate/differentiated, 17 (n. 33),
    71, 82 (n. 96), 85, 94
discernment, xv, xxv, 87, 91–92, 94,
    95–96, 100, 104, 107, 109,
    114, 121, 122, 123–24, 136,
    151 (n. 9), 154–55 (n. 24),
disembedding, 10, 14–15, 16–19,
    21–26, 28, 29 (n. 20), 91, 104,
dissent, 40, 42, 85, 109–10
Drane, John, 22, 27, 29 (n. 22), 30
    (n. 25)
Erickson, Millard J., 73, 78 (n. 67), 82
exodus, 4–5, 7, 8, 39–40, 41, 46, 49,
    59 (n. 54), 95 (n. 16), 163 (n.
    33)
exile, 8, 163 (n. 33)
Fiddes, Paul S., 76, 78,
Freire, Paulo, xxii–xxiii, 110 (n. 20),
    125, 127, 128, 149, 150–51
    (n. 7), 151 (n. 8), 154 (n. 22),
    160, 161, 166–68
Giddens, Anthony, 10 (n. 6), 11, 16–
    23, 27 (n. 14), 31 (n. 34)

Scripture Index

OLD TESTAMENT

Genesis

Exodus

Leviticus

Numbers

Deuteronomy

1 Samuel

Scripture Index

Acts

1:8	57
2	61
2:17–18	157
13:22	47
20:28–31	62–63
20:28	54
20:17	62
20:28	62
20:35	63

Romans

12:2	6–7, 136
12:16	119
15:5–6	119

1 Corinthians

1:10	119
4:16	63
9:7	54
11:1	53, 63

2 Corinthians

4:17–18	138

Galatians

3:28	157

Ephesians

4:1–12	94
4:11	38, 54, 63, 95
4:12–13	54
4:12	27, 63, 96

Philippians

1:3	xviii
4:8	170

1 Thessalonians

1:6	63

1 Timothy

2	157

Hebrews

12:2	30
13:20	54, 60

1 Peter

1:1	59
2:11	59
2:19–25	60
2:25	54, 59, 60
5	53
5:1–4	63–65
5:2ff	95
5:2	54, 64
5:3	47, 53
5:4	54, 60
5:8	60
5:10–11	60

Revelation

2:27	55, 60
6:9–11	60
7:9	60
7:14–16	60
7:17	55, 58, 60
12:5	55, 60
19:15	55, 60

Made in the USA
Las Vegas, NV
28 November 2022

60573886R00115